The Other Mother

LIVING OUT
Gay and Lesbian Autobiographies

Joan Larkin and David Bergman
GENERAL EDITORS

Midlife Queer: Autobiography of a Decade, 1971–1981
Martin Duberman

Widescreen Dreams: Growing Up Gay at the Movies
Patrick Horrigan

Eminent Maricones: Arenas, Lorca, Puig, and Me
Jaime Manrique

Taboo
Boyer Rickel

The Other Mother: A Lesbian's Fight for Her Daughter
Nancy Abrams

The Other Mother
A Lesbian's Fight for Her Daughter

Nancy Abrams

The University of Wisconsin Press

The University of Wisconsin Press
2537 Daniels Street
Madison, Wisconsin 53718

3 Henrietta Street
London WC2E 8LU, England

1   3   5   4   2

Printed in the United States of America

Library of Congress Cataloging-in-Publication Data

Abrams, Nancy.
The other mother: a lesbian's fight for her daughter /Nancy Abrams.
282 pp.   cm. — (Living out)
ISBN 0-299-16490-X (cloth: alk. paper).
ISBN 0-299-16494-2 (paper)
1. Abrams, Nancy.   2. Lesbian mothers—United States Biography.
3. Lesbian mothers—Legal status, laws, etc.—United States Case
studies.   4. Custody of children—United States Case Studies.
5. Visitation rights (Domestic relations)—United States Case
studies.   I. Title.   II. Series.
HQ75.53.A27   1999
306.89—dc21   99-13125

For my Little Goose

Contents

Acknowledgments

Many people helped me to see that this story had significance beyond my own personal challenges: I would like to thank JP for suggesting I keep track of it all; the readers from Dodge who showed me that I had no choice but to write this down; Jane Howard who asked me to write about a party and who always wanted to know the interesting details; and Le Anne Schreiber who suggested I start at the beginning.

I would also like to thank Kathryn Kendell at the National Center for Lesbian Rights for the help she has given me and for the work she does on behalf of lesbian mothers across the country.

I am grateful to David Bergman, Joan Larkin, and Raphael Kadushin for their dedication to publishing gay and lesbian autobiography.

I owe a debt of gratitude (or at least a really big gift certificate to a really expensive department store) to Veronica, whose generous spirit is unmatched.

This is a book about family, and I owe a lot to my own. I would like to thank my mother who has been there every step of the way for me, and who has also been the best grandmother I could wish for my daughter. Both my parents taught me that happily-ever-afters can start anytime, and that families can take many shapes.

And to Whit, for everything.

Author's Note

I once heard Grace Paley say that any story told twice is fiction. I believe that statement wholeheartedly. And yet, what follows is not fiction. It is the truest rendition I could give of my experience. Nonetheless, I have created many fictions in order to tell this story. I have changed the names of characters and places to protect the privacy of the real people about whom I have written. At times I have condensed conversations or events, or altered them slightly for the sake of clarity. I have chosen details to include, and to exclude, sometimes consciously, sometimes not.

Almost all of this work is based upon my journals in which I have recorded bits of conversation, impressions and emotions. What hadn't been recorded is reconstructed from my memory, and with help from people who were close to me at the time the events took place.

I wrote this book during the years when I had no contact with my daughter. Reconstructing our lives together—how she came to be and how I came to lose her—was, in effect, my only way to spend time with her. It was also my way of making sense of what happened to our family, and what I saw happening to other families like ours around the country.

Of course this story would be very different had any other party involved been the one to tell it.

All that said, I have tried to follow another of Grace Paley's aphorisms in writing this down. When asked how she knows when a story is complete, she answered: When it is as honest as it can be.

I have tried here to write as honest a story as I can, using fictional techniques at times, but always holding to the truth as I experienced it.

The Other Mother

Searching

Yesterday someone asked me when I last saw you. I tried to come up with an answer, but as soon as I began to mentally roll back through time my mind slid off a cliff into clear white space. I had to say I didn't know.

When you were born, we counted first the days, then weeks, then months that you were with us. "Can you believe she's a whole week old?" Norma would ask, staring at your eight-pound body wriggling in my arms. At nine months we had a miniature birthday party for you to commemorate that now your lifetime outside of the womb equaled the time you had spent inside. On your first birthday, relatives traveled from New York City and New Hampshire to celebrate with us in Cambridge. When you were about eighteen months old, I heard a friend who had no children tell someone else that you were "about two." I scolded her later. "Don't you know that until a baby is twenty-four months old, you count her age in months? Eighteen months has nothing to do with two years old."

Now six months or six years makes no difference to me. You are someplace else. I can't see you or speak with you, so why bother counting? If I really try, I can come up with this statistic: I have missed five of your birthdays, and all of the seconds, minutes, and hours in between.

The story I am about to tell you is one I wish I never had to recount. I'd rather fill these pages with tales of your childish antics; running just for the sake of it, turning things over to find out what's on the bottom, spilling things just so they could be refilled, bringing rocks, weeds, and blueberries home in your pockets as presents. But there is more that you must know and I must say. The way that I came to be your other mother is an unusual tale. The way I lost you, more so.

Telling this is a painful task. I approach it as I would combing the tangles out of your windblown hair. I start where there is some order, high on the scalp, drag the comb through what is smooth and easy to sort: to the right, to the left. Stop at the knots. Take a small section and find what separates easily. Try again.

You should know that even now, sometimes when I dress for work, instead of finding the agate earrings I am searching for, I come across one of your barrettes, like the plastic one with a yellow rabbit in the center. Then the whole morning at work I think about the barrette you left behind on one of your visits long ago.

I should record the fact that before you and your mom moved away, you gripped me in your arms, told me I was your prisoner, and wouldn't let me say good-bye.

These stories tell themselves over and over in my sleep. They are the stories that live in the short silence I hope you never have to hear, between the question "Do you have children?" and my answer: sometimes "yes" and sometimes "no."

Here's what my daughter wore to day care on June 15, 1993: a short-sleeved shirt with pale pink stripes and matching pants, white socks with pink stitching, and her 101 Dalmations sneakers.

It was the last day I saw her. That's why I remember the details: How I poured Cheerios and milk for breakfast. How I tried to make it just another morning. I didn't even pack her suitcase until after my partner drove her to day care. Then I got dressed, and went to court.

Every time a new friend or acquaintance visits my house and sees along the mantel a parade of photos of a little girl starting at birth and stopping abruptly at age four—like a time-lapse photograph of a flower whose petals never open all the way—they ask, "Isn't there something more you could have done?" My gut lurches at the question. As it does when anyone asks how long it's been since I've seen her. Four and a half years. A lifetime, literally, when you consider: She was four and a half years old that last day. Nine now.

The day I went to court, my daughter forgot to put on her silver ring, the one with a turquoise stone the size of one of those sugar dots on paper strips she loved to tear off with her teeth. I found the ring on the edge of the bathtub. Next time I cleaned, I moved it into the bowl where we keep hair ties and barrettes.

I'm wearing that ring now. On a chain around my neck next to a sterling silver symbol I received as a gift, which in some ancient alphabet is said to mean fulfillment. I wear that necklace, and I hope. Fulfillment of this desire seems a simple wish.

But I know now that what's simple, what's easily achieved, is the emptiness of longing. Fulfillment is not.

I

It was 1986. I was twenty-two years old, and I felt my heart had been broken one too many times. Six months earlier my last lover had pulled away from the curb on her Honda Rebel 250 motorcycle. Now I was ready for someone new, and I demanded a replacement relationship the way some people insist on a first-class seat on an airplane: It was available, so I had simply to request one for myself and agree to pay the price.

My romantic desperation had not been earned. I'd had a handful of boyfriends in high school and college, but in those days I tended to be the one doing the leaving. Since becoming involved with women I'd had two romances I considered substantial and a few flings. No one had warned me that a relationship was something that had to be built. If I was too sensitive to disappointment, it was because I hadn't bargained on the time it would take to create "happily ever after."

My friend Samantha had come over to eat dinner and watch MTV. As I spooned mounds of steaming rice and lentils onto our plates, I couldn't resist breaking into one of my frequent laments about being single. And Samantha couldn't hold back from offering her stock reply: "You can't rush these things."

"But it's already been so long," I said, stroking my cat, Ahab, who had climbed into my lap.

"You haven't even gotten over Evel Knievel yet."

"She has a name."

"It wouldn't be fair to your future girlfriend to get involved now, you're still pining." Sam was forever practical. Everything about her, from her perfectly straight hair that fell just past her shoulders, to the parallel lines made by her thin eyebrows and level mouth, seemed studiously planned and carried out. Life was a science to her, and there were right ways and wrong ways to do everything, including cooking rice and falling in love.

"The next one, whoever she is, is for keeps. I can't take another heartache," I said. I may as well have affected a swoon for all of the melodrama in my voice. But that was how I felt back then, eating dinner from mismatched bowls in front of the television as the fading late-autumn sun threw stripes of light across the room. Michael Jackson was singing "Billie Jean" when the phone rang. Ahab scrambled to the floor as I stood to answer it. It still seems too convenient that in the middle of that conversation with Sam, someone should have called to ask me out. But that's how it happened.

"What's that grin for?" Sam asked when I came back to the living room.

"Who says you can't always get what you want?"

"Who was it?"

"Amy, from my karate class, the one I told you had been flirting with me last week. She asked me to a movie."

(That's how things seemed to be for me then. I made demands, and they were answered. Friends have said to me, "You're so lucky," or "Your life seems charmed." Someone said it to me just recently, when the job I'd had my eye on for several years suddenly opened up just when I was back on the market for a new position. I did get the job. But what does that really mean about luck? About a charmed life?)

Two nights later, Amy and I had our date. After a movie and a beer at a new café in Harvard Square, she invited me to her apartment. Despite a valiant effort, I felt nothing more for Amy than I had when I taught her how to curl her fingers into a proper fist in the beginners' karate class where she was my student. I was beginning to think Sam was right. Maybe you can't just grab for love like that.

As we climbed the porch steps to her apartment, I tried to think of an excuse to go home early. But in the endless moments while Amy fumbled with her keys, I dropped my eyes and noticed a canvas that someone had left on the porch to dry. It was a picture of a black horse stampeding through a cabbage-colored landscape. Somehow the dark colors appeared bright, making what might have been a portrait of doom into something beautiful. The paint was applied so heavily it had ridges almost wide enough for a fingertip to ride through, like the folds in a bowl of just-whipped cream.

"Like it?" Amy asked, clicking on the porch light. If she had painted this, there must be more to Amy than I'd discovered that evening. "My roommate painted it," she said.

"Roommate?"

"Yes, Norma."

It was another week before I met Norma. Amy brought her to the next karate session. "This is Nancy Abrams, the one who liked your painting so much," she said, introducing us.

A nervous smile spread across Norma's lips. My eyes accidentally locked into hers, making me uncomfortably aware that we were exactly the same height. As if I had purposely intruded, and she was warning me away, Norma looked off to the side. Or maybe it was a sign of her insecurity, shyness, a desire for privacy.

Norma Jean I wanted to say, letting myself take in her flawless skin, her sad mouth. But she told me her name was just Norma. Norma Friedman. As she spoke she smiled. Her eyes, although not sharply focused, challenged mine—to flirt or fight, I couldn't be sure which. The extra-large T-shirt draped over her birdlike frame gave her the appearance of being helpless. Still, something proud in the way she held her neck convinced me that she was a match for anything the world could offer. As she learned to punch and kick, Norma threw her arms and legs as one might toss a scarf around one's neck; with a looping, casual sweep.

One night after class, Amy offered to give me a lift home with her and Norma. I wasn't sure whether Amy was still interested in me, or if she sensed my attraction to Norma. But in that moment I wasn't worrying about Amy's motives. I accepted the ride.

Norma sat in front beside Amy, never looking back to ask me a question or add to the conversation. While I struggled to keep up with Amy's patter, I listened to the silence surrounding Norma. Aloofness never scared me away. Its curious emptiness always drew me in, as it did that night.

"Why don't you come by our apartment for a cup of coffee?" Amy suggested. We had stopped at the light where she'd turn if I declined. But curiosity about Norma made me say yes.

When we arrived at the run-down Victorian house where they occupied the first floor, Norma slipped into a bedroom off the kitchen, saying she had a phone call to make. I tried to hide my disappointment and drank from the cup of peppermint tea Amy made me. For an hour I took delicate sips while Amy tried to engage me in conversation about the karate class, cooking, coming out, everything except what I wanted to talk about—her roommate.

Finally, giving up any hope of seeing Norma again that evening, I rose to leave. "I could give you a ride home," Norma said, emerging at last, wearing a black scarf and knit hat pulled down to her eyebrows. "I'm going to Store 24 for some ice cream anyway." Nothing seemed to move as Norma stood there in the doorway—except for the great waves of energy in her green eyes.

I followed Norma into the convenience store, saying I wanted to buy a newspaper. I already had one delivered to my house, but I wasn't telling. In the store, I discovered a different side to Norma. On every shelf she seemed to find something amusing. She made the fluorescent-lit aisles feel like a playground. She shook a box of macaroni-and-cheese mix so that it sounded like a set of maracas. "I love this stuff, don't you?"

"Macaroni and ice cream?" I asked. "Doesn't do anything for me."

Finally she laughed. I did too. She picked up a quart of Ben and Jerry's Cherry Garcia ice cream. Sitting in the parked car with the heat turned up, we ate our ice cream with flat wooden spoons.

Besides her taste for packaged pasta dishes and unusual ice cream flavors, I learned little about Norma that night. Like me, she had graduated from college the previous spring. She had majored in art history, but was now working at a pizza shop. I was putting my liberal arts degree to an equally useful end: I was managing a health food store.

Amy called a few days later. She, Norma, and some friends were going to drive out to Springfield to go to a new bar Friday night. She wanted to know if I'd like to join them.

"All the way across the state?"

"Sure, it's an adventure."

Friday morning I woke to the sight of snowflakes drifting past my window. It'll be an adventure all right, I thought. The sky was an impenetrable gray; there was no chance the weather would change soon. Norma called to announce the obvious: Everyone was backing out because of the snow.

"I guess this isn't exactly road trip weather," I said.

"Road trip weather? That's a funny thought. Wouldn't this be road trip weather if we took a road trip in it?" she asked.

"You mean you still want to go?"

"Don't you?" A snowplow scraped along the street below. Now that it was just the two of us, I realized I did want to go—more than ever.

"The only problem is that my car is no good in the snow. I don't have the right tires, and my windshield wipers get stuck all the time," Norma was saying.

"I'll pick you up, then."

"You think it will be okay, don't you? I mean with the snow and everything."

"Of course I do. We'll be fine." In that moment, my confidence seemed genuine, even to me. I hardly noticed that I was convincing Norma of the solidity of her own rash plan, that I'd made an about-face in the minutes since I'd picked up the phone.

I called in sick to work, telling myself that the store would be quiet anyway. That freed me to spend the rest of my day choosing an outfit and cleaning out my car. The weather report came on and confirmed what I already knew: The snow was not about to let up. This is crazy, I told myself, as I drove to Norma's place.

Less than an hour into the trip, what had been snow turned to icy rain.

"I knew we shouldn't have done this," Norma said. By now it was as though the stormy drive had been my idea from the start.

"Come on, this is perfect road trip weather if you ask me." I meant it, too. Inside the car it was warm and smelled of our damp sweaters. Outside, the world was suffused with a gentle, faraway glow. Norma told me about herself and her family. She didn't speak to her parents much, but she said she was very close to her older brother, Eli. Even though she was working at a pizza shop, Norma had ambitions. She had applied to graduate schools and she planned on becoming a lawyer. "An artist needs a practical profession. Something to fall back on," she said. "Besides, I'll need to support a family someday." Those sounded like far-off plans. I was more interested in what she told me about the present. She said she was trying to get over a string of bad relationships. The women she'd dated recently seemed to be using her for sex, she said.

Stay with me, and no one will ever hurt you again, I wanted to tell her.

About thirty miles outside of Springfield we saw a car that had skidded off the highway and crumpled against a guardrail. "Why don't we pull off here? We don't have to go all the way to Springfield just to get a drink, do we?" I asked.

Norma agreed and I pulled off the pike in Sturbridge. We found a pub and went inside. "See, it's even more of an adventure this way," I said. "Who knows what we'll find."

The bar was decorated with prints of old cars, tired brass railings, and green walls. "It reminds me of this place my father used to bring me to," Norma said. The way her voice sounded I couldn't tell whether the atmosphere seemed friendly or sinister to her. "It was dark and cozy like this," she said. "I must have been fifteen years old. I remember I always ordered a strawberry milkshake, and my father would say, 'You're a cheap date, kid.' " Norma stabbed a french fry with her fork. "There was this woman who would come to the tables to tell people's fortunes. She must have had a dozen bracelets on each arm and she moved her hands a lot when she talked. I loved the sound those bracelets made." As though she were suddenly conscious of her own voice, Norma paused. I tried to think of something to say that would encourage her to continue. I was mesmerized by the steady clicking of her carefully pronounced words. But I didn't have to encourage her. "My father bought me a cup of tea one night even though he knew I hated it," Norma said, picking the story up again. "The fortune-teller told me I had to drink it all if she was going to see my future. I still hate tea."

I had nearly finished my burger and had ordered another beer. Norma had taken only a few bites of hers. Instead she collected french fries on her fork and shuffled them around, making trails through a puddle of ketchup on her plate. She held her burger for a while and put it down without eating any.

"What did she say?" I asked.

Norma smiled, a wistful, child's smile. "I don't remember all of it." For a moment I thought that was the end of the story. But then Norma continued. "She said I'd die young. I remember that."

"That's horrible. What kind of a person would say a thing like that to a child?"

"I still believe her," Norma said.

"Don't be ridiculous. We make our own destiny. There are always choices."

"But don't you think some things are meant to be? I got that feeling when we met. Didn't you?"

"Yes," I said. "I'm glad we met."

In the near-empty pub we sipped our beers and talked about everything. The only world that existed was the one lit by the green glow of the candle in the netted glass on our table. The waiter came by, asking if we wanted refills. From the sweep of his eyes around the vacant tables I knew he wanted us to leave, too. I asked if he'd heard a weather report.

"Where are you heading?"

"Back to Boston, we hope."

"I wouldn't try it. The pike is pretty bad," he said.

"What?" Norma asked. "You mean we might not get home tonight?"

"We could try. I think we'd be fine."

The waiter suggested a motor lodge a few blocks away and went off to write our check.

"Maybe he's right We'll just wait it out here." Norma said. I tried to contain the happiness in my voice as I agreed.

I drove the car through the deserted streets and slid into a parking spot. The motel lacked charm or character, but covered in snow it looked inviting. The room was typical: small, anonymous, and just clean enough.

"This is pretty funny, isn't it?" Norma asked.

"It's not so bad." I pulled off my shoes and spread my damp socks along the radiator to dry.

"I don't have any pajamas," Norma said, and she giggled again. She sat at the edge of the bed still wearing her coat and hat.

"That's okay."

"But we just met."

"Oh well," I said, trying to make light of her concerns.

"I don't want anything from you, you know."

"Don't worry. We just got stranded," I said. But I was disappointed. I wanted her to want a lot from me.

"I just don't want it to turn out the way everything else has turned out lately. You know, like I was telling you . . ."

"With those other women?" I turned on the television, and sat back on the bed. "We'll watch a movie and go to sleep. It'll be like a slumber party."

I kept my word, staying on my side of the double bed. But that night it was as though Norma's warm scent was a living presence, rolling against me, keeping me awake.

In the morning we found a diner and ordered pancakes.

"You know what my theory is?" Norma asked.

"About what?"

"About love."

"What is it?"

"I think if one person has a crush on the other, the other usually has one in return."

As I poured syrup onto my pancakes, I wondered what to answer. I didn't say right then that I wanted to test her theory.

Two weeks later Norma and I went out dancing with some of my friends in celebration of my twenty-third birthday. Even Amy came, having resigned herself good-naturedly to the way things were turning out between Norma and me. My friends switched partners and danced in groups, but I danced only with Norma. We laughed when we accidentally bumped knees and hips. Each time our dance steps collided I was reminded of how new our knowledge of each other was.

We all returned to my apartment for champagne. Norma looked beautiful in her vintage dress and Bakelite earrings. I thought that the modest, old-fashioned neckline made her look all the more sexy.

After my friends left, I drove Norma home and gave her a slow kiss good night. We hadn't spent a night together since our chaste evening in the motel and I'd resigned myself to taking things at a snail's pace. "Call you tomorrow," I said.

"Don't you want to come inside?" Norma asked.

"Of course I do." But before the words were out of my mouth, she had hopped out of the car and was pulling my door open.

I woke the next morning under a quilt, two comforters, and a batiked cotton bedspread. The blankets were all new and brightly colored, but they held the warmth of the night the way old things seem to do.

Cold air had crystallized on the single window above Norma's bed, letting in a dull glow that reminded me of the candlelight we had made love by the night before. I propped myself on my elbow and looked at Norma, who was still sleeping. Her curls lay flat against her scalp. Her dark hair contrasted sharply with her pale skin. Awake, she'd surely put on lipstick in some shade of purple, and blue-tinted mascara. She might wrap a green scarf around her head. Her hands would punctuate her sentences with jabs at the air. I felt privileged to know her sleeping, naked face, and leaned down to kiss her. From the intentional way her eyes opened, I suspected that she had been awake for some time, feeling me watch her. She kissed me back and I fell into the soft, easy world of her embrace.

"You'll be late for work," I said.

"What about you?"

"I'm in even worse shape. I have to stop home and pick up some clean clothes."

Norma slid out of bed, and crossed the painted floorboards to the closet in one long stride. She wore a black cotton camisole and matching underwear, which she immediately covered up with a pink terry robe. "Here," she said, throwing me a long knit sweater decorated with flamingos and palm trees. Next she produced a pair of red leggings, short purple boots, and thick gray socks, the only neutral color in the ensemble. "You can wear these," Norma said.

"No I can't, Norma," I said, holding up the sweater. "Don't you have anything a little more subdued?"

"Oh come on, Nancy, you can't go through your whole life wearing nothing but plaid flannel and blue jeans. Live a little."

"But I'm going to work."

"So?"

"Well, these aren't work clothes."

"It's what I wear to work."

"Yeah, but you can get away with it. I don't have your flair."

Norma turned back to her closet and fished out a turquoise tunic with a black zigzag stripe around the shoulders, and she traded the red leggings for a black pair. "There, this should suit you, it's got black in it," Norma said.

"It's still a little adventurous, but it'll do," I said.

Norma gathered the clothes I'd rejected into her arms, and went to the bathroom to make herself up and get dressed.

"You look great," Norma said returning to the room. "They won't even recognize you at work."

"I hope not," I said. But I felt pleased. Normas was right, after all. I hadn't worn anything so colorful in years. I'd bought into the lesbian antifashion aesthetic of the early eighties, and wore mostly flannel shirts and denim. When I had to dress up I ironed a blouse, wore a cardigan sweater, and put on pleated trousers and cowboy boots instead of sneakers.

Kissing Norma good-bye that morning before we each went to work felt oddly familiar, as if we'd been waking up together forever.

In the months that followed, Norma and I created some of our own routines. We spent most of our time at my apartment, since I had no roommates. Norma cooked our dinners—macaroni and cheese out of the box, or ravioli from a can—and I supplied our desserts, pints of ice cream, the most unusual flavors I could find. We liked to watch sitcoms in the evening and imagined ourselves in some kind of lesbian farce. We were two girls together, helpless when lightbulbs needed changing and when fuses inevitably blew. We had fake arguments about who was the butch. Meanwhile we raided each other's closets and jewelry boxes. There was a silliness that surrounded us and made us happy.

One evening Norma turned up at my apartment by surprise, a shopping bag in each hand. "Happy Anniversary," she said, handing me her packages.

"Anniversary?"

"Four months today."

"Really?"

"Well, I'm not sure exactly, but I needed an excuse. How's this? Happy Thursday!" I laughed and peeked inside one of the bags. "They're for you, do you like them?" I pulled out a green silk blazer that shimmered in the light and slipped it over the sweatshirt I was wearing. "Keep going," Norma prodded. There was a mustard yellow blouse and a pair of black stirrup pants.

"This is so wonderful. Thank you."

"Keep going, there's one more."

At the bottom of the second bag was a package gift wrapped in newspaper. Norma had written across it in blue, orange, and pink crayon, *A rainbow of colors to brighten your world. All my love.* Inside was a dime-store paint set and a box of colored pencils.

"Do you like it?" Norma asked.

I opened the paints, licked my thumb, and rubbed it in the purple. I smudged the paint on Norma's chin and kissed her. "I

love you." As soon as I said it I giggled, as if to lighten the seriousness of what I was feeling.

Norma pulled me toward her. "When you laugh like that, it
sounds like crying," she said.

One night, after I had returned home late from a concert, I called
Norma. I knew that she stayed up past midnight, so I was in the
habit of calling her at any hour. At first when there was no answer, I thought she might be sleeping. But her phone was right
next to her bed; she would hear it ringing, and she would know it
was me.

My next thought was to be jealous; maybe she had someone
else over. It was irrational, but I couldn't put the thought out of
my mind. The next day when I drove by her house I didn't see
her old Toyota in the parking lot. I was convinced she had spent
the night out. When she finally called me a day later, she wouldn't
answer my questions about where she had been. That confirmed
my suspicions, and I told her I couldn't continue seeing her.

When she finally broke down and told me that she had gone to
Emergency Services because she had been feeling suicidal, I was
sure it was a far-fetched excuse. Only when she rolled up the
sleeve on her heavy wool sweater and showed me the scratches
running across her forearm did I believe her. Seeing those raised
red lines on her skin and the storm building behind her eyes
didn't make me want to turn my back and forget Norma. It made
me want to help. I wanted to be with her all the time so she would
never feel that desperate again. Next time, I wanted her to call
me, not some stranger at Emergency Services.

There's a scar on my arm, too. It starts at the bend of my wrist
in the shape of a long, messy teardrop, then narrows into a line
that runs dangerously close to a bold blue vein. It fades out a
couple of inches above my elbow. Mostly, I forget about it. But
I'm reminded of my scar when I'm talking to someone, and the
person confesses to me that he or she, or a sister or brother, once
tried to commit suicide. Or she admits having thought of suicide.
Or understanding it. And then looks at me, a little too seriously.
Then I remember the scar, and I feel guilty.

Truth is, I'm too curious to kill myself. It's the reason I stay at
parties or movies, even after I can see that nothing is going to happen; it's a dud. But it might get better. The end might make every-

thing that came before seem more interesting or meaningful. Someone might arrive. If I leave now, surely I'll miss something.

My scar is from an accident that happened when I was four years old. I wanted to close the storm door to the kitchen, which was blowing open and shut in the wind. It wouldn't stay closed. So I punched it. And the glass shattered. That's what I told my parents. It made perfect sense to me then. But now, remembering how I refused to let the cut go unbandaged, even after the stitches had long since been removed and the rawness healed, I wonder. After my mother refused to let me have more gauze, I arrived at nursery school with toilet paper coiled down my arm and Scotch-taped into place. It was the year my grandmother died. My mother was distraught. I already knew what my father's temper looked like, and I knew it was ugly. My parents' marriage, I know now, was already beyond repair. My hand through glass was my first serious broadcast. It's the reason I know a call for help when I hear one. Mine echoed for years against the walls of my childhood home, unanswered. "She was trying to shut the door," my parents probably told friends who asked about my bandages. A child debating the wind with her fist—how stubborn!

If Norma was calling for help, I wanted to answer. I thought I knew how.

I started by asking Norma more questions about her past. I listened more carefully to the stories some of her friends told about the times in college when she had overdone it with drugs and drinking. It seemed that before we began dating, Norma's peaks of hilarity had been matched by frightening valleys of depression. Amy said that Norma had told her of a time when she had contemplated suicide on a daily basis. And Norma admitted that this hadn't been her first trip to Emergency Services. But in the months that we had been together, this was the first evidence I'd seen of a serious problem.

As I rolled back through the weeks we had spent together I searched for signs, but all I could come up with were the quirks in her personality that I found appealing, or the extremes in her moods I chalked up to an artist's temperament. I was an adult, but somehow I had preserved the magic thinking of a child. I didn't doubt that I could impose my vision of our relationship over the reality of it. I believed somehow that by loving each other we would fix each other, and that by my wanting things to work out we could make them work.

In any case, the good things we brought out in one another were more important in my mind. I was beginning to see the world the way an artist does, squinting at the most ordinary sight to see a sensuous palette of soft colors instead of mundane objects. I had always been organized and focused, a Jew with a Protestant work ethic. Norma insisted on playing.

Seeing my wardrobe now as the creative opportunity Norma had insisted it could be, I bought a new gangster hat, white with a black band, at a secondhand store. I stopped by Norma's apartment to surprise her and get her reaction. It had been only a week since she had had her crises, but already I'd put it behind me.

Norma answered the door with a sketch pad under her arm. "I was just going to call you," she said.

"Well, here I am."

"We have to talk."

I sat opposite her in the small living room. No lights were on, but the bright blue afternoon lit the room well. "I'm leaving," Norma said.

I felt as if an ocean wave had just crashed on me. "What are you talking about?"

"I was accepted to graduate school."

"That's great," I said, trying to sound as though I meant it.

"It's a very competitive program. Yale."

"You were accepted at Yale? They have an art program?"

"Law."

"That's amazing. I'm so impressed."

"But I have to move away. It's too bad, but . . ."

"Wait. That doesn't mean it's over with us. I can move, you know, I'll come with you."

"It's too soon for that kind of a commitment."

For nearly an hour I insisted that following Norma to Connecticut was the right thing for me to do. After all, what did I have to hold me back? Just a job schlepping crates of tomatoes around for five dollars an hour. Finally, she agreed.

The next day I ordered subscriptions to two Connecticut newspapers. I began bringing the classified section to Norma, and together we looked for a job for me and apartments for the two of us. Norma suggested we drive out to New Haven and start looking around. I had her convinced.

Then one night over dinner she announced that she'd sent Yale a letter declining their offer.

"Why would you do that?"

"I got into a teaching program at UMass."

"Teaching? But what about law?"

"Well, it doesn't really fit with my plans. It takes so long, and I want to have a baby."

"A baby?"

"I've told you this a hundred times already. I want a baby. I've always dreamed of being a mother."

"I thought that was a fantasy. You're a lesbian. You can't just decide you're having a baby."

"What about Robin and Beth? They did it."

Beth was in our karate class. Her daughter, Emily, sometimes slept in her car seat in the corner of the dojo while we worked out. I'd written them off as oddballs and regarded their daughter as part curiosity, part invader. Our friends were mostly women around our own age who seemed to relish their independence. Now, suddenly there was a baby among the lesbians. It seemed horribly out of place to me to see a woman with a crew cut, in workboots and jeans, with a cloth diaper slung over her shoulder, a baby bottle in one hand and a rattle in the other.

"This is very serious, and if you don't like the idea it really doesn't matter. It hardly concerns you."

"But we were talking about us."

"I was talking about me."

What was I doing? I barely knew this woman, and already I'd offered to move with her to another state. Now I was entering into family planning. "You're right," I said. "But what if you and I do decide to make a life together, someday?"

"Then you'll be a mommy, too."

The thought sounded preposterous on so many levels. Being a lesbian seemed to have few tangible advantages in a world full of sexism and homophobia. Here's how it looked to me back in 1986: As a lesbian you resigned yourself to a life with no male income in the family (women still earned sixty cents to the male dollar). There would be no spousal benefits at work, and then there was the harassment in the streets, confrontations with drunken punks if you held your lover's hand in the park, and so on. But as I saw things, there was at least one perk: Sex without consequence, no unwanted pregnancies.

"If you really want a baby that badly, I suppose no one's going to stop you. But what's the rush?"

"I've already been waiting for this for a long time."

"But the world is such a mess. In Denmark they can't even drink cows' milk because they've been contaminated with the fall-out from Chernobyl."

"So people should stop having babies?"

"Yes. If we can't guarantee them a safe world," I stammered. "Why plan to bring a child into such an uncertain future?"

"Are you saying that people should just give up hope?"

"I'm saying people should act responsibly."

Norma's cheeks flushed. "Why is everything so impersonal for you? You act like we're talking about some obscure political issue. This is my life and my decision!"

"I'm sorry," I said. "I didn't mean to upset you."

"Actually, I don't care whether you approve of my having a baby or not. It's none of your business."

"Maybe not, but . . ."

"And in addition, what do you know about responsibility? Who are you to preach?" Norma pulled herself up straight. Pride, or something as sharp, shot from her eyes.

"I wasn't preaching. I . . ."

Suddenly Norma's expression changed. Her rational arguments crumbled into a mountain of sobs. She was crying so hard she couldn't catch her breath. I put my arms around her and held her tight. "I'm sorry," I said.

"This isn't about you," she whispered. "It's just . . ." Her hands dropped to her lap like two downed birds. "I had an abortion once."

I stroked her hair. "It's okay. We can talk about it when you feel calmer."

"With Glen. You know, the boyfriend I had in college. He wanted to keep the baby but I couldn't face it."

"I'm sorry. I didn't know."

"I want my baby," she wailed. "I want my baby."

It was a week or so later, and talk of babies, for the time being anyway, had receded. Norma and I were soaking in a warm tub of water which we scented with lilac. I rested against Norma's body in perfect bliss. "Being in a bath is like wearing worn clothes," Norma said. "It's where I'm completely myself."

I wouldn't have moved when the phone rang, but Norma thought it might be her brother, who was traveling in Europe at the time. She'd given him my number and told him to call as soon as he settled in.

Ahab sprang from where he was curled on the radiator, and followed at my heels as I ran to pick up the phone. A minute later Norma appeared, wrapped in a towel. "It's my mother," I whispered. "She wants to visit for the weekend." Ahab crawled into Norma's lap and kneaded her towel with his paws.

"Mom, I have some news," I said, mopping the drops of water that had fallen onto the phone. "I have a new girlfriend. You can meet her when you come." Norma looked down and smiled shyly as I stroked her bare shoulders. "You'll really like her. She's an artist." Norma kissed the back of my neck. Her lips felt like little flowers blossoming down my spine. "She's unbelievably smart, too. She was accepted into Yale's law program, but she turned them down." Suddenly my back was cold. Norma had left the room. My mother was saying that she couldn't wait to meet her. We made our plans, and when I hung up I went to find Norma.

I knocked on the bathroom door. "Hey, are you okay in there?"

There was no answer. I could hear the sound of water rushing in the sink. "Norm, is everything all right?"

"Leave me alone," she said. I tried the door. It was locked. "Just go away, would you?"

Before I could wonder what I had done to offend her, the door eased open. "If I tell you something, will you promise not to hate me? And promise you won't tell your mother, either."

"Of course," I said.

Norma's voice tightened into a determined staccato. "I lied to you. I don't know why. I just thought I had to impress you or you wouldn't love me. Why would you love me anyway? So I had to. I just made a little something up. I didn't think you'd believe me. I never did anything like this before. I feel so stupid."

We were standing in the doorway like neighbors exchanging gossip on the stoop. Norma's arms were crossed in front of her, I was holding my towel around me with one hand. "What, Norm? What is it?"

"I never got into Yale. I never even applied."

For some reason, I laughed. I knew I should be appalled, but I wasn't. After all, it wasn't as though Norma had cheated on me. She hadn't committed a crime. It didn't hurt. I expected a lie like that to actually cause me physical pain. My father had always said that the worst thing I could possibly do was lie to him or my mother. The truth had become almost a religion for me. But this blasphemy was thin as air. And the absence of pain was like a joy in itself. So I laughed.

"It's not funny," Norma said, although she was laughing too. But haltingly, as if she'd stop suddenly if I did. "You're not going to leave me, are you?"

When we stopped laughing I looked into Norma's face. It looked different. For the first time I noticed that her right eye was slightly wider than the left. One nostril was fuller. Her mouth tugged slightly to one side. It was a barely visible asymmetry, but I wondered why I hadn't seen it before.

"What are you looking at?" Norma asked.

"You," I said. "Just you."

Norma and I had known each other for about six months by then, and already I wouldn't consider leaving her. My parents met at a football game one fall, and were engaged to be married by spring. That wasn't unusual in the fifties.

It wasn't until after I, the youngest, was born that my mother says she knew for sure her marriage wasn't going to be happily-ever-after. It took another decade for her to even consider doing anything about it. No one plans to repeat the mistakes their parents made.

But do we dare to consider that maybe mistakes aren't mistakes while they're happening? They're love that went too deep, too quickly. They're your soft spot for someone crying, or your deep surprise at finding that someone knows how to comfort you when *you* cry. They're physical passions you couldn't resist. It's only in retrospect, in the eyes of outsiders, that our misguided turns are written off as mistakes. Or we do it ourselves. We put a chapter of our lives into a box and label it: Too Young, or, Too Crazy. We flatten everything we know beneath a cartoon steamroller. We lose the smells, the shapes, the textures. We forget that even a love that goes wrong may hold its own brand of healing.

II

As Norma and I headed for the Cape, rain drenched the windshield. It was as if we were driving through the set of a low-budget movie, and some overzealous stagehand was dropping buckets of water onto our car.

"Do you think this is some kind of an omen?" Norma asked.

"The rain?"

"Every time we try to take a trip the weather turns. Maybe it's a sign that this relationship isn't meant to be."

My foot involuntarily tapped the brake, causing the car to lurch. Out of the corner of my eye I could see Norma flinch. I couldn't tell if it was the sudden movement that made her react, or if she was registering the impact her comment had on me. Could she mean what she had just said? Everything had been going so well.

"Last time, you were the one who said the blizzard was road trip weather," I said, trying not to sound hurt.

Norma smiled. "You were so funny that night. You were nervous, weren't you?" Our relationship was less than a year old, and already, reminiscing was one of our favorite activities. So I knew that even if Norma had at first meant to call our future into question, she had already changed her mind. Relieved, I joined in her instant nostalgia.

"Me? Nervous? You were the one who wouldn't even take your hat off to get into bed!"

"No, no. You were all serious and stiff." Norma squared her shoulders and pulled her chin in tight. "Like this," she said, and began to giggle. I pried my eyes from the highway to sneak a look at her impersonation of me. It was only a second, but it was just long enough to distract me from the traffic slowing in front of us.

"No!" I heard Norma yell, as she braced herself against the dashboard.

I slammed the brakes which caused the car to fishtail on the slick road. The sound of our car crashing into another was oddly distant and muffled beneath the sloshing sounds of falling rain. Before I even let myself look at the damage, I wanted desperately to undo it.

"It hurts, it hurts," I heard Norma cry. She was bent over, clutching her knee and wailing. There was no blood, no broken glass. I could breathe again. I pried Norma's hand from its grasp on her bare knee. The skin was red where it had bumped the dashboard. "You're okay," I said, hoping it was true. "Let's see you bend it."

There was a tapping on my window. A young man, probably our age, stood without a raincoat or hat, his long hair dripping onto the car. "You're okay, baby," I told Norma, before rolling the window down.

"What the hell is the matter with you? Look at my car!" His yellow Volkswagen bug was crumpled like a tin can.

"I'm really, really sorry," I said, hearing the ridiculous inadequacy of my words. It was only then that I remembered that I had been driving Norma's car. She'd be angry when the shock was over, I told myself. And that outweighed this stranger's wrath.

"She all right?" a police officer asked, pushing up against the window where the young man had been.

"Yes, sir. Mostly scared, I think."

Norma nodded, still sobbing. He asked to see my license and registration. I fumbled in Norma's glove compartment for the papers, while she stared out the windshield, rubbing her knee.

A tow truck brought us to an auto mechanic's shop. The rain stopped as quickly as it had started, and a hesitant glow of sunlight appeared over the tops of the scrub oak and pitch pine that defined the landscape. "I'm not insured for a second driver," Norma said, as we sat on a bench just inside the shop.

"Don't worry. I've got enough to cover it." I did. I had been saving money to buy a word processor. I had decided that it was time to start taking my writing more seriously.

The mechanic came out, wiping his hands on his thighs. "I bent that wheel rim back into place. Oughtta get you home, but then you should bring it in to someone, get a new one. I'm not saying that tire couldn't blow if you went over something just the right way." We had to have the alignment checked, and to fix the right fender, which was badly dented, he said.

"You're sure it's okay to drive now?"

"Well, I wouldn't go to California tonight. Especially not until you get those headlamps replaced."

I thanked him, and wrote out a check. "I guess we'd better go home and get all of this taken care of," I said to Norma as we walked out into the lot.

"No way," Norma protested, suddenly happy again. "We're on vacation. We'll worry about it when it's over."

"But Norm—" I couldn't tell if I was reeling from the sensation of skidding cars which kept replaying in my bones, or the sudden change in Norma's attitude.

"Forget it. The car still goes and we're almost there."

"But we should be talking to the insurance company and we don't have any headlights. Besides, I'd like someone to look at your knee."

"It's better. Just a little sore. And the insurance company isn't going anywhere. We can report the accident from a pay phone, and deal with the rest next week."

"And the lights?"

"If we hurry we'll get there before night. We won't need them." Norma didn't wait for an answer. She was already opening the car door and entering the passenger side.

"Slide over," I said. "You're driving."

"I want you to drive."

"Norma, I'm shaking like a leaf. That scared me to death."

"You seem perfectly calm. I can't get over how well you handled everything."

I held out my hand. "See, like a leaf. You drive." The sun was starting to sink. It was probably dinnertime already. We had both left work early and had planned to be on the beach by now. "Besides, how can you trust me after what just happened?"

"I trust you. Come on, get in."

I sat behind the wheel—buoyed by Norma's trust or too tired to argue, I don't remember which. In any case we had an hour's drive to the hotel, and I wanted to beat the sunset so we wouldn't end up stranded in the dark with no lights, on top of everything else.

"It's like getting back on the horse," Norma said as I fastened my seat belt and turned the ignition.

"I know all about that. When I was twelve I fell off a horse at summer camp."

"And . . ."

"I never rode again."

She gave me a self-satisfied smile and crossed her arms over her chest.

I drove slowly, with Norma coaxing me forward, reminding me to breathe deeply and reassuring me that she trusted me completely. Finally, I pulled in front of our hotel. The sound of the parking lot gravel crunching under out tires was music to my ears. Norma gave me a hug. "See, now aren't you proud of yourself? You did it!" We left the battered car in the lot and found our room at the top of a well-worn flight of stairs. I lay across the four-poster bed, staring at the pale pink ceiling, while Norma soaked in the claw-footed bathtub. When she emerged, wrapped in her terry robe, she sat behind my head and massaged my temples. "Everything's okay now. Don't think about the car, or the insurance. No one was hurt and we're on vacation."

"I'm trying. I'm just shaken up. I keep hearing that crunch the cars made when they hit."

"Stay right there," Norma said, and fished around in the knapsack she used for luggage in search of something. She pulled out a sketch pad and a tin decorated with little calico cats. "Let's draw," she said, as she popped the lid off the tin and took out a handful of watercolor crayons.

"Draw?"

"Yeah. Draw what you're feeling. Draw anything."

I slid off the bed and sat on the floor facing Norma, the crayons heaped between us. "Draw a picture of yourself, and how you're feeling," she suggested.

I took out a peach-colored crayon and began to outline a face. Norma stepped behind me and reached over my shoulder. "Let me show you," she said, crouching down. She replaced my crayon with a cornflower blue one and moved my hand in wide arcs across the paper, filling the whiteness with every sweep of motion. "Be bold. Start with colors. Later you can fill in the lines. Think of light and shade, not shape," she said.

My hand took over, blending colors, bearing down hard, then lightening to make quick, confident strokes. I changed colors instinctively, and when I was nearly finished, I pulled out a magenta crayon and outlined a face. The woman I had drawn was colored in shades of blue and green water. Her eyes were hot red, and her mouth was pressed shut.

"I love the wild colors," Norma said. She slid her paper across to me. "I drew you, too." In her picture I was seated as I was, curled over my own piece of paper. But instead of the paper, Norma had drawn an ocean. There were diamonds falling from my eyes into the water. The edges of my brown hair glittered, as if more gems had fallen onto me from the sky. "It's about how your tears are blessings, and your feelings make you beautiful," she said.

I had never thought of feelings as beautiful. Anger was the monstrous red of my father's rages. Fear was cold, sharp, and familiar. Sadness, frustration, and hurt were scribbled balls of gray that blurred the landscape. But now, my tears felt clear and clean and welcome; crying was a joyous relief.

It was too late to go out, and besides, we didn't want to. We climbed into bed, our colors spilled across the rag wool rug beneath us. I forgot the car crash and everything else, except our whole, happy bodies. I fell asleep that night feeling loved as I never had before.

Perhaps it was because this feeling of contentment seemed so new to me that I thought back to a long-ago visit from my father's parents. Because they lived half the year in Maine and half in Florida, we saw them only about four times a year. My grandmother must have just entered the kitchen a few steps in front of my grandfather, who would have been carrying in their suitcases. There was a plate full of ruggalach on the kitchen table, and the smell of hot coffee from the Mr. Coffee on the counter filled the house as it always did on the evenings when we waited for them to arrive from the airport. I loved my grandmother. She had that clean sweet smell of medicine about her, and her lipstick-red mouth burst into a smile whenever she caught sight of me. I loved that she baked a special batch of tollhouse chocolate chip cookies for me the way I liked them: without the chips, but with plenty of crushed walnuts in their stead. I loved that she knew songs and poems by heart, and I loved the way she pursed her mouth when she recited. But when she asked me for a hug that night, I could not move my arms. I had grown as cold and square as the gleaming white refrigerator that loomed at my back. I did manage to dispatch a kiss, however, with mechanical efficiency.

Why had this image stuck with me all these years? Why had this become my personal proof that I had a childhood void of affection? It can't have been that bleak, I told myself. And I searched my memory for moments when there was physical warmth between members of my household. My parents must have clasped hands, or at least exchanged warm knowing glances in my presence. There must have been loving truces in the shoving and shouting matches between my sister, brother, and myself. Maybe my memory was flawed. Maybe my parents did lounge in each other's arms, she leaning back into his embrace while they watched television in the den, or for a moment in the kitchen after the last dinner plate was dried and put away. But I couldn't remember it. And I did remember the way my body froze when my grandmother reached out her arms to me, and I wanted to retreat into the crisp warmth of her belted blue raincoat. I wanted to hug her. I simply didn't know how.

In the morning Norma and I woke, and set about filling our week's vacation with bicycle rides in the dunes, walks to the beach, and dinners in crowded cafés along Commercial Street. We snuck off to buy each other gifts of postcards, dresses, and headbands. We lay on the beach with the ocean before us and dunes at our back. At night, we made love on the beach, lulled by the sound of the waves. It was then that we decided to live together. We fantasized about an apartment with a painting studio for Norma and a writing room for me.

"And a room for the baby," Norma said.

"Of course," I agreed, not wanting to spoil the perfection of the moment. But just as quickly, I pushed the thought of babies aside.

That night Norma fell asleep with her head on my shoulder. I dreamed that we were living together. I was sitting at a desk, typing. There was a baby sleeping in a Snugli on my chest. Even in the dream I was surprised that it felt right to be weighted down like that.

But in the morning my certainty burned away. When Norma spoke of babies I convinced myself that this idea of hers would be a fleeting one and that she would come to her senses. But her determination only increased. In the months that followed she talked about what she would name the baby, and picked up infant clothes she found at tag sales. "We're too young to start having babies," I'd argue. "By the time my mother was twenty-three she had two," Norma countered. "We don't have enough money," I said. Norma was going to go to UMass on a fellowship and I was making under ten thousand a year at the health food store. "People with a lot less money have children all the time," Norma said. "But we haven't even been together for a year. Don't you think we should give our relationship more time before we take on such a big challenge?" Norma wouldn't hear of it. "Straight couples have babies right away. Half the time brides are pregnant at the altar." I couldn't think of a response.

When I was about ten years old I walked into my older sister's bedroom while my mother was explaining the facts of life. "You might as well hear this, too," my mother said. She had a box of sanitary napkins on her lap and was giving a dry speech about sperm and eggs, and what a mommy and daddy do when they love each other very much. In the end that speech explained very little to me.

Despite my mother's preparatory talk, womanhood caught me off guard. I first discovered my period in a bathroom stall during the six-minute break between seventh-grade English and social studies. My body, I realized with a shock, was preparing itself for motherhood.

I associated having babies with sticky jelly prints on the refrigerator and frustrated aspirations. A straight-A student in eighth grade, I worked for a C in typing because I feared that if I memorized the q-w-e-r-t-y alphabet, I could only become a secretary. On similar grounds I refused to learn how to use the washing machine or dishwasher. No one would want a wife who couldn't do housework, I reasoned. I wouldn't put so much as a toe onto the path of womanhood, which I assumed would inevitably lead to babies. The way I saw it then, the fewer female skills I possessed, the less likely I would be to land in any of the female traps as I had naively identified them: Wife, Mother, or Secretary. I wanted to be something as yet undefined, but definitely different. By the time I fell in love with a woman at college, I had learned that women could be more than just wives. I admired female writers such as Virginia Woolf, the Brontë sisters, and Emily Dickinson. None, I discovered, had ever had children. The trade-off seemed implicit.

Later I would find my maternal grandmother's diary. In 1928, at the age of nineteen and with a constant stream of gentleman callers, Frances Abrams had written: "Love just leads to marriage and children and I don't want anything to do with that."

I met Louise in the cafeteria on my first day of college. We were both in the line for vegetarian entrees, and while we waited for the metal tub to be refilled with meatless lasagna, I invited her to share a table. Louise was a good four inches taller than me. Her long straight hair was casually combed. I instantly began a *Seventeen*-style makeover for her in my mind. She should trim those split ends for starters, and buy a good conditioner. A cut with bangs might help break up the excessive length of her face. I wasn't one for makeup, but even I could see that a little eye shadow wouldn't hurt in her case. It would accentuate her best feature, her hazel eyes. As for clothing, the bulky chamois shirt she was wearing did nothing for her figure, which I could hardly make out beneath it. And judging from the dollops of sour cream she'd heaped on her potato, I guessed either she didn't care about her weight, or the shirt was meant to hide it.

We set our trays on a table overlooking the apple orchards which were part of the rural campus. The minute Louise's eyes rested on me I felt weightless and insufficient in my India-print cotton skirt and white T-shirt. For some reason, before we even finished eating our dinner, I no longer believed that Louise was the one who needed a makeover. I longed to be as solid and unself-conscious as she was. I wished I could take a second helping of dessert with the genuine enthusiasm that she did, but I couldn't curb my habit of ticking off the number of calories each spoonful would cost me.

Louise and I talked about everything that evening, or so it seemed. We compared notes on religion and discovered that we both believed spirit existed in nature more than in churches or synagogues. We both called ourselves feminists, and studied the utopian visions of Marge Piercy, Ursula K. LeGuin, and Charlotte Perkins Gilman. I told her about my boyfriend back home, and she, for a reason I didn't yet understand, began talking about a camping trip she'd taken with her best girlfriend in high school.

After dinner we took a walk across the school's playing fields, toward the woods at the far edge. "Look, there's a hiking trail," Louise said, leading the way. To my suburban eyes the woods looked deep and threatening.

"We'd better not, it's getting late."

"Oh, we'll be back before dark," Louise promised.

One evening, as I sat cross-legged on the single bed in Louise's dorm room, I spied, pinned to her bulletin board, a button with interlocking women symbols. My naiveté came crashing in on me. The girlfriend Louise had talked about at dinner had been her lover. How obvious. What was less apparent to me was why my first reaction was to feel jealous.

"You're a lesbian," I said, sounding more matter-of-fact than I would have believed possible.

"Of course," Louise said. "Didn't you know?" If I'd managed to sound unperturbed with my question, she sounded downright nonchalant with her reply. "What about you?" she asked.

"I told you," I said impatiently, "I have a boyfriend."

"So?"

"So . . . of course not!" Now it was all I could do not to shriek.

"Of course not?" Louise's smile unnerved me.

"Do I seem like a lesbian?"

"What does a lesbian *seem* like?" Louise was sitting on the floor, leaning back against a set of desk drawers, her elbows resting on her knees.

"Well, they smoke cigarettes, drink beer, and play pool."

Louise shook her head. "How can you say that?"

"You're the one who accused me of being a lesbian."

"Listen to yourself, Nancy. I didn't *accuse* you. We're not talking about a crime."

What were we talking about, and why? Why wasn't I running from the room? Why didn't I just make another friend? "I'm sorry," I said instead. "I don't know why I said those things. But I really am straight, you know."

That weekend Louise went home to visit her girlfriend, and my boyfriend came up to visit me. At night while he held me I dreamed that Louise and I were silver gulls soaring through the sky. I tried to graft the feelings I was having for Louise onto my boyfriend. I wondered why I'd never felt so strongly about him.

When Louise came back to campus I told her I needed to talk to her. We took a walk through the woods but I couldn't bring myself to tell her my feelings. It was getting dark and cold, and Louise hadn't brought her gloves. She curled her hands into little balls and pulled the sleeves of her sweater down over them. "Here," I said, holding my hands out. I pulled my gloves off one at a time, and took Louise's cold hands between mine. After I'd rubbed them warm again I meant to hand her my gloves. Instead, I just kept holding her.

A few months later I called my mother from the pay phone in the basement of my dormitory to announce that I was in love. "Her name's Louise," I said.

"Isn't Louise your friend that I met during parents' weekend?" my mother replied. "She seems like a lovely girl."

Having seen my mother wake up to feminism after her divorce some four years earlier and transform herself from a doting housewife to a radical rabble-rouser, I was a lot less surprised by her reaction than my friends were when they asked how she had taken the news. (My boyfriend at the time—known for his dry wit—was almost as calm. "Well, I guess this changes the nature of our relationship," he said.) But my mother wasn't all smiles over my newly found sexuality. "The only thing that makes me uncomfortable about this," she said after some thought, "is that you'll miss out on having children." I didn't tell her just then that this was a relief to me.

Louise and I were lovers for a year, until I took a semester off to travel across the country alone. Louise still says she didn't realize that when we said good-bye we were breaking up for good. But I knew that we were. That first love came on me with such supernormal force, it terrified me. Emotions had always seemed to elude me, but now that I'd let love through, anger and pain came with it. I said I was traveling to test my wings, but I knew I was running away. I was trying to put as much distance between myself and the source of my feelings as I could; three thousand miles before I finally hit ocean. Finally I realized there was no running away, and turned around and came back. By then Louise had found someone new.

III

The apartment Norma and I rented was too small for all our dreams. We made one bedroom into Norma's studio, covering the wood floors with paint-splattered tarps. We wedged my writing desk into the second bedroom, with a futon on the floor and crates stacked for shelves because we had no bureau. The small living room doubled as a dining room, since the kitchen was too small to hold a table. Ahab would have to stay inside because the lease Norma convinced me to sign forbade pets. She thought that if the cat was inside, no one would ever know we were harboring an illegal tenant. So I built a climbing structure for him in the living room, hoping it would keep him entertained. Instead he ignored it, and the wooden monstrosity just added to the clutter of the room.

One night I came home to find Norma huddled by the living room window, wrapped in her bathrobe. She clutched her head in her hands as if her neck was too weak to hold it up for her. Her back heaved up and down.

"What is it?" I crouched down on the floor beside Norma, and tried to take her hand in mine, but I couldn't pry her fingers from the side of her head. "What happened?"

"I just want to die. Just let me die," she wailed.

"Baby, baby, it's okay. Tell me what happened."

"You'll hate me," she said. "You'll leave."

"I'm not going anywhere," I said. When I pulled her fingers back, they loosened easily. She had been hiding a bald patch the size of a fist she had shaved above her left ear. "Now, that's a funny haircut," I said, trying not to sound horrified. "Are you going to start a new trend?"

Norma choked on a sob. She fell into my arms and I rocked her. "I don't know why I did it," she said. She began talking about her childhood, telling me how chaotic her household was, and how tempers would flare at unexpected moments. She talked about never feeling in control. "I guess sometimes I do these crazy things just to prove that I'm in charge now," she said. I turned off the lamp over our heads. Maybe I just didn't want to see too much.

Norma always looked particularly beautiful when she woke the day after one of her crises. On this morning she had tied a satin scarf around her head, making her look like a bright-eyed gypsy. We decided to make this a special day. We would drive to the mountains, and Norma could make all of the decisions: where we would stop, what we would eat, what station we would listen to on the radio. That way, she could feel in control without having to do anything she would regret. Later, she said that was the best day she'd ever spent.

But it wasn't enough. Another night, as we were getting into bed, I noticed red streaks down Norma's back. I ran my finger across them but she pulled away. "I must have made the shower too hot," she said.

In those early months when we lived together I would sometimes wake to find Norma's side of the bed empty, and I would hear the sound of water rushing in the bathroom. At first I assumed she was washing her face, and was coming right back to bed. I'd go back to sleep and forget to give it any more thought. But one night I couldn't fall back asleep, and the water kept streaming and slapping. Maybe she was taking a shower. But why would she be doing that at three in the morning? I got out of bed and knocked on the bathroom door. I thought I heard Norma coughing.

"Hey, are you okay in there?"

The water stopped. There was silence. "I'll be right out," Norma called.

When I asked what she had been doing in there for so long, she said it was nothing, she was just using the bathroom. Her tone of voice didn't invite further questioning.

As I lay awake trying to put the pieces together, I remembered a friend in high school who ended up being hospitalized for bulimia. In the morning I asked Norma if she were having a problem with food. I told her I suspected she had been throwing up last night.

"Of course not," Norma protested, looking so disgusted that for a moment I believed her. "I was just washing up."

"In the middle of the night?"

"I wasn't throwing up." Norma buttered the bagel she had just toasted and began to search the refrigerator for some orange juice.

Her tone of voice and her cold, precise movements frightened me. But I persisted. I wanted to get to the bottom of this. "Okay, but if you were, if there is a problem . . ."

Norma slammed the refrigerator door shut, but her words came out calmly. "You're right. Now are you happy? Food is the only thing I can control in this world. It's all I have that's mine."

We sat at the kitchen table, each taking bites of the bagel she had set between us on a paper towel. I told her about my high school friend. Norma seemed to know all about the condition, and even agreed when I suggested she see a therapist.

"To tell you the truth I've considered calling a psychiatrist," Norma said.

"A therapist would probably be less expensive, and they're just as helpful," I offered.

"But therapists can't give you something, you know, medicine to make you feel better." Norma's voice was getting smaller and smaller, so that now she sounded like a little girl.

"You don't need drugs. You just need someone to talk to, someone who knows how to help you deal with your feelings."

"Some people need more than that. Some people need to be institutionalized for a while." Norma's face was shifting again, the parts seemed to slide slightly up, down, left and right. A chill ran through me. I wondered if she were really as sick as she claimed to be. But I didn't let myself stop there. I pulled us both back up with my optimistic insistence. "No, Norma," I said. "You just need a little help, and maybe some rest. But you can do it all right here without men in white jackets and Thorazine. I know you feel pretty bad right now, but you're going to feel better. I promise."

"Really?" Norma looked as though she believed me. "How do you know?"

"Because I've felt the way you do now. I've wanted to hurt myself too. That's why I used to drink so much—to dull the pain."

It hadn't been that long ago. My first year in college I began therapy. The emotions of coming out and the process of confronting the tangle of myths my family had woven were all too much for me to handle. I remembered how my first girlfriend used to let me cry in her arms all night long. She stood by me through therapy and she loved me through a year of the most intense self-searching and growth I could imagine possible. Finally, I began to see a clearing in the gray swirl of depression, confusion, and misguided emotions. I had to admit that part of my attraction to Norma was that as bad as they were, my problems paled in comparison with hers. With her, I felt more stable, more sure than I really was.

I wanted to be there for Norma the way Louise had been there for me. Norma could cry into my strong arms. I would stay with her through all of the sadness. She would feel better, and I could help.

I felt this was my duty. I felt I owed it—to someone.

Early autumn sunshine peered through the window and warmed our faces and bare feet.

"I'm going to start charting my cycle this month," Norma announced, as we cuddled on the futon folded against the living room wall. "I need to know if you're with me on this or not."

Had Norma not pushed, I might never have made a decision as to whether or not I was ready to become a parent. Or, maybe I would have decided that I simply was not. But she insisted on an answer and she insisted on promptness.

Our discussions on the subject had been going on for months. We argued about whether to have a baby while we took walks along the Charles. We argued about it at night in bed. We argued seated on the white leather couch of the couples counselor Norma's new therapist had recommended that we see.

The counselor was in Norma's camp. "If Norma wants to have a baby so badly, there's nothing you can do to stop her," she told me. I wondered whether this was what marriage counselors tell husbands who are reluctant to become fathers. But husbands at least have a little more control than I did when it comes to the mechanics of starting a family.

But that afternoon Norma insisted that it was time to decide. If she was going to get pregnant it would take a long time. We'd have to research the ins and outs of artificial insemination, find a donor or sperm bank, and then wait like any other couple for the pregnancy to take. She laid down her ultimatum: the baby or the relationship. In that case, I said, I would move out. And I began to cry.

I didn't want to end our relationship, but I felt trapped. How could you leave someone while you were still in love? It seemed unreasonable. And if I loved Norma so much, how could I deny her the opportunity to fulfill her dream? Somehow it didn't occur to me at that time that if she loved me, she could compromise, too. At least we could have waited.

Instead, the next day I told her I would give it a try. I would become a mother.

My mother started out like everybody else's in our suburban Long Island neighborhood. PTA meetings, Jell-O molds, cocktail parties for father's associates. And I, her youngest, was just the daughter she expected. I charmed my teachers, served hors d'oeuvres to her guests, and wore the dresses and ribbons she bought me.

But then it happened. She changed. We changed.

My mother went back to school when I was in sixth grade, the same year I observed the first sign that my body had a life of its own and that its will had become much stronger than mine. I stood in front of my bedroom mirror naked and appalled. Somewhere I learned to be ashamed, not proud, of what was happening.

At about the same time I began to change on the outside, she was changing from within.

Before then my mother seemed to fit into a world where women wore lime-green golf skirts, shopped at Bloomingdale's, and had a "girl" who came in once a week to clean. But from what she says now, nothing could be worse than living out that cliché. "Not having money is far preferable to having it under those circumstances," she told me recently when I was brooding over my bank balance and wishing I could have some of the luxuries she did at my age. Her "lifestyle choice" came with its own compromises: submitting to the rule of a demanding husband, submitting to the rules of a society that demeaned women by relegating them to the world of the trivial.

My mother had gotten a marriage certificate instead of a diploma. She married my father after her junior year in college, the summer she had planned to travel abroad with friends.

Whatever her dreams of achievement may have been, her job as a young wife and my mother was to be prettier than all the other mothers, to help us with our homework, and to have dinner ready on time so my father would have no reason to yell. As far as I was concerned then, that was enough. The woman she had been before she married—and the woman she might become beyond her marriage—were equally alien to me.

I remember coming up the kitchen stairs after fourth grade one day, and although I don't remember what I was saying, I know that I was demanding something unreasonable of her. She stood at the top of the flight looking down at me. "Have you ever stopped to think that I'm a person, too?" she fumed. I hadn't. The light shifted at that moment, as if the sun had gathered its strength. My mother was transformed for me, her face came into focus. But of course for her it wasn't a sudden transformation. She had been growing up, just as I had been, slowly.

Within a year or two, she had decided to go back to school, to finish up that prenuptial promise to herself. Deciding to study history was my mother's way of putting an end to the charade her marriage had become. My father worked long hours, often returning home after I had already gone to bed. My mother immersed herself in her schoolbooks, and went with her new university friends to lectures and political marches that my father disapproved of. But still, when there was a graduation or bar mitzvah to attend we all pulled together and behaved like a happy family. It's just that I was still too young to have figured out that we were acting.

But then the jig was up. One afternoon I returned home from sixth grade anticipating Hawaiian Punch and Devil Dogs served on the small round table in the blue and white kitchen. Instead I found *him* there. Red hair exploding to his shoulders, his face a jungle of beard and glasses. "What is *that?*" I demanded.

My mother knew everything my question implied. But she answered politely, ignoring my choice of pronoun. "This is Pat, he's my professor at school." He would also become her lover and—more easily than I would have expected—my friend.

The next year I had a stomachache that turned out to be menstrual cramps, and childhood was gone.

What was lost in all of this was a time of order and predictability. Get up. Wash, brush, dress. My seat at the dinner table. Drying the dishes: my chore afterward. A mother at home, a father at work. Sister in the small bedroom to the right. Brother in the more spacious room on the left. This order was comfort then. Its dissolution had the power of an earthquake—something large and unstoppable that will never let the landscape revert to a familiar shape.

When I was in junior high, my mother bought a subscription to *Ms.* magazine. The word "Ms." had just been coined. It was an ugly word, hard, like the unkempt women pictured on the magazine's pages. Catching a glimpse of that magazine on my mother's bureau, I felt almost as ashamed as I had been when I found a *Playboy* in my grandfather's study. Strong and ugly or kitten-soft and voluptuous: I was sickened by my options.

That summer my parents announced they were getting a divorce. The sun was shining on the patio stones which were keeping my bare feet warm. I couldn't help wondering how the world had so easily deceived me.

My father's leaving was a slow, draw-out process. It started well before the announcement. I remember him teasing me: "Do you ever wonder if your mother and I are actually one person? Think about it: You never see us both at the same time, do you?"

The first thing we tried to do together as a broken family was to see my brother, Todd, off to college. My father, who had moved into a one-bedroom condominium thirty miles east on the highway, came back to the house for the event. There was a screaming fight in the driveway as we loaded into the station wagon—my sister, Julia, slammed back into the house, refusing her consent in the family's silent pact to pretend nothing had changed.

I, on the other hand, was in no rush to face the facts. When friends visited on weekends, I said my father had gone to work or that he was away on a business trip. In eighth grade my best friend and I agreed to exchange our deepest, darkest secrets.

Hers was that she'd let her boyfriend put his hands down her pants. This revelation seemed trivial to me. I told her my parents were divorced. I think she felt cheated, too.

My mother insisted on her independence. She refused to take alimony payments from my father, and for the first time they wouldn't accept our charge at Bloomingdale's, or anyplace else. We were shopping in Lord & Taylor one evening, as we often had before. Only this time, in the dressing room my mother checked the prices of the sweaters we'd just tried on. "Sorry," she said, "they're much too expensive." My sister and I pulled our shirts back on without a word. Then my mother's face lit up. "Let's just take them," she said. "You mean steal?" my sister asked. "Let's," my mother said. It was a giddy moment in which we simultaneously acknowledged our shift in economic standing and decided it could be an adventure rather than a sentence. It was the moment when I knew we'd stepped over the line between insiders and outsiders. I felt the grief of banishment, and the possibilities of freedom that come with being cast out. But the moment passed, and consequences and right and wrong reordered themselves. We handed the sweaters back to the salesgirl, and left the store.

When I entered ninth grade my sister left for college and I made a new friend. Joanie was the only girl my age I knew of whose parents were divorced, too. She was also my only friend who lived in an apartment, not a house.

She and her brothers lived with their mother in a run-down complex on the main drag through town. We smoked pot in her living room even when her mother was home. But her mother never emerged from the darkened bedroom where she seemed to be always getting over a hangover or creating one. The next summer Joanie moved away, and my mother sold our house. It had become too expensive for her, and too empty for me. She found us an apartment. I recognized it immediately. It was Joanie's. My mother took Joanie's mother's bedroom. I slept in the one Joanie's brothers had shared. I knew they had hidden a litter of kittens in the closet of that room, and that their mother never even suspected they were in the house. We had a lot of cleaning to do.

When I was in high school my mother stayed out far later than I did on weekends, so naturally our apartment was the place to hang out. The parties were tame, though. We drank some beer, made out some. Mostly we talked, watched television, and made messes in the kitchen. When we went to someone else's house one of the boys would walk me home and come inside with me until the emptiness of the rooms stopped thudding so loudly.

Yellow legal pads covered with notes for my mother's Ph.D. dissertation spread across the dining room table. Weeknights, I fell asleep to the tapping sound of typewriter keys. Pat, no longer my mother's professor but still her lover, invited me to join his college students for discussions and protest rallies. He introduced me to my first real boyfriend, a guy who owned a motorcycle and a beat-up Nova with a handmade bumper sticker Scotch-taped to the rear window that read "Sandinista."

My father had always said how alike my mother and I were. "Look at them, Big Sue and Little Sue," he'd say as we sat side by side watching television or reading. It was a phrase that used to fill him with pride. Now my mother and I were the same size in everything, and when my father would visit he'd be more likely to say, in a voice mixed with wonder and something less glad, "Look at you. Just like your mother."

As soon as I agreed to be a mother, Norma proposed we start a savings account. This was to be our first show of commitment to the plan. We would deposit ten dollars each week, guaranteeing that by the time the baby was born we would have saved at least five hundred dollars. After we left the bank Norma ducked into a florist shop and came out with a single red rose. "Happy Mothers' Day," she said, handing me the flower.

My friend Sam was shocked when I told her I'd decided to become a parent. "What about your feelings about bringing more children into this world?"

"Norma's going to do this with or without me. Don't you think I should at least be supportive?" I felt I couldn't tell Sam about the abortion, Norma's secret reason for wanting this baby so quickly, and so desperately.

"Supportive is what you are if your lover wants to apply for a better job, or come out to her parents. If you don't want a baby, you don't agree to have one just to be helpful. A child is for keeps."

"I know that."

"What about your own goals and plans? How supportive is Norma being of those by insisting on having a baby so soon?"

"Look, Sam, I didn't expect you to understand, but this is between Norma and me. Can't you just be a little happy for us?"

All I could do was end the conversation. I couldn't convince either of us that what I was doing was right. But maybe it wasn't wrong.

After all, Norma's way of doing things often netted happy surprises. Like the day she talked me out of doing errands, and we spent all afternoon making sculptures out of Fimo clay instead. Or the time we decided to go to California for a week on a whim even though we couldn't really afford it. Somehow everything seemed to work out. It had so far, anyway. Maybe this would too.

"What kind of a mother do you think Norma would make?" Sam asked.

I was still thinking about Norma's colorful, playful side when I answered. "I think she'd be a blast to have as a mother. Besides, I'll be like the father. I'll be there to balance things out."

Sam nodded. I thought I had convinced her. In any case, I was doing a good job of convincing myself. The truth was, I was becoming increasingly dissatisfied with my life. The thought of change gave me hope. I was bored with my job, had no ambitions or plans to change it, and had already had what I considered to be more than my share of unsuccessful relationships. Painful togetherness or freedom through divorce was the choice of options my own family taught me. Maybe stress was the price one had to pay to endure a long-term partnership, I reasoned. In spite of everything, I didn't want to give up the way my parents had. My only choice, I thought, was to ride out the bumps and settle for security, if not total happiness.

Norma decided that since I was such a reluctant parent-to-be, I might need some training. She enlisted the help of a friend who had had a baby as a single woman through artificial insemination. This new mother needed help with her infant, and I needed help learning about the joys of motherhood. So we volunteered to baby-sit for little Ava on Sunday afternoons. "Operation Mommy" was underway.

The baby was small and pink and full of smiles and endearing cooing sounds. I learned to change her diaper, give her a bottle, and strap her into a baby backpack so we could go out for walks.

Something inside me softened. I started asking friends if they knew a man who would donate sperm for us. I went with Norma to a meeting of lesbians who were considering motherhood. I still had my doubts, and my case of baby fever was fed by a very low flame compared with the inferno that fueled Norma's desires. But it was there nonetheless, burning gently in my heart, warming me to the sight of bassinets and baby carriages—sights that had once made me squirm.

September marked two new beginnings. Norma began graduate school and she began preparing to get pregnant.

Perhaps in another culture, in another time and circumstance, we'd have readied ourselves to make a baby by offering prayers to Cybele, Dagon, Fortuna, or any other god or goddess of fertility. We might have carved a statue of Aku'aba and rubbed her high stone forehead with our thumbs. We might have planted myrtle, cypress, or pine as offerings to Astarte, or lit candles or even Beltane fires. But I doubt those gods and goddesses had powers over women who didn't also worship the phallus, or at least employ one. Besides, ours were more pragmatic times. And despite the Virgin Mary's good fortune to conceive, there's only one God now, and we didn't expect His help.

Instead, Norma bought a basal body thermometer which would show the minute lurch of her body's temperature caused by the activity of her luteinizing hormones. This would indicate when ovulation occurred. She drew a chart on graph paper to study the pattern of her readiness to conceive. Along the top she numbered the days of the month, along the vertical she wrote: "Temperature." She taped this page above her side of the bed and began to plot. Upon waking, even before she spoke a word, Norma would pop the thermometer into her mouth, read the results, and record them on her chart.

We should have posted a chart on my side of the bed, too. Mine would track my emotional readiness to become a parent. But while Norma's graph evolved into a tidy row of peaks and valleys, mine would have resembled a child's scrawl. My emotions about becoming a parent didn't follow anything like the regular hormonal rhythms of Norma's body.

For one thing, Norma's chart in and of itself caused my feelings to short-circuit. It represented the first tangible sign that she was dead serious about having a baby. The money in the bank account could always be spent on a vacation if we changed our minds, I reasoned. But there was no reason to plot one's basal body temperature except to become pregnant. Some days I found myself clinging to strange hopes, like perhaps at her annual checkup the doctor would find some medical reason that Norma could not get pregnant. On other days, I would see a small child in a stroller and couldn't wait for us to have our own. Maybe Norma would have twins, one for each of us to take care of. One day I would pray that Norma would be one of those women who took years to get pregnant, and the next I would reassure myself that her previous pregnancy, the one that led to her abortion, proved she was abundantly fertile.

Meanwhile, Norma ovulated like clockwork. In fact, her hormonal rhythms seemed to be the most regular aspect of her life.

That winter, on our first anniversary, Norma and I went out dancing at a club in Boston. I had to work myself into a celebratory mood as I'd been feeling run-down and had a sore throat that had been hanging on for weeks. As the night wore on Norma and I sipped our beers and talked about everything, just as we had on our first date a year before.

Now that Norma was in therapy, she was more open than ever about discussing her childhood. She'd start out in a lilting tone of voice, as if about to recount a charming tale. But the stories were never happy ones. Although she grew up in a well-to-do family, there was nothing secure about her childhood. It was as though she'd been raised in a gilded mansion with no doors or windows to keep trouble out. She'd begin the story of an outing to the zoo which would end in a description of one of her parents' bitter fights. She'd describe a witty, debonair friend of the family whom she called Uncle, and end by explaining that he had molested her. There was a babysitter who had been her favorite, until the night he chased her and her older brother, Eli, around the living room with a kitchen knife threatening to kill them—and worse if they told their parents. It got to the point where any mention of Norma's past would make me flinch in anticipation of another tale of quiet horror.

"Uncle and I used to dance just like this," Norma told me as we swayed to a slow song. I felt as though the joy of our celebration had suddenly been spilled. Norma kept talking, but I was having a hard time listening.

My sore throat did not go away. At work I began to dread the groaning noise that announced the arrival of the delivery truck. When I heard the semi rumble around the corner, I knew there would soon be twenty-five-pound bags of granola and five-gallon buckets of tofu and molasses to haul. Normally I would look forward to a miniworkout in the middle of my routine. But now I found myself taking advantage of my status as manager and changed the rules so that I was no longer responsible for checking in deliveries.

Smaller and smaller tasks became difficult. I couldn't keep up with my karate workouts. I stopped swimming at the YMCA on weekends. Some days I couldn't walk two blocks without needing to sit down. I used two hands to roll down my car window.

I went to several doctors, but none could find anything wrong. An allergy specialist determined that just about everything in the environment, from dust to cats to oranges, was making me sick. I discounted his diagnosis and didn't buy the hundreds of dollars' worth of pills and vitamins he prescribed. I read about the "yuppie flu," and asked another doctor if that could be what I had. Even if it were, she told me, there was nothing I could do about it. There was no test for it and no cure, she said.

Whatever it was, it kept me exhausted and discouraged. I still wonder if it wasn't part of the reason I didn't have the strength to resist more effectively when things began to move more quickly that spring.

In May, I overheard Norma on the telephone with a friend from college. She was asking if she could get her old boyfriend Glen's phone number.

"Why are you trying to track down Glen all of a sudden?" I asked.

"Sperm," she said.

Chances

I worry that you will find your beginnings marred. Certainly you will meet people who were the result of something that went on in a petri dish, in a laboratory, or on the crackling paper of a doctor's examining table. I want to tell you that you are not like them. That your beginnings were not so sterile.

And yet, against my will I believe there is a proper way to conceive a child. The most important thing, I find when I examine this prejudice, is that at the moment new life is prodded into being, there should be no air between the parties involved. The passage of sperm to egg should be achieved in warmth and wet and darkness.

But that wasn't at all how it happened for us. There were vast cubic miles of cold New England air between our donor, the host of the invisible fish—and Norma, into whose womb they would swim.

Your warm skin, moist mouth, strong bones, and blood—as full of life as any other child's—all exist in protest to my narrow notions of the proper recipe for making a baby.

I

Karla Fischer came to the store at least once a week and filled her basket with jars of organic baby food, Nature-O's cereal, and sweetened soy milk. She was my age, and her baby was one year old. I'd met Karla when she was pregnant. She was a vegan, she explained, and didn't eat any animal products, including milk and eggs. So she asked me what nondairy foods I could recommend that were high in calcium. I helped her load her basket with bunches of kale, broccoli, and bags of sesame seeds.

On this afternoon, Karla hoisted her groceries onto the check-out counter while her son dozed in the baby backpack she wore. I slid jars past the register and punched in the prices. "You always seem so content," I said. "Being a mother suits you, doesn't it?"

Karla's porcelain-white cheeks became drenched in rose, her eyes glinted. "Having a baby changed our lives forever," she said. "David and I wanted this little guy more than anything." As if she couldn't resist, she reached behind to stroke the baby's delicate head. "It's great. You should definitely try it."

I bagged Karla's groceries and said good-bye. Norma had called earlier that day to say our friend Marcia had found a donor for us. We would inseminate that month.

I can't count the number of times people have asked me, on hearing that I had a baby with another woman, how exactly she was conceived. When I'm feeling strong I tell them that it's a private matter. When I'm feeling facetious I wonder what would happen if I asked exactly how *their* children were conceived: Who was on top that night? Did they do anything kinky? Most of the time I simply say, "A.I.: artificial insemination," and I try to end the interrogation there. Of course the real story is much more interesting than that.

Norma and I laughed as she plucked the jar of artichoke hearts off the supermarket shelf. That night we ate the tight-wound leaves with special pleasure, having purchased them with an unusual purpose in mind. We needed a low glass container in which to transport the sperm. The ideal jar would be shallow with a wide opening. These proportions would make it easier on the man who would help us, and on me when I would suck up the slight contents with my syringe (needle removed, of course), careful not to lose a drop between jar and womb.

There was intense concentration broken by fits of hilarity as I tested my instruments at the kitchen sink. I deposited a quarter inch of Paul Newman's salad dressing in the bottom of the jar and lined up the syringe alongside the insemination tool of lesbian lore: the turkey baster. I was thus prepared for the squirt test. I filled each instrument, then took two backward paces. I shot streams of Italian dressing across the kitchen in order to measure which method produced the farthest reach. The winner, without question, was the syringe. In the bargain, I impressed Norma with my scientific approach.

But filling the jar with salad dressing proved much easier than filling it with the real thing. For months I asked every man I knew whether he would be willing to make a small donation. Working in the natural foods store, I knew a lot of men who wore their long hair loose and their Birkenstock sandals all year round. I thought that made them alternative thinkers, and thus more likely to agree to my unusual request. "Or perhaps you have a friend?" I would ask when one man after another turned me down.

I couldn't believe how many men had moral reservations about parting with a secretion they would otherwise wash down the shower drain without a thought. On the one hand I could understand the responsibility men said they would feel for the offspring created by their genetic product. On the other, I had very little patience. "Did you call every woman you've ever had sex with, even a one-night stand, to make sure she didn't end up pregnant? Because God knows your genetic product might already have multiplied." I felt self-righteous at the time. In the years when I had boyfriends I don't recall any asking me if I was using protection. It seemed that as long as they were deriving pleasure from the act, they were unconcerned about the grave, moral responsibilities and repercussions that suddenly emerged when I asked men if they would do it into a jar, as a favor, pretty please.

Now the issue seems a lot more complicated to me. I often wonder what our donor would think about the way his act of charity turned out. I have often wished I could find him, and ask him for help.

In our search for "Mr. Right," our main concern was that he should be heterosexual and not involved in casual sex with multiple partners or intravenous drugs. It was 1987, and we were well enough informed to know the dangers of inseminating with untested fluid. But because we had yet to experience the actual deaths of real people from AIDS, we allowed ourselves to believe we would not get hurt at this dangerous game. Ruling out the number-one and number-two risk categories became our sole screening process. Other women we knew opted for safer routes of insemination. Local doctors sold tested frozen sperm and the service of inseminating it for some two hundred dollars a shot. It could cost six hundred or more each ovulation cycle, as the chances of getting pregnant increase with the number of inseminations during the fertile period. Another friend made her own arrangements with a donor, as we were attempting to do. But she insisted he be tested for HIV, then agree to remain abstinent until she became pregnant. Miraculously, she found someone who complied. We thought sperm banks were too much money, and getting a donor to be tested on our own would be too difficult and too time-consuming. In retrospect we were amazingly lucky that our gamble turned out as well as it did.

After months of being turned down by friends and acquaintances, Norma and I developed a strategy. We appointed our friend Marcia to be our go-between. We gave her name and phone number to everyone we knew, and asked them to ask everyone they knew if they knew a man who would donate his sperm. Having Marcia as the intermediary meant that we would remain anonymous to potential donors, and they to us. That eliminated one cause for reservation men had voiced: that we might one day come after them looking for child support money. Marcia would keep the donor's name and address in a sealed envelope, in case our child would want to contact him when she reached adulthood. She screened the candidates and presented their profiles to us for final approval. Although we started out with a long list of preferred characteristics—our donor should be Jewish, dark-haired, and green-eyed (in the hopes that we might create a baby that looked at least a little like me)—we were finally thrilled to have the cooperation of a Christian, monogamous, heterosexual, blond, blue-eyed stranger.

Until this time I had never contemplated my own conception—never wondered whether I was sparked into being on a night of bright passion that swept my parents into each other's arms. Had my father begun wanting her early that evening, when he saw her sweeping her blonde hair back in two matching tortoise shell combs, then dabbing some scent onto her neck in front of the makeup mirror? And had his desire been building all night, as she entertained his associates with cocktails and cheese puffs downstairs in the living room? At the end of the night did she undress slowly, in front of the television? Or was it altogether less romantic than that? Had the prelude to my life begun some night when my mother was tired from my brother's tantrums? Had she just returned to bed, having been jostled out of sleep by my sister's late-night cry, to find my father wanting something, too? Did she turn toward him only to avoid that hurt, rejected look in his ice-blue eyes? Did she scoot reluctantly past the break between the single beds hitched together with a hook and eye at the boxsprings, and let him have his way? He could have been drunk and thinking of someone else's wife. She could have been bored and wondering whether she could convince a friend to go shopping with her the next afternoon.

I cared more whether she loved him the day they were married in her father's backyard. I cared that the white Navy uniform he wore on their wedding day made him look like a prince. I cared to know when she began to love him. Was it in the bleachers at the college football game where they met on the arms of other dates? Or was it later? Did she fall in love with her handsome fiancé who wrote her letters from Japan while he was stationed overseas? Did she love him the year they lived in Coronado, California, where she read books on the beach all summer, determined to plow her way through the literary alphabet—Austen, Brontë, Cather, Dostoevsky . . .—to ease the loneliness she felt looking out over the wrong ocean?

This is how I've come to understand things: Each person's history begins with a night of passion, submission, or something less defined than that. We break through at conception onto the scenes of other people's lives.

My mother has told me that he hit her once while she fed me my bottle. I imagine it as a slap across her face. A snapping sound. A clap like the sound of wood hitting wood on a movie set. "Roll 'em!" Let the bad times begin.

I was setting up a holiday display at work when Norma called. The day had been long, and I was beginning to feel the increasingly familiar bone-weariness of my still-unnamed illness. I was filling wicker baskets with assorted herbal teas and all-natural fruit spreads, leaving the task of dragging out heavy sacks of grains and restocking the bulk bins for one of my healthier co-workers to undertake in the morning. That night in particular, I had reason to pace myself.

Norma and I were planning to inseminate when I returned home. We had done it once the night before, and planned to do it three times during that month to increase the odds of having our efforts pay off.

Norma hadn't become pregnant the previous two months. Now all she could talk about was the condition of her cervical mucus, sperm motility, and the symptoms and sensations her pregnant friends were experiencing. As if it would help ease the grief of her unpregnant state, Norma came home one afternoon with a stray dog. "We can't keep him," I protested. Our lease said no pets. "As it is we're pushing our luck by having the cat in this apartment. We'll definitely get caught if we take this dog." But Norma insisted we take the chance. So that's what we ended up naming the little mutt with a black coat and a white patch over one eye: Chance.

"Marcia just called," Norma was saying over the phone. "The donor had an accident. He's in the hospital."

"An accident? That's awful."

"He went skiing in Vermont for the day and he broke his leg."

"He went on a ski trip when he knew he had to donate to-night?" I knew I was being unreasonable. Actually, I was more upset for Norma than for myself. She had inseminated once al-ready, after all. She could be pregnant for all we knew. "Well, at least it's just his leg. He won't be out of commission for long."

The cashier's voice came through the intercom. "How much for the organic cheese gift baskets?" I barked some answer into the speaker, and returned to Norma. "We'll talk when I get home, honey. It'll be okay."

"No," she said, and I could hear that she was sniffling. "To-night's the best night. Last night was early. It's day fourteen and I always ovulate on day fourteen."

"The sperm can last up to seventy-two hours. It can still work."

"Please, tonight's the night."

"Honey," I said, laughing now, "there's nothing I can do about this. The guy is in the hospital."

"Get us another guy," Norma pleaded.

"It took us months to get the skier. What do you expect me to do, get a guy to jerk off in the back-stock area?" I looked out over the store. Maybe I could do it, after all. The thought made me laugh again. "I know how you're feeling, but we just have to wait," I told Norma.

"Please," Norma wailed.

The intercom squawked again. Someone wanted to use a one-hundred-dollar bill to pay for a dollar-fifty tube of aloe lip balm.

"Norm, I'll call you later."

"Promise you'll try. Promise me."

"You have to be kidding."

The cashier tapped on my office window. I could see the line of waiting customers growing longer behind her.

"Just try," Norma insisted.

"Okay, I'll try," I said, and hung up the phone. The problems at the cash register were much easier to solve than Norma's.

As I was closing the store that night I heard someone knocking on the front door. I walked up front expecting to see Norma. But the woman, whose face was half hidden behind a red scarf, was Karla. "Sorry, Karla," I said, pushing the door open just an inch. "I'm closing up."

"I know," Karla said. "But I need a favor."

I remembered the favor I had promised to do for Norma. I hadn't asked a single man for sperm that night.

"Dave's brother just turned up at our doorstep with three of his buddies from college. Unannounced! I need to get some food . . . please?"

"Karla, I'm sorry, I've already counted out the deposit for tonight. The registers are all closed up."

"I understand." She tightened the knot on her scarf. "Men," she muttered.

Men! "Wait a minute," I said, catching Karla by the elbow. "On second thought maybe we could make a trade—a favor exchange."

I explained my dilemma, and to my surprise Karla was enchanted by the request. "What a blast. And I thought we'd be stuck watching TV tonight!"

"But don't have Dave do it, that would be too weird. I know him." I scribbled a makeshift questionnaire on the back of the weekly specials flyer. "Ask them about these things first. Whoever isn't in any of the risk groups is our man." I handed Karla a jar of baby food and instructed her to empty it and sterilize the container in boiling water. I explained about keeping the sperm warm, and gave her directions to our apartment and our phone number. "If this works, I'll owe you a million," I said. Karla was so giddy about the adventure she nearly forgot to buy her food.

As I charged up the steps to our apartment I felt like a victorious knight. I looked into Norma's tear-swollen eyes, and for once I knew I could make it better. "Have no fear," I crowed. "I found one."

"A man?"

"But of course, a man!" I covered Norma's face in kisses. We were embracing on the living room couch when Karla called.

"I've picked one who fits the bill," she said. "He's perfect—handsome, smart, and monogamous."

"Don't forget, we want this to be anonymous, so don't tell him who we are, and don't tell us who he is."

"Don't worry, he's from Colorado. Anyway, he's in the bathroom right now, so I guess I'll be there soon."

When I hung up, Norma reminded me that she already had used the skier's sperm once that month, so if this worked, there would be no way we would ever know for sure who the baby's father was. This was good news to me. I couldn't help perceiving the donor as direct competition. I was jealous of this mystery man, for if he ever entered the picture, my role, I feared, would be even more ambiguous.

I was perfectly happy about our anonymous procedure, but we also had to consider how our child would feel about it. We knew that one day he or she would ask about daddy. In the meantime we were getting plenty of practice phrasing answers to all kinds of curious questions, because we were constantly being interrogated by friends and family, straight and gay. What would it be like for a child to grow up in a home with no father? they wanted to know. Well, we reasoned, that happens all the time. Fathers have been known to abandon their children. Or they die. The tragedy is the abandonment or the loss, the sense that the family is no longer complete. Our child would be born into a whole family unit—complete according to our needs and desires. This would be a two-parent family, we explained again and again. The fact that we were both women would simply be a given in our child's life.

A friend who was adopted talked about her longing to know about her birth parents, and suggested our child would want the same. I could understand her feelings. Presumably, for an evening or an afternoon in the backseat of someone's car, or somewhere at some time, her birth parents shared an intimate, maybe even a loving moment. There was history there, however brief. There was a story.

Our child would have a donor, not a father. The only mystery would be about whether this man's family had a predisposition to heart disease or a tendency to diabetes, we thought.

When asked about the issue of male role models, we vowed that our child would have plenty of men in his or her life. There would be uncles, for sure. Norma was very close to her brother Eli, and my brother would surely take up the role of uncle with enthusiasm. Then there would be grandfathers, schoolteachers, principals, guidance counselors . . . So, where's the problem? we asked our interrogators.

Anyway, what we were about to do was nothing new. People had been conceiving babies through artificial insemination since the late nineteenth century. Modern estimates said that every year there were some thirty thousand babies conceived at sperm banks, and who knew how many more transactions between friends and friends of friends like the one we were about to engage in?

Still, there were no studies about how it all turned out for the children, or at least none that we could turn up. What little research was available seemed to be about children born to heterosexual couples who used A.I. because the husband was infertile. That, we reasoned, was a whole different ball game.

In the midst of all of these explanations and rationalizations stood a simple truth: We wanted a baby, and this was how, as lesbians, we could get one. In the absence of scientific evidence to prove that what we were about to do would work out in the long run, we armed ourselves with what we had. Hope and determination.

Within a half hour the doorbell rang. Norma retreated to the bedroom and I climbed down the hall stairs to find Karla waiting in the foyer. She was fishing a bulging wool sock out of her down parka. From the sock she pulled the jar of sperm. "You said to keep it warm," she said, handing me the goods.

I grabbed the jar, thanked Karla, and said good-bye. The sooner we used the sperm, the better chance of its working. Like a runner in a relay race, I dashed upstairs to where Norma was already waiting in bed.

We had heard that after insemination, a woman can help the sperm move quickly to the egg by lying with her hips raised for an hour or so. According to this theory, gravity would help slide the sperm down toward the egg. Unlikely though this sounded, I helped Norma prop her hips up on a stack of pillows, and sat by her side for an hour trying to distract her from the discomfort of her ridiculous slouch.

Two weeks later I woke at four in the morning to find Norma kneeling above me, bouncing up and down on the bed. The drugstore pregnancy kit said we were having a baby.

"Aren't you happy? Why aren't you happy?" she was asking, as I forced my eyes open in the dark.

II

Norma's pregnancy was difficult from the start. It didn't take us long to learn that morning sickness was a cruel misnomer. Her "all-day" sickness meant we could not take a car ride without Norma having to pull over to throw up by the side of the road. We couldn't go out to eat because the smell of mayonnaise or fried fish or even something as innocuous as burnt toast could make her nauseous. I stopped cooking altogether, totally frustrated because it seemed that no matter what I prepared, Norma couldn't stomach it. We were back to packaged macaroni and cheese.

We made an early appointment at the medical center to see if our nurse-midwife might be able to offer some advice. The nurse who would see us through this pregnancy turned out to be a trim gray-haired woman with glistening slate eyes. "I'm Rhetta Franklin," she said, extending a wiry hand toward Norma. Norma introduced herself, and me: "This is my partner, Nancy," she said.

"Partner?"

"We're lesbians," Norma said. Lesbian sounded harsh in the pale room decorated with pastel pictures of babies and maps of women's insides. I wished Norma had said we were lovers, instead.

"Well, this will be a first for me. I hope that doesn't bother you," Rhetta said.

"As long as it's not your first baby," I said, trying to keep things light.

"So you'll be, like, the father?" Rhetta asked me.

"I'll be the baby's other mother."

"How interesting. How nice. Two mothers." Rhetta wrote something on one of the pages in the manila folder spread open in front of her.

"About the morning sickness . . ." Norma said, steering the focus back to the purpose of our visit. Rhetta answered her questions, and suggested she keep a box of crackers by the side of the bed so she could eat some as soon as she woke each morning. That should help ease the discomfort, Rhetta said. She checked Norma's pulse, weighed her, prescribed some prenatal vitamins, and declared that all was "right on track."

We were putting on our coats when Rhetta asked, "What will you do if it's a boy?"

I saw Norma's neck stiffen. "We'll buy him little blue outfits instead of pink," she answered. The chill in her voice told Rhetta she had made a serious misstep. We both bristled at the assumption that because we were lesbians we hated boys and men. In fact, Norma had always pictured herself having a son, and while I preferred the idea of having a girl, I didn't feel strongly about the gender question.

"I guess that was a stupid thing to say. I'm sorry." Rhetta leaned forward in her chair, as if by bridging the physical space between us she could regain a sense of intimacy.

"You might want to do a little reading about lesbian families," Norma stated flatly.

I wanted to erase the painful silence that followed. "It's okay. I guess you don't meet families like ours every day," I said.

"No, Norma's right," Rhetta said. "I will do some homework. I'll see what I can find."

A few weeks later Norma began to bleed. We called the advice nurse at the hospital who said it could signal a miscarriage, or on the other hand, she added, with the medical establishment's knack for covering every base, it might be nothing. To be safe, Norma should lie down, and we should wait it out, she said.

"Did anything like this happen the first time?" I asked Norma.

"What first time?"

"The first time you were pregnant. You know, by Glen."

"Oh, that. I don't remember. It was three years ago."

"You'd remember if you had gotten sick, or if you bled, wouldn't you?"

"Why do I have to think about that now?" Suddenly, Norma looked very weak as she leaned against the pillows on our bed.

"I need to know. Just answer and I'll leave it at that."

Norma staggered to her feet and left the room. "If I lose this baby, you're to blame," she said as she tucked Chance under her arm and walked out the backdoor. I wondered where she could be going on such a cold night. I knew I should feel cruel for upsetting her like that, but I didn't. I felt determined. I ran out to the hallway and called after her. "It's just a simple question." Norma turned to look at me. "C'mon," I pressed. "Just say 'yes' or 'no.'"

To my surprise, Norma came toward me, unbuttoning the winter coat she had thrown on over her sweatpants and T-shirt. She slipped the winter boots off, and I saw she had no socks on. "I guess I don't know where I was going," she said, hugging the dog to her chest. I settled into a chair in the kitchen, suddenly afraid I was going to get my answer.

"There was no first time," she said.

"You mean you were never pregnant before?"

Norma seemed to grow a little taller, as if she had literally been relieved of a heavy weight. I too felt light, as if there was nothing holding me to that kitchen, its white cabinets and white walls. I took a breath and everything regained its weight, I settled back into my chair and braced myself for whatever was coming next. "What else? Just tell me what else isn't true," I said.

For a couple of weeks after that, Norma seemed to be trying extra hard to avoid conflicts. She came home with small gifts for me, like a new pen set and a beaded choker. I let myself forgive her. But I also let myself hope that the pregnancy wouldn't stick. I wanted more time to sort out what I was learning about Norma. I wanted a chance to decide again. Instead, as though I was too dizzy to do anything else, I decided to leave our lives in the hands of fate. I had spun the plastic arrow on a child's board game, and now I was waiting to see which colorful wedge of direction it would wobble to a stop on: Move ahead three squares. Move back two. Pick another card.

And so the world kept spinning, further and further out of our control. I was running a fever nearly every day. The store where I worked was preparing to lay off employees. And Norma and I received an eviction notice in the mail. The maintenance man had reported to our landlord that he had seen us enter and exit the apartment with a dog on several occasions. We had violated the terms of our lease.

I called my friend Beth, thinking she might provide some guidance. After all, she'd been through what I was just embarking on. She was the only person I knew who had a child as a lesbian co-parent, so I asked her if she would mind my coming by to talk about babies.

When I arrived at her house in Jamaica Plain, Beth was straddling the roof beam of the backyard shed she was building.

"Hey, come on up," Beth called, waving her hammer toward the metal ladder. "You can help me drive in a few nails before it gets dark."

"What's this going to be for?" I asked as I climbed the rungs.

"Storage. Now that Emily is getting bigger we're running out of room." Beth handed me a hammer, and I made a few lame attempts at driving nails into the slanting roof boards.

Beth's baby, Emily, was the first I had met within the lesbian community. She was also the first newborn I'd ever gotten a close look at. I remember staring at Emily's tiny fingernails, utterly amazed at how delicate and vulnerable this creature was. But I was equally amazed at the fact that two women I knew had voluntarily sacrificed their freedom to tote this little bundle around with them to brunches, to the park, and to anywhere else they might want to go.

Beth and I had many interests in common. We both played the flute, she well and me badly, and we both practiced karate. But now, all I wanted to talk with Beth about was motherhood. Beth, it turned out, had initially been as skeptical as I was about the idea of having a baby. And her partner, who was as gung ho on the topic as Norma was, convinced Beth to go through with it. This, it turned out, was our strongest link.

"So, you didn't plan to have kids?"

"When?"

"You know, when you were younger, when you were planning your life."

"Did I think about kids when I was drinking in the gay bars?" she said, laughing. "I think I sort of unconsciously thought I won't have kids because I'm a lesbian," she said. "I remember I saw this talk show on TV and there were these lesbians talking about being parents. I was just staring at the screen thinking, you can't do that. If you're a lesbian you can't have kids."

Then along came Robin, and Robin's determination to have a baby. Like me, Beth went along for the ride. She pulled out the power of attorney she had tucked into her billfold. It authorized her to oversee any medical decisions on Emily's behalf. "I guess dads don't have to carry this around," she said, as she refolded the deep creases of the page.

"Have you taken any other legal steps. Have you gotten guardianship papers or anything like that?" I asked.

"Nah. Robin wants to do it, but I'm too paranoid." At the time, lesbians and gay men weren't even allowed to be foster parents in Massachusetts. "I mean, what if we went to a judge to get the paperwork done, and they took Emily away?" She began sweeping a pile of nails into her hand, and slipped them into a pouch in her tool belt. "It would probably be okay. I'm just too scared to risk it."

We climbed down the ladder and went inside. Robin was putting a bowl of potato salad on the table, and Emily squealed when I inadvertently sat at her place at the table. "My chair," she said, trying to eject me by pulling on my knees.

"Now that's not very nice," Beth scolded. "We like to share with our guests." Later, two-year-old Emily and I made up, as she sat on my lap and I demonstrated again and again how to tie a shoelace.

While Robin put Emily to bed, Beth and I talked about what I could expect as a parent. "It's exhausting," Beth said. "But I guess it's worth it."

"How do you handle not being exactly the mother, and not being exactly the father?" I asked.

"It's not always easy," she said. "Once during a therapy session I brought up something about Emily. I don't remember what it was—a discipline problem or something. The therapist just looked at me and said, 'She's not your kid.' " Beth shook her head. "I mean this was someone I was going to for support."

"And?" I asked. "Then what?"

"Well, I never went back to her again. But that's not the point. I realized I can't depend on other people to understand. And I definitely can't depend on other people to validate me. Or to help me figure out what my role is."

"If this is supposed to be encouraging, it's not," I said.

"But it's true. You see, you just have to define your own role, then insist that it's a good role to be in. If you look around you'll see how many parents are kind of in-between, like stepparents, or adoptive parents, or aunts who are raising their sisters' kids. If you make a big deal about how different you are, you'll feel really awkward. But if you just accept that it's another variation on the theme, it goes easier."

It was one thing to become a parent. Suddenly I realized I was being asked to become a pioneer. And that wasn't necessarily so bad. I had always been better at politics than personal interactions. As frightening as what Beth had told me seemed, I felt better prepared to try to change the world than I was to change a diaper.

Little did I know what it means that babies grow much faster than social and political attitudes evolve. Or how tragic it can be when one so swiftly outpaces the other.

We hadn't planned to tell our families that Norma was pregnant until her first trimester was over and the threat of miscarriage had passed. But our first lesson in pregnancy and parenting was already unfolding: We were no longer in control.

My mother, who knew Norma had been trying to get pregnant, was suspicious right away. "You haven't mentioned how the plans for starting a family are coming," she said over the phone one Sunday.

"They're coming. Nothing new," I said.

"You know your voice gets squeaky when you lie," my mother said.

"Jeez, is this some maternal sixth sense I'm gonna get when our baby is born?"

"So she *is* pregnant," my mother crowed.

"Ma-aa . . ."

"Just let *me* be the one to buy the layette. Norma's mother won't mind, will she?"

"What's a layette?"

"See, I'm right. How far along is she?"

"Okay, you're right. But you have to promise not to tell anyone." I knew this plea would be in vain. My mother isn't good with secrets.

"Why can't I at least tell your sister and brother?"

"We don't want to jinx this. The pregnancy has been hard so far." I explained how Norma had been cramping and that she bled a little.

"Oh, that happened with me every time. It's probably nothing."

"Well, we hope so," I said. But at that point I honestly didn't know what I was hoping for. I kept wondering if there were more things about Norma that I thought I knew but would one day learn were just more lies. Norma swore there was nothing else, but now I had to curb my instinct to probe every piece of information she presented. I'd try to coax stories from Eli when he called, to see if her brother's version of their past matched

Norma's. I began asking him about where they had lived and how their parents had behaved. But I didn't find any significant discrepancies between his recollections and what Norma had said.

Meanwhile, my mother's inability to lie even by omission became obvious. Word of Norma's pregnancy had leaked, and we knew that my mother was the source. My aunts and uncles, my sister, even my grandfather, were logging in with their congratulations.

The card we received from my grandfather was accompanied by a check for twenty-five dollars, with which we were to begin a college fund for the baby. Grandpa Abe's nonchalance about our decision to become parents had already become legendary in our household. One evening, months before when we were visiting Grandpa Abe for dinner, Norma took him by the elbow and led him to the kitchen. We had just decided to start a family, and for some reason, Norma felt he should know. "Nancy and I are going to have a baby," she said. Then approaching eighty, but still maintaining a look of steely agelessness, he eyed Norma, then me. He looked troubled, maybe even angry. "You girls can't do that," he commanded. I could see Norma straightening her spine in preparation for our already well-worn speech about how gay people had the same maternal and paternal instincts as anyone else, and could be just as loving as parents.

"Why not, Grandpa Abe?" I asked.

"Because," he said shaking a stern finger, "you, Nancy, are working in a grocery store, and Norma here hasn't even gotten her degree yet. You need good jobs to have a baby." Where my grandfather picked up his live-and-let-live attitude when it came to my sexuality I never figured out. But when it came to work and money, the man had fixed standards.

Remembering this, I unfolded his card and read aloud: "It's wonderful you girls are having a baby. Adoption is an admirable pursuit," he wrote. Norma laughed as I handed the card over to her. "I guess your mom didn't mention the particulars," she said.

"Well, he'll see for himself soon enough," I said.

Around that time my sister called. She told me that she had had a dream that I was taking a trip to someplace far away on a train.

"Just because I'm going to be a parent doesn't mean I'm going away from you," I said.

"It was just a dream!"

"So you don't feel worried that the baby will take me away from you?"

"I guess I do," Julia admitted. "Besides, I always thought I'd be the first to have a kid."

"Well, you are older. Not to mention straight. I guess I'd have put money on your being first, too."

Then Julia told me that my father was hurt because I hadn't told him about the baby myself.

"I didn't tell anyone about the baby except Mom. She blabbed it," I protested.

"He's still upset."

"I guess that's why he hasn't called."

"So you call him," Julia said.

"He'll just say what a horrible idea it is, and how he doesn't approve of my lifestyle, and all that crap."

"But he's your father," Julia said.

"It's been five years since I came out to him. When is he going to just get used to it? I don't want to hear his ranting anymore."

"Who says he's going to rant? He just wants to talk," Julia said.

When I was in grade school my father used to say, "Let's talk," and I would suddenly feel important and honored. Talking in this context was not the casual exchange that commonly occurs between two or more people. Talking, when he said it that way, was an invitation to a near-sacred ritual. He would usually say it after dinner, when my mother was washing dishes and putting leftovers into Tupperware bowls, and my sister and brother were upstairs playing some game I was too young for. I would follow my father, trying to be as grown up as he, although my eyes barely came up to his belt loops. He would sit in one of the stern, high-backed living room chairs that no one ever used, and I would be lifted onto his lap. I'm sure he asked me about school, and that I answered. But what I remember from those talks are his stories about his life before I was born. He told me about how when he was in high school he got a job selling Scripto pens to earn pocket money. Summers he would set out wearing a pressed white shirt, tie, and good trousers. While other boys would get bored of selling and congregate on a Brooklyn stoop, my father wouldn't stop until supper time. At the end of the summer he won the award for making the most sales. "You see, I wasn't the best or the brightest, but I came out on top because I worked hard," he explained. "Be the best at what you do, kid," he would say, patting my shoulder.

I like to think of my father as that determined boy who carried boxes of Scripto pens between his sweaty palms, believing so blindly that it worked.

Now I wished my father and I had learned more from those talks; that we had practiced discussing what was important and difficult to say. I wished we hadn't stopped talking when we began to disagree.

For the time being, I let the subject of the pregnancy slide.

Norma was two months pregnant on our second anniversary. The cramps and bleeding had passed. But now that the physical problems had subsided, Norma's moods had become more intense and unpredictable. I found myself depending more and more on my conversations with Beth to get me through. "Don't get drawn in by her hysteria, it's probably just hormones," Beth advised. "Look at this pregnancy as a science experiment. Take a step back and observe the human body's remarkable capabilities and tricks," she said.

I tried to follow her suggestion, but it didn't always work out. When Norma was about three months pregnant and we were preparing to move out of our apartment, we got into an argument about household chores. There was a lot for me to do. In addition to my own share of the work, I had to take care of those tasks a pregnant woman shouldn't perform. For instance, I was responsible for spraying the dog with flea repellent and repainting the windowsills and doors so we wouldn't be charged by the landlord for the scratches my cat, Ahab, had made. But I had health problems of my own. I was still getting fevers and sore throats so often I was never sure if I was sick still, or again. So I suggested Norma take on some more tasks like calling real estate agents, and following leads on apartments. This led Norma to accuse me of not pulling my weight and not taking her pregnancy seriously. "I nearly miscarried once already and you still keep making these demands. If you don't want a baby why don't you just leave now? Don't make me lose this one!" she yelled.

The argument slid in a downward spiral until we were accusing one another of ridiculous breaches. Norma stopped talking to me, convinced that I was out to sabotage her pregnancy. For two days the silence between us grew. On the morning of the third day we had an appointment with the midwife. Without speaking we got in the car and drove to the medical center. We exchanged only as many words as necessary so as not to alarm Rhetta.

Norma lay down on the examining table and Rhetta smeared thick clear jelly across her stomach. "Listen to this," Rhetta said, and pressed a small amplifier against the gel.

"Oh my God. I can't believe it." Norma motioned me closer. "C'mon," she said, "listen." Her voice was warm enough to thaw my resentment. I took a step toward her and Norma grasped my hand. We fell into a hushed silence, listening intently as if we were receiving a message from the world beyond.

"Isn't it beautiful?" Rhetta asked.

It was more than beautiful. It was miraculous. Stupendous. Nothing short of the most wonderful sound in the entire world. That little thumping sound had plowed a field of peace that Norma and I could meet in. When we left, we didn't mention the fight. We just loved each other again.

That week my supervisor called a mandatory staff meeting at the store. I had known for a long time that the business was failing. The natural foods market was oversaturated in our area. Now there were entire supermarkets dedicated to health foods in Cambridge, and general supermarkets were carrying natural foods lines as well. Our small specialty store was being crowded out of its own niche.

We met one morning before the store opened for business, and studied the dismal sales charts and discussed shrinking profit margins and overdue bills. But nothing could get me down. I was having a baby.

I had to tell somebody, so when the meeting was over I cornered Mark, my co-manager, who was in the office sliding loose-leaf binders stuffed with sales figures back into their places on the shelves.

"Wanna hear some good news for a change?" I leaned back against the desk, and instinctively began sorting through stacks of mail.

"Sure could use some."

"We're having a baby."

"Congratulations," Mark said, abandoning his books and throwing his arms around me. Then he stepped back. "What about Norma?"

"What do you mean?"

"How does she feel about you . . . you know . . . getting pregnant?"

"It's her baby," I laughed.

Mark looked intently at my abdomen. "How'd you do that?"

"Do what?"

"How'd Norma get you pregnant?"

"I got her pregnant."

"I must be old-fashioned or something—I don't get it."

"Ever heard of artificial insemination?"

Mark nodded enthusiastically. "Why didn't you say so? My grandfather was a farmer. He did that to the cows all the time."

Karla had asked right away if the sperm had worked. I told her no, because we hadn't been ready to make the pregnancy public knowledge yet. But now that Mark knew, I wanted to tell Karla before someone else did. She came to the store that week, as usual, and I took her into the office to break the news.

"I've been thinking a lot about you since that night," she said. "I think you're really brave."

"Brave?" I asked, shoving my hands into my apron pockets.

"Yeah, brave, to do something so bold, starting a family like this. I really admire you."

"That's nice, but it doesn't have anything to do with bravery, you know."

"Of course it does. What you're doing is new and untested. You'll have to face all these obstacles from society, but you're going ahead and doing it anyway. And you'll show the world that there are all kinds of ways to make a family."

I thought about what Karla had said as I walked up and down the aisles with my clipboard, taking inventory of the cereals and grains for my weekly order.

Once when I was traveling cross-country by bus, I met a woman who invited me to stay at her place overnight in Chicago. I felt I had gotten to know her in the eight hours during which we had been sharing a seat, so I accepted her offer. When we arrived at her apartment she showed me her collection of exotic reptiles. I was too groggy from traveling to bother asking about all of the lizards and snakes she kept in immaculate aquariums. "Come, we'll take this guy out in the sun," she said, draping a thick snake over her shoulders. We swapped notes about our lives over glasses of iced tea. When the phone rang, my new friend asked me to hold the snake while she ran inside to answer it. She placed its muscular heft over my shoulders and instructed me to hold still while she was gone. "Try to relax. He doesn't like sudden moves," she said.

When she returned from her call she took the snake back. "Boy, you're really brave. Most people would be much more nervous about holding a boa constrictor."

I had no idea the snake was a boa. Had I known, I would not have let her leave it on my shoulders. I would not have been brave.

Whether or not I'd have taken on the challenge of being a lesbian co-mother if I could have known then what it would eventually mean is an academic question and unanswerable. One thing is for sure though: Knowing what I know now I would at least have agreed with Karla. Courage was indeed required. But even more than that, if I were to draft a list of necessary characteristics for the potential nonbiological lesbian mother today, above courage, I'd put faith as the number one attribute.

We began our childbirth class on a spring night when Norma was about five months pregnant. Her belly was tight and round like a basketball beneath her floral print maternity jumpsuit. The other women in the room were outfitted in equally snazzy outfits designed for the eager mother-to-be. I wore my after-work uniform, jeans and a clean sweatshirt. Like me, the husbands were also dressed in casual attire, khakis, deck shoes, polo or T-shirts. The teacher sitting opposite us was the only unpaired woman in the room, and the only woman besides me with a flat stomach.

"Let's start by going around the circle and introducing ourselves," our perky leader suggested. In each couple the pregnant woman went first.

"I'm Marianne, and I'm due in August."

"I'm Marianne's husband, Al. Not quite sure I'm ready to be a dad, but, well, what the hell!"

"I'm Sarah. I'm six months along. This is my husband Pete's second baby, but my first."

"Like she said, I'm Pete. And the first time around, with my previous wife, no one invited us husbands to childbirth class. So this is a new one on me."

Norma and I exchanged glances as the discussion moved

around the circle, closer to where we sat. Finally it was her turn. "I'm Norma and this is my partner, Nancy," she said motioning toward me. "This is our first baby, too."

For the first time the leader interrupted. "Isn't that nice. That's just great," she said, her smile straining to maintain itself. "And you are . . ." she said, looking past me to the pregnant woman sitting to my left. I opened my mouth to speak at the same time as my neighbor. "I'm Lois," she was saying, as I croaked a bit louder, "I'm Nancy, Norma's partner. I'll be our baby's other mother." There was an awkward silence. Lois eased a little closer to her husband. The leader looked pained. "That's all," I said, feeling foolish and a bit triumphant.

During the break at the midway point, the women gathered on one side of the room and compared notes about maternity clothes and exercises for their sore lower backs. The men gathered in another corner, complaining about how their wives hogged all the pillows on the bed now, and how unpredictable the mothers-to-be were with their moods. I stood awkwardly between the two knots of people for a moment. I could hear Norma telling the women about a mail-order catalogue that sold all-cotton nursing bras. She was perfectly at ease, holding court with the other expectant mothers.

My attention jerked to the other side of the room. One of the men was saying that he was tired of his wife's one-track mind these days. "She used to care about my business, or our garden. Now she's just got her nose in those baby books."

I took one step closer to where he was speaking. "I know what you mean," I said as I joined his circle. "If I hear one more word about the pros and cons of natural childbirth versus epidurals, I think I'll scream."

The men nodded in agreement. Suddenly we were all talking at once, and the ten-minute break flew by.

In the second part of the class we practiced breathing techniques. "Okay moms, stretch out in a comfortable position on the carpet." The women lowered themselves onto the floor. "And dads, you kneel down by mom's head."

"You mean partners," Norma said, propping up on one elbow.

"Well, yes, of course. In this class I suppose we'll say partners."

On the drive home I swore I'd never return to childbirth class. But Norma insisted. "You were great," she said. "Besides, we can't let Suzy-cheerleader get off so easily." She was right to make

us stay with it. By the last session our teacher had stopped trip-
ping on the word partner, and the friendships Norma and I made
with the other couples soon grew to include friendships between
our children.

The day after Norma's graduation from her teaching program,
our lawyer called to set up an appointment. Our powers of attorney and Norma's will had been drafted, and were ready to sign.
We had decided to have the documents drawn up as a means of
protecting our family in case of Norma's death, or if my right to
parent the baby should one day be challenged by a hospital or
school. Occasionally we discussed what would happen if our relationship ever broke up. "I'd never deny your right to see our
child," Norma would say. "Whatever becomes of us, you'll always
be the other mother."

In the will, Norma stated that the baby should go to my guardianship in the case of her death. The powers of attorney gave me
the right to make decisions for Norma or the child if medical
treatment were ever necessary. The lawyer had explained that
there was no way to guarantee my legal status as a parent, but that
these documents could help establish our intent.

Norma and I had discussed the idea of pursuing more binding
legal contracts. For example, a couple we knew of who had a
three-year-old daughter had gone before a judge to have the
nonbiological mother deemed the child's "co-guardian." It was a
simple procedure in probate court which gave the co-mother the
legal standing to take the child out of school for a medical appointment or family emergency, to obtain visitation rights in case
her child was hospitalized, and so on. This status wouldn't guarantee that if her partner died, the baby would automatically go to
her custody (even though her partner's will specified that that
was her desire). The child's blood relatives, her grandparents and
aunts and uncles, still had more legal standing than she did. Co-
guardianship didn't grant her the same entitlement as if she were
the child's *father*. But, as our lawyer had said, "It's just one more
legal document the court would have to tear down before they
could deny you your status." It was something we thought we
might try after the baby was born.

We also considered the idea of my adopting the baby in a so-
called second-parent adoption. But at the time, no judge in Massachusetts had yet granted a lesbian couple this status, which was

becoming the preferred legal arrangement for lesbian-headed families in California and a few other states. A two-parent adoption would allow the co-parent to legally adopt the child without the birth mother's having to surrender her rights. Norma and I had discussed trying to pursue such an adoption, which would mean ours would be the test case. But with the antigay fervor that had been stirred up over the foster parenting issue at that time, we doubted we'd succeed. (Five years later, Dr. Susan Love and her partner, Dr. Helen Cooksey, would become the first in our state to be granted this status.) For the time being, our lawyer suggested we put off pursuing such an option at least until the baby was old enough to speak for him or herself, maybe in a few years. In light of all of this, the short stack of papers we were about to sign seemed like a very good start.

Our lawyer's trim, tidy receptionist led us into a small library that was dominated by a large cherry table. Shelves of leather-bound tomes lined the walls. After Norma and I had taken seats at the vast table, the receptionist placed a folder in front of one of the empty chairs. Attorney Carlton entered and picked it up. "Let's see," she said, thumbing through the pages. "Before I call in the witnesses, why don't you tell me if you had any questions regarding the final draft I sent you?"

"No," I said, "it looked good."

"Norma?"

"It all looks fine."

"All right then," the attorney said, and pushed a button on the intercom. The receptionist returned with a young man. "George and Carolyn will be our witnesses." The room was weighted down with the silence that accompanies formal rituals. Papers were shuffled back and forth and signatures were put in place.

"I feel like I should kiss the bride," Norma whispered when we were left alone.

"I know what you mean. It feels like we've just been married." We folded the documents into the stiff paper envelope the receptionist handed us and left the office. That half hour in our lawyer's library had been the most formal acknowledgment we had had of our relationship.

The next afternoon Beth and I were practicing a duet on our flutes. Beth had been trying to convince me to play more so I could join a women's marching band she was part of. I had no intention of signing up, but I liked playing music with Beth, and I particularly enjoyed the conversations about parenting we had afterward.

Beth put her flute on her lap. "So, how is that science experiment going?"

"You mean Norma?"

"That's the one."

"Oh, she's been a little better. I hear the last trimester is easier." I pulled my flute apart and began to wipe down the sections before putting them back in the case.

"Sometimes. Robin mellowed out then, too. But don't worry if it's still a little rocky. It will all be worth it when you've got that little baby in your arms."

"You know, I keep forgetting that that's what all of this is for. Sometimes I don't believe there ever will be a baby."

"There will be."

"But what if the baby arrives, and I don't feel like I'm its parent?"

"This sounds like a bad case."

"A bad case of what?"

"A bad case of denial. The whole world tells you you can't have a baby and become a mom, and now you're starting to believe it."

"Well, it's true. I have a hard time imagining that this is all going to happen and that I'll be as much a parent as the dads in our childbirth class."

"You know, sometimes I still have trouble believeing that, and Emily is two years old! But you have to work at it. If you don't, it will make a wedge between you and the baby, and that's not fair to her." Beth swabbed out the headpiece of her flute with a handkerchief. "As a matter of fact, you've got to start now. Get in the habit of thinking like a parent. Dream some dreams for that baby."

A few days later Beth called me. "How about you give me a pep talk for a change?" she asked.

"A pep talk?"

"Tell me that having a baby is worth all this shit."

"What happened?"

Beth's voice cracked. "I hate this. I hate being a dyke and trying to be a mother. I pay for half of everything and I can't claim Emily as a tax deduction. Robin always wants more from me, and the baby always wants Robin. If you asked me today whether you should have a baby I'd say get out now while you still can. You're going to hate this, too."

I didn't know what to say, except that it was already too late for me. Now the sight of babies and children made my heart yearn. I couldn't wait to be a parent.

My mother invited Norma and me to come to New York so we could shop for the baby's layette together. I hadn't been shopping in Bloomingdale's since I was a teenager and had nearly forgotten the ostentatious opulence of the store. Walking between the circular racks of designer dresses made me aware of how much my life had changed since I left New York bound for college. But my discomfort couldn't survive the force of my mother's excited anticipation as she led the way to the baby department.

As we approached the racks of tiny shirts and overalls a smiling saleswoman approached us. "Your daughter?" she asked, peering over her half-glasses at Norma's pregnant belly. "This is my *daughter-in-law*," my mother said, putting an arm on Norma's shoulder. "She and my daughter" (her other hand reaching for mine) "are having a baby together." The saleswoman may as well have let out a gasp. I could feel the color of embarrassment rise to my cheeks, too. Until, that is, I saw the pleasure her surprise was giving to my mother, who gave me a sideways glance, a half wink as if to remind me to keep a sense of humor. After all, we'd be surprising people quite a bit in the months and years to come.

Back home Norma and I placed the blue-and-white-striped bassinet in a corner of the bedroom and filled it with the miniature white undershirts that snap around a diaper, red corduroy booties with rubbery slip-proof soles, and more towels and washcloths than we thought any small person could ever need. In just a few months there would be a real baby to replace the heaps of clothes, towels, and blankets that were folded inside it.

But first we had a lot of work to do. It took Norma and me three months to find a new apartment, and we couldn't help wondering if Norma's blossoming belly and our insistence that we needed only two bedrooms had something to do with the sudden "shortage" of apartments. It seemed we'd be getting along perfectly well with potential landlords until they suggested that perhaps we'd want a third bedroom for when junior got a little older and more active. "You may not mind rooming with the little one right at first, but soon enough he'll need his own place," they'd say to Norma, who couldn't help but correct them. She'd explain how the bedrooms would be divvied up: a nursery for the baby, and the larger bedroom for us. Then the deal would start to fall apart. The people who looked at the place that morning had changed their minds, the landlords would say, or they would suddenly be reconsidering whether they were going to rent the unit at all. Maybe the paint in the room we'd settled on as the nursery was lead based. An inspection would be too costly, they'd say.

The apartment we finally found through an ad in the paper was perfect. The landlady didn't bat an eyelash when we explained what we wanted. "I have a niece out in California who had a baby that way" she said. "Cutest kid you ever did see. Smart, too."

"I've been thinking," Norma said as we worked in the kitchen, wrapping our dishes in newspaper. "This baby has taken over my body long enough. When it's born, I don't want to breast-feed."

"What?"

"My mother didn't."

"But we agreed. It's the most nutritious way to feed the baby."

"It's my body and I don't want to."

"But it's my baby too, and I think it should be breast-fed. At least for a little while."

"I'm not doing it. Not even for one day. Nine months of sharing my body is long enough."

I was filled with rage. She'll play this control card every chance she gets, I realized. Now it's *her* body. Next it'll be *her* baby, not ours. But this time, the fissure in my composure opened a new view and the anger was short-circuited.

"All right. I'll nurse the baby then," I said, folding down the flaps on a full carton.

"You?" Norma put an unwrapped dish down on the counter and dangled a handful of newspaper at her side.

"Sure. I've got breasts."

"But you don't have milk. That's the key ingredient."

"I bet I could get some."

Norma returned to wrapping the dishes. "If you think you can give the baby milk, go ahead. In the meantime I'm going to start researching which brand of formula is the best."

The next week, after we had settled into our new apartment, I called our midwife. Rhetta said she had heard about adoptive mothers who nursed their newborns as a way of bonding with them. They used a device with a plastic pouch full of formula and a tiny tube that could be placed against the nipple for the baby to drink through. The contraption encouraged the baby to keep sucking at the dry breast.

"So the woman doesn't actually produce breast milk?"

"No, but it's a great way to get close to the baby," Rhetta explained. She gave me the phone number of a local LaLeche League representative so I could order the necessary equipment.

I called the woman from LaLeche and asked again if it were possible for me to make breast milk without giving birth. "You might produce a small amount of milk," the woman explained, "but the main emphasis for adoptive mothers is the nurturing that breast-feeding can offer." I explained that the baby would be nurtured plenty, I was hoping to actually feed the child. Apparently impressed by my determination, she directed me to yet another midwife. This woman, Peg, was thrilled to hear about my idea. Yes, she was quite sure it would be possible for me to make milk, she said. "Your baby will be in good company, too. Moses had a wet nurse of course, and so did King Tut," she said.

A wet nurse? I didn't like the sound of that one bit. But Peg's outburst did reassure me that it could be done. Had been done in the past. "But hadn't those women given birth to their own babies, so they could nurse the others with the leftover milk?"

"Well, true, this will be a bit of a challenge, but I'm sure we can do it." We set up a time to meet, and next thing I knew I was sitting in a crowded coffee shop a block from the women's bookstore, watching the door for someone who looked like a midwife who was armed with the ancient secrets of King Tut's nurse. The restaurant was the kind of place that served breakfast all day long. Peg was easy enough to pick out of the mid-morning crowd of grandmotherly women wearing pink lipstick and jogging outfits. The glass door swung open and there stood an earth-mother type whose cascading red hair fell over her green velvety tunic. I waved and she sauntered over. A chunk of rose quartz strung on a satin cord around her neck, and a pair of silver earrings shaped like fertility goddesses, bobbed enthusiastically as Peg slid into the booth across from me.

"I dug up some information for you," she explained after the waitress had taken our orders. "You don't have a lot of time to get ready before the baby arrives. You should start preparing your breasts right away."

"Preparing them?"

"Yes. You can produce milk but you have to work at it. And you still might have to supplement your supply with formula. Especially at the beginning." Peg cupped a hand around one of her ample breasts. "You should knead your nipples like this," she said, pretending to pull at the aureole which was hidden somewhere beneath the folds of green cloth. I looked around to see if anyone was watching. No one seemed to be, but I told Peg I got the idea, hoping she'd put her prop down. She did. "You might also want to rub your nipples with a towel a few times a day," she said with her mouth full of scrambled eggs. "Toughen them up." I wondered if the woman who nursed Moses subjected herself to this torture. But before I could ask, Peg was giving me recipes for herbal tinctures. These concentrated solutions of dill and fennel soaked in a small solution of alcohol should help stimulate lactation, she said. I could also boil fenugreek and drink the resulting tea.

Finally, she added, I should let a newborn suck on my breasts before our baby was born. The heavy suction would encourage the milk to come down, she said. I told her I didn't have a candidate for this job, so she said I could use an electric breast pump instead, several times a day if possible.

In addition to following Peg's instructions, I ordered the device my midwife had described, a so-called supplemental nursing system. That way, when the baby arrived she wouldn't get frustrated and stop sucking if I didn't have enough milk right away. As strange as the plan seemed, I became fascinated by the possibility that I could actually nurse the baby.

I stopped by the health food store where a going-out-of-business sale was underway, and picked up the herbs I needed along with a few boxes of Mother's Milk tea. I bought more than enough. Who knew, maybe one day we would have a second child.

I explained the fine points of my plan for producing milk to Norma as I boiled herbs and prepared tinctures. She watched me tug and massage my breasts, and asked if I was sure formula was really bad enough to warrant all of this fuss.

"You watch. I'm going to make some milk."

"I wish you could just take mine," Norma said. Already her heavy breasts were beginning to leak.

Eight weeks before Norma was due to give birth, we accepted an invitation from friends to attend a James Taylor concert at Great Woods. We were just settling onto our blanket on the lawn when Norma clutched her belly and groaned. "What was that?" she asked, as if we could all feel what was happening inside of her.

"What was it like?" I asked.

Norma smoothed her T-shirt over her belly. "I guess it was nothing. But it felt kind of like a contraction."

All around us people were huddled together on blankets swaying as bars of "Handy Man" drifted through the air.

"Maybe we should go home," I suggested. But Norma insisted we stay. "It can't be anything serious," she said. "It's too early."

At intermission Norma went to the restrooms. When the concert resumed, she still hadn't returned, so I ran up the dirt path to the bathrooms to find her. "Norma," I called into the large room line with stalls.

"I'm in here," Norma squeaked from inside one of them.

"Are you okay?" I asked, leaning on the door.

"I think we'd better go home."

I told her to wait and ran back to get our friends. One woman went for the car, and three of us went to get Norma. We debated calling an ambulance, but Norma insisted she was feeling better. She got into the backseat and slept most of the way home. But when we turned off I-95 and entered the city, Norma asked to go to the hospital. Our friends waited in the reception area, and I followed Norma into the emergency room.

The last time I had accompanied Norma to the hospital had been shortly after we had begun living together. That day, the admitting nurse had cornered me with a pile of paperwork while Norma was whisked through a set of doors to be examined. I promised Norma I would follow as soon as the forms were completed. But when the nurse learned I was Norma's "roommate," she refused to let me in. I argued, whined, and nearly cried. Finally, when she was busy checking someone else in, I trailed another nurse through the locked door where I found Norma. Her diagnosis that day had been endometriosis. Scar tissue had lodged in her reproductive system, causing the extreme pain that had brought us in that day.

Now I was wiser. I had a power of attorney that said I could make medical decisions for Norma if she was unable, but I wasn't taking any chances on whether or not it would hold up for premature labor. Besides, the piece of paper was back in our apartment. So I told the admitting nurse that I was Norma's sister, and as though I'd uttered the secret password, I was ushered inside without question. Within minutes, a nurse named Sunny arrived and hooked Norma up to an intravenous unit. It could have been dehydration that caused the contractions, she said, but she wanted to keep Norma overnight, just in case.

Our midwife arrived next and asked if I'd like to stay the night in the room with Norma. Sunny interrupted. "We don't usually let siblings stay," she said.

"Siblings?" Rhetta asked.

"That's what I told the lady at the front desk," I explained sheepishly.

"They're partners," Rhetta explained to Sunny, as though she had frequently negotiated overnight accommodations for lesbian couples in the maternity ward. "Nancy is the baby's other mother."

Norma and I stayed the night in separate hospital beds. In the morning Sunny checked Norma's pulses, and the baby's heartbeat. "You can go home, but you'll have to stay in bed for at least six weeks."

"Six weeks? No way!" Norma protested.

"This is serious. Even if your baby was a normal size, birth would be chancy at this point. But your baby appears to be very small for this stage in its development. If it were to come now, there's no guarantee that we could save it." She quoted some depressing statistics about infant deaths due to premature labor, and medical complications for those that survived. "You must stay in bed, and no cheating," she said.

After Sunny left the room I listened to Norma's complaints about her diagnosis. "I can't do that," she said. "I'll go crazy."

A few minutes later Sunny returned with a copy of *Newsweek* in her hand. The magazine was folded open to a photo spread about premature babies. "This one was born seven weeks early," she said pointing to a creature that barely looked human. "Now, will you promise to stay in bed?"

Norma cried all the way home. I repeated Sunny's tips for making bed rest manageable. "You can do light exercise," I said, imitating her singsong delivery. "You can point and flex your toes, and do neck rotations to your heart's content." I managed both to make Norma laugh, and to keep my own fears buried. I felt responsible, as if because of all my uncertainties about having this baby I had somehow caused this situation. I remembered Beth's words: I had to start dreaming for this child.

I scrubbed the dried ramen noodles off the stove top, and washed all of the dishes. It was the end of Norma's first week of bed rest, and already it seemed interminable. Wrappings from the clay Norma had used to sculpt figurines, and the empty bag from the chips we had eaten in bed while we watched television, were strewn around the apartment. In an effort to make order in what was beginning to feel like our jail cell, I sorted the mail into piles. I found an unopened envelope addressed to Norma and me and brought it into the bathroom where she was soaking in the tub.

"Mail call!" I said as I walked in.

Norma was rinsing her hair with cupfuls of water. The top of her pregnant belly rose above the bathwater like an island. "Did you see this?" I asked, holding the envelope out for her to examine. The return address was from her brother Eli in New Hampshire. I pulled out the card and showed her the picture of a teddy bear on the front. "Just to let you know I'm thinking of you—all three of you," Eli had written.

"That's so sweet," Norma said.

"Hey, you're crying," I said, wiping the outer corner of her eye.

"I don't know if there will ever be three of us," she said.

"Norma, stop that." I sat on the milk crate we kept by the tub. Norma padded it with an inflatable bath pillow and used it to sit on when she took showers now. In addition to everything else, the pregnancy had brought out varicose veins that hurt when she stood for too long.

"Don't you worry?" she asked.

"I refuse to worry," I said. "Now you have to stop it. It's not fair to the baby to give in to fear like this."

Norma quieted a little, so I reached across and pulled a bag of green powder from the shower basket.

"What are you doing?" she asked.

"It's the relax-a-bath powder. I think you need some." I stuck my arm into the warm water and swirled the tiny crystals into a little green storm.

"Want me to finish rinsing your hair?"

"Okay." Norma handed me the plastic cup and I poured tap water over her head again and again. I ran my fingers through her scalp, not even noticing that my dungarees were soaked through from leaning against the tub's slippery edge. "What are you smiling about?" Norma asked.

I didn't tell her that I was wondering how it would feel to wash our baby's hair.

In the weeks that followed, a heat wave grew so intense it was as though the streets were humming with the mounting strain. I was officially unemployed by then and Norma had quit her most recent job in the children's room at a local library. So we spent the humid summer days closed into our bedroom, which was cooled off with a twenty-five-dollar air conditioner I'd found at a tag sale. Norma's legs ached from her varicose veins, even when she reluctantly wore the rubber stockings the doctor had prescribed. As if to compensate, she dressed in elegant ample sun dresses. She managed to make the idea of bed rest look as romantic as the term sounds.

Norma convinced me to spend more time practicing the flute now that I was unemployed. "You keep complaining that you're not musically inclined. Well, you have to work at it," she'd say. "Practice." She didn't seem to mind my mistakes. She just kept encouraging me, and clapped when I made it through a song. Occasionally we defied doctor's orders, moved off the bed, and took a picnic to the river where we'd spread a blanket on the grassy bank. We tried to convince ourselves that the slight breezes from the water were healing enough to make up for the pressure such a trip might be putting on Norma's cervix.

With all that time on our hands, we found ourselves with the leisure to worry. When we were alone we let ourselves feel the doubts we didn't permit in front of others: Would the baby one day resent us for bringing it into the world in such an unconventional manner? What if our answers to questions about who daddy was weren't satisfying? Could our families have been right; should we have waited until we had more money?

I had my own concerns as well. Most pressing at the moment was Grandma Ruth. My father's mother, the strict, Orthodox voice of morality in our family, was the only one who still didn't know we were expecting. And she was the one whose unlikely blessing I most wanted.

Whenever I thought of broaching the topic, I was stopped by this memory: Once, when I was about twelve years old, I was riding in the backseat of the car with Grandma Ruth. My parents were probably driving us to a restaurant for lunch, or to the store to shop, I don't remember. What I do remember is that somehow we got on the topic of having children. I told my grandmother that I intended to adopt children when I grew up. My grandmother, a tiny woman who stood less than five feet tall, loomed above us all with her strict Jewish interpretation of right and wrong and the tenacity she inherited from her immigrant parents. "No you won't," she said. "You'll see, when you grow up you'll want children of your own."

"But they would be mine." This was the first time I'd told an adult my plan, and since I didn't know anyone who was adopted, I have no idea where I got the idea to begin with.

"You can't love an adopted child the way you love you own." My grandmother's wrinkled face was set, her small pink mouth clamped tight. When I tried to argue she just insisted. "You'll see, Nancy, there's nothing like blood."

My grandmother's reaction shocked me. She had always bragged how smart I was. I couldn't stand that she wouldn't see this my way. If she disagreed with me so strongly, maybe she was right. Maybe I hadn't thought this through enough. I searched my mind for facts with which to argue my case, but all I could come up with was a childish retort: "You'll see, Grandma."

Another memory only furthered my case for putting off full disclosure. It was the only other time I remember coming to a dead heat with my grandmother. I was probably about fifteen, and was reading *Rubyfruit Jungle,* during a visit to her house. I had a boyfriend at the time, and was only reading the lesbian coming-out tale because my cousin, who loved to read as much as I did, had recommended the book to me.

"What's that story about?" Grandma Ruth asked as she set the table for lunch.

I told her it was about a girl who grows up and becomes a lesbian. My grandmother froze, one dairy plate suspended above my place at the table. "Why would you read a thing like that?" she asked, lowering the plate with an unusual effort. She walked toward me, wagging a pile of paper napkins a few inches from my face. "Those people scorn God," she said, almost hissing. I had never heard my grandmother speak that way before. She was the one who taught me that prejudices weren't natural, that people had to be taught to hate.

By the time Norma was pregnant, my grandmother had known for years that I was a lesbian. Although her first reaction was to promise my father she would "straighten me out," she came to at least accept me and my relationships. But I couldn't bear to tell her that now Norma and I were having a baby. My grandmother was nearly eighty years old, and I convinced myself that she couldn't understand such a new concept. But with less than a month remaining of Norma's pregnancy, I knew I couldn't hold off any longer. My grandmother was living in Florida by then, so we rarely saw her. I picked up the phone, wishing this didn't have to be so hard. Just as I did when I was twelve years old, I still wanted desperately for my grandmother to love me and to approve of my decisions. This time it seemed impossible.

"How could you have waited so long to tell me this?" she asked. Although I knew that now my grandmother had trouble walking, and spent most of her time watching television with her live-in nurse, her voice was as strong and insistent as ever.

"I don't know, I guess I thought you might not approve."

There was a long silence. "Of course I don't approve. How could I approve?" She went on to say such a thing was unnatural. "It's against God's law."

"God's law?" I asked. "Does it say in the Bible that lesbians shouldn't have babies together?"

"Don't be wise, Nancy," she said. "You're too smart to talk like that." The bottom line, she said, was not her approval but God's. And God wouldn't approve of a family like the one Norma and I were starting. By this time both my grandmother and I were choking on sobs as we argued and explained back and forth. After what must have been a half hour of this, I said, "But Grandma, I pray to God every night, and I feel his love. I think he does approve."

"Is this true?" my grandmother asked. I could imagine her lips pursing and her eyebrows raising with the lilt of the question. "You pray?"

"Of course I do, Grandma." I did pray, although mostly in English, saying only the traditional Sh'ma in Hebrew at the end.

And my God was not the bearded man from the Old Testament, but something closer to an androgynous, robed monk or high priestess. A kind of Buddhist-Pagan-Jewish hybrid deity.

"And you feel right about this, you feel right with God?"

I told her I did.

"Okay, then. Okay. You're a good girl, Nancy," she said.

Several months later when the baby was born we brought her to see my grandmother on Hanukkah. My grandmother held her on her lap, and handed Norma and me an envelope for the baby containing Hanukkah *gelt,* the traditional gift of money she had given to each of her grandchildren for all of our lives.

One morning, toward the end of Norma's period of bed rest, I was massaging my breasts in preparation for nursing when I saw a yellowish bead of liquid on my nipple. "Norma, come look," I said.

"That's the colostrum," she said. "That's the first milk."

"I can't believe it."

"Now the baby will get a double dose," Norma said.

"What do you mean?"

"I decided I'm going to nurse the baby, too."

Had I known that would be the case, I wouldn't have bothered with those months of preparation. If Norma was going to nurse, why should I have gone through these elaborate rituals? But it was too hot to argue, so my anger burned inside me, instead. But it wasn't just the heat that melted my will to react. I had become aware of an invisible wire running like a tightrope under my feet. Perhaps it was a thin line of panic about starting a family with Norma. No, it stretched back farther, to my own family. Whatever it was, so much concentration was going into moving slowly along it that I missed what was going on around me. By walking the tightrope that stretched across the divide, I would finally become something—a parent. A *good* parent. Pride was twisted into my determination to continue forward, too. I'd bullied the world into believing I could be a parent even though I was a lesbian, and even though my own childhood had been deeply flawed.

Just before the birth, my friend Sam asked me again if I was sure that having this baby with Norma was the right thing to do. This time I said no, I wasn't sure anymore. "You know you can get out of it, it's not too late," Sam said. This time I knew that it was too late. It wasn't only a matter of making the best of the situation anymore. Now, finally, I wanted to know the baby that was growing inside Norma's womb. Delicately, carefully, I slid my foot forward along the taut rope which I was convinced was my destiny. And when I groped for reassurance and support, it was Norma who was there.

As for the question of breast-feeding, I convinced myself that it was just as well that Norma had changed her mind. I probably couldn't produce enough milk to feed the baby all it would need to grow, anyway. I could still feed her once or twice a day, and Norma could do the rest. It was a compromise, and potentially a very convenient deal. If Norma went out, or was busy or sleeping, the baby could still nurse. How many couples could boast a thing like that?

III

Like any other couple, Norma and I spent late nights, long dinners, and obsessive afternoons trying to arrive at just the right name for our baby. We also spent hours, days, and months during the pregnancy deciding what the child would call me. Who would I be to this child?

From the moment Norma and I first began discussing whether or not to have a child together, I knew my role was tenuous at best. The first realization, of course, came when Norma threatened to have a baby with or without me. She could get pregnant just as easily either way. But assuming I was in the picture: Then what?

When we joined a discussion group for lesbians who wanted to become parents, I learned that others in my position—the co-parents-to-be—had various interpretations of how they would define their relationship to their babies-to-be. One woman thought of herself as the baby's aunt. Another came to meetings only occasionally and seemed not to care what her role would be. One considered herself to be just as much a mother as her partner—equal billing.

The summer before our baby was born, Norma and I got serious about finding our own answer. We went to the library and researched ancient Greek, Indian, and Latin words for mother. We had heard that some African cultures have kinship networks that allow for more than one type of mother per child. We tried on different variations of the word mother: Norma would be Mommy, and I would be Mama, or Mami. Finally we decided that since we were Jewish, our child could call me Ima (pronounced *ee-mah*), Hebrew for mother.

I loved the idea. Ima was a label that would let me be mother both in word and in deed. Ima was a foreign word but still familiar. Others in our family and community would understand it. Yet it acknowledged our difference as a family—my distinction as a mother—without feeling alienating. It signified that while I was to be a female parent, I would not be the same kind of mother as Norma would be.

That was not the end of our name game, however. Further elaboration would be needed. Now we had to decide what the rest of the world would call me. For example, would we one day tell the director at our child's day care center that I was our child's Ima? Even if the director turned out to be Jewish, she wouldn't necessarily get the whole picture. One future day, when Norma and I would show up at the doctor's office, would we explain that Norma was the biological mother, and I was the *non*-biological mother? I didn't like the sound of that. I am as biologically sound as anybody. Yet lesbian parenting books and articles we had read often used that unwieldy and unattractive term to refer to moms like me. For my tastes the term was too sterile. Besides, it wasn't true.

Co-mother, a term accepted in most liberal circles, sounded too much like co-pilot to me. I was more than just an assistant. Since the heterosexual couples we knew called the parent who did not give birth the father, I even considered that. But this, Norma argued, would be too confusing for our child, and of course I agreed.

Sometimes we jokingly referred to me as "the other mother." It was descriptive, after all. No one questioned that Norma would be the baby's mother. And as the other female parent, I would be, too. But the label quickly lost its charm. I began to feel that referring to myself glibly as "the other mother" was a little like a man's mistress appearing at a social function on his arm, and introducing herself as "the other woman."

While families living openly with two lesbian mothers are a relatively recent trend, "other mothers" have been around in various forms forever. Every adopted child has a birth mother and an adoptive mother. Yet the birth mother, until very recently, was erased from the family's consciousness to make the child's family fit the acceptable pattern.

For decades, the picture we've had of the birth mother in such a situation has been of an irresponsible, immoral woman who misbehaved and had to pay the price. When a woman admits, even today, that she is going to give a baby over for adoption because she knows she cannot provide enough emotional or financial support, she is suspected of being "cruel" or "heartless." Witness the homes for pregnant women that still exist today, where women who have decided to put their children up for adoption can carry their pregnancies through in secret.

As a society we have no fond feelings for other mothers. It is difficult to even utter the word "stepmother" without wanting to put the adjective "evil" first. Maybe that's why some lesbian couples choose to refer to the nonbirth parent as an aunt, or simply by her first name. But this seemed to me like an unearned demotion. Having helped make the decision to start a family, maybe even having considered bearing the child herself, having been present at the child's birth, awake for night feedings, and having changed her share of diapers, this woman deserved a better title, I thought. After all, the child knows this family member is her parent, and has probably even tried to call her "Mommy" on occasion.

But for all of my research, my interviews with other lesbian couples, and my social and political analysis, it would be the baby herself who would be the architect of my role.

During her pregnancy, Norma thought we should talk to the child growing in her womb. Not being the sentimental type, I thought the idea was hokey. But I was roped in. I sat facing Norma's abdomen and played lullabies on my flute. Each day I would lay a hand where the baby was kicking and yell silly greetings, like, "Hello, in there," as if I were calling down a rabbit hole.

When our daughter was born, and Norma and I were surrounded by nurses and a midwife, all of us talking at once. The baby's wide eyes seemed to focus selectively—on Norma and on me. She knew whose she was from the start.

As the years have passed, and our lives have become increasingly complicated, I have had to think back again and again to that look in my daughter's eyes in order to see myself as she sees me.

Amelia

I've often thought that one day I would laugh and tell you that you were born a virgin birth on Virgin Mary's birthday. It's true. Both parts. You were conceived with no man present. And the woman who cut my hair the day you were born confirmed the part about the birthday. As it turns out, you, Mary, and the hairdresser all share the same one.

Stripped down to these facts, your birth is a fairy tale in which you are the enchanted one. A new nativity play, in which Norma is Mary, and I am Joseph, Josephine perhaps, or just plain Jo. It wasn't quite a manger where you were born. The hospital had a birthing room with all of the so-called comforts of home. I think it was the rocking chair no one sat in that the hospital brochures alluded to when they touted the virtues of the cozy room. Norma said it best: "We could have been in the middle of a four-lane highway for all it mattered." She was right. We were braced for and focused on one event only: squeezing you into our lives.

I have to admit, I couldn't imagine that our antics, Norma's and mine, could really produce something as serious as a baby. Maybe the fact that I didn't believe accounts for why you didn't stick to my life. Perhaps there is truly some fairy dust released by the act of believing, and without it, well, you know what happened. You have to dream to have dreams come true.

I

After threatening to arrive prematurely, Amelia was born nearly two weeks after Norma's due date. I slept through the first contractions. Then, sometime around midnight, Norma woke me to update me on her progress, and we both went back to sleep. In the morning she was still feeling the gripping sensations, dull and painless. After one false labor, and countless tugs and pains that Norma mistook for contractions, we had grown so used to trips to the hospital and phone calls with midwives that I think we were beginning to believe pregnancy was a permanent state of being. It was easy to forget that there was really a baby coming, and not just more false promises.

We decided to go to Norma's acupuncturist, who had offered to give Norma a special treatment when the baby was on its way to make her labor go smoothly. After that we decided to go shopping and get haircuts. "I want to look good for the baby," I said, only half joking.

We walked to Harvard Square to do our shopping, unconcerned about spending money on things we didn't really need, despite the fact that my unemployment checks only went so far. We were also acting quite blasé about Norma's condition, despite the fact that now and then she'd pause to hold her belly and assess the strength of the contractions.

I bought a pair of low brown leather boots. Norma bought a pair of sandals at an end-of-summer sale. By the time we got to the hair salon, Norma was having to sit down on occasion and wait out a contraction. Neither of us suggested going home, though; we were having a great day. At the hairdresser's, after our shampoos, we were each led to neighboring chairs facing mirrors. "How do you feel?" I asked, as a young woman who must have been just out of beauty school combed my long, wet hair.

"Pretty good, but they're getting stronger," Norma said, still smiling into the mirror. The man who held scissors poised above her head had a puzzled expression on his face.

"She's in labor," I said, and Norma and I both laughed.

Looking back on the day we waited for our baby to be born, all I can see is the lightness. Even the walk home from the hairdresser, during which Norma collapsed against the sides of buildings we passed by, was always funny when we retold it. She made it up the flight of stairs to our second-floor apartment one step at a time, with me coaxing her along. But I also remember that I was feeling guilty by the time I settled her onto our bed. I should have taken her condition a little more seriously, I thought.

With so much time to prepare we should have been ready. The bags should have been packed. I should have known what was coming. Soon we would have a baby to take care of; a helpless person who would need all of our attention. This was no time to wonder if we could handle it. I called the midwife. Her answering service promised to track Rhetta down. Meanwhile, I ran back and forth between comforting Norma and repacking the bag we had never attended to after the hospital stay ten weeks earlier.

The midwife could not be found, the woman from her answering service told me. We should wait a little while, surely they would locate her. I tried to hide the panic in my voice when I told Norma that we were to stay put for a few more minutes. Finally, I called the service and informed the operator that we were on our way to the hospital, midwife or no midwife.

Norma and I trudged down the stairs even more slowly this time. The contractions wracked her body and each step was a major advance. Finally we made it to the curb and I lowered Norma into the car. I was practically hyperventilating and Norma was moaning loudly by the time we arrived at the hospital. At the emergency entrance I convinced a nurse to bring a wheelchair to the car for Norma. This stout woman in her white uniform clearly did not consider childbirth an emergency worthy of special attention. It would have taken a detached limb or cardiac arrest to elicit any sympathy from her. But to keep me quiet, I suppose, she helped Norma into the chair. "Now you'll have to calm down," the nurse ordered as she wheeled Norma into the hospital.

"You hear that, honey?" I said. "You need to take it easy."

"I was talking to you," the nurse snapped, bobbing her chin in my direction.

Norma and I got a lot of laughs out of that one, too. When we retold the story time and again, Norma would break into giggles when she described me in my green hospital-issue scrub dress, with my argyle socks and new leather shoes adding to my anti-style statement. To this day I caution expectant fathers not to wear new shoes to a birth. "All those hours on your feet will break them in quickly all right, but it's not worth the pain."

Rhetta finally caught up with us on the maternity ward, where Norma was already being wheeled into the birthing room. She explained that she had been on the ward all along. She had fallen asleep in one of the rooms after delivering her fifth baby on her unusually busy shift, and of course nobody knew where she was. "We must have set some kind of record today," she said, as she examined Norma. Norma clutched my hand so tightly that I had to remove the engagement ring she'd given me the year before, because it was cutting a blood-red gully into my finger. "Oh my, you're pretty far along," the midwife said, one hand reaching inside of Norma. "I can already feel the head."

"You can? What color hair does the baby have?" I asked.

Norma was still able to laugh. "She said *feel,* not *see.*"

"Of course," I said, trying desperately to get hold of myself.

Two hours after we entered the hospital, the midwife was lifting a baby's head out of Norma's body. I was sliding ice cubes across Norma's forehead at Rhetta's request, and watching the hands of the clock as midnight approached, wondering what day our baby's birthday would be.

"Come see the head," Rhetta said between contractions. "Don't you want to see your baby's head?" I didn't want to. At that moment the baby seemed to be a cruel tormentor. That head was doing nothing but causing my lover intense agony. Looking back, I am in awe of how strong my loyalties to Norma had become.

The next thing I knew, the midwife was holding up a long scrawny creature. Nurses appeared in the room out of nowhere to clean and swaddle the baby. Up until the last minute, Norma and I debated what girl's name we would use. Just moments before we had switched from Amanda to Amelia. "It's prettier," I said. Norma nodded and almost smiled.

The midwife placed Amelia in my arms first. What had been a misshapen dangling creature moments before suddenly transformed itself into the most beautiful being I had ever seen. Looking down at Amelia's face I felt calm for the first time that night.

I had always imagined that being born would be a horrible ordeal—being forced from a dark watery cave into the bright commotion of a hospital room. But to look at this infant's calm, inquisitive gaze, it was clear that she saw the moment as the beginning of a fantastic adventure. She must have cried when she took her first breath, but I remember Amelia's first moments as perfectly quiet. She looked around the room with an expression of awe, as if she were overjoyed by the new territory she had come to explore. She looked at me and captured me. Captivated me. Activated a longing I didn't know I had.

I handed Amelia to Norma who was laughing and crying all at once. She immediately put the baby to her breast, and one of the nurses helped Amelia find her first suck of food. Another nurse put her arm around me. "Congratulations," she said. I recognized the woman whose arm was draped across my shoulders as Sunny. She had been the nurse who took care of Norma when we were in the hospital for the false labor. What amazing luck, I thought, that she should be the one on duty that night. Her presence meant that I wouldn't have to be treated like a friend of the family in my first hours as a mother.

The night Amelia was born I slept on the maternity ward in the single hospital bed next to Norma's, and Amelia slept in a clear plastic bassinet in the nursery across the hall. In the morning, Norma and I couldn't wait to see her, as if we needed confirmation that her existence was not just a dream we had shared. I walked across the hall and asked to take Amelia. An unfamiliar nurse looked up at me. "We can only release babies to the mother or father," she said. I hadn't thought about the fact that Sunny might have gone off duty while we slept. So, for the first time ever, I made my case. "I *am* one of her mothers. She has two." The nurse gave me a suspicious look. I tried my best not to look like a kidnapper as I strode across the row of bassinets to Amelia's. "Thank you," I said, as I wheeled her out. I felt the nurse's gaze on my back the entire time, but she didn't protest.

I was nervous handling the baby. When I was a child I was so afraid to pick up animals that I don't think I held a kitten until I was an adult. I was sure that what appeared to be a darling creature on the ground would squirm and scratch if I dared lift it. But Amelia didn't resist my efforts to pick her up. I immediately fell in love with the warm solid feel of this little being. I handed her to Norma, who put Amelia to her breast. We commented on everything about her. Her eyes were the dark but uncertain blue that meant they would soon change. Her nose was wide and flat, which, the nurse told us, was a result of her passage out, and would change in the next couple of days. We were particularly awed by our baby's fine blonde hair. In our own baby pictures Norma and I both had full heads of thick brown hair.

"Here, you try it," Norma said, pulling Amelia off her breast and handing her to me.

"No, that's okay," I said. "Not here in the hospital, anyway. What if someone walks in?"

"Who cares?"

"Wouldn't they think it was strange to see me nursing the baby?"

"Go ahead. If we're going to worry what other people think, we're going to have a lot of worries."

I drew the privacy curtain around the bed and lifted my sweatshirt. I nudged the baby's cheek with one of my nipples and she turned to grasp it with her mouth.

"Wow, she's strong," I said.

"Like a little vacuum cleaner."

Amelia sucked contentedly, then fell asleep in my arms. As we lay nestled in bed, me in my jeans and favorite green sweatshirt, Norma in a hospital gown, and Amelia dozing between us, our pediatrician walked in. We had met Dr. Hogan only once before, during a brief introduction in his office. He had explained that since the baby was to be delivered by a nurse-midwife, he would have to come to the hospital and check on the newborn, as was required by some statute. That had been the beginning and the end of our introduction.

Now Dr. Hogan was standing before us, as promised. I didn't move my arm from around Norma's shoulders, or make any motion to sit up when he entered the room. "What a beautiful family portrait you three make," he said. With those words, Dr. Hogan endeared himself to us forever, and guaranteed that he would be the one we would call when Amelia had her first rashes and ear-aches. He sat on the edge of the bed and looked over at Amelia, who had drifted into sleep. He asked us a few questions, then said he'd let the baby rest for the time being. "Everyone seems to be doing fine," he said.

For the time being at least, we were.

The blank birth certificate form Norma and I received in the hospital on the morning after Amelia's birth was the first taunt. There were spaces for mother's name and father's name, but there was no room for my name. Our way of addressing the situation was to give Amelia my last name and Norma's joined by a hyphen. That little dash was as strong, I hoped, as a drop of Krazy Glue. It was the only bond, beyond Norma's and my best intentions, that secured me in the family.

Two days after she was born, we brought Amelia home from the hospital and settled her into the blue-and-white-striped bassinet that was waiting for her. Chance crawled under the bed with his favorite chew toy and sulked because of all the attention the baby received, and the cat perched on the edge of Amelia's bassinet looking down at her with a hungry smirk.

Still recovering from an infection that resulted from the birth, Norma stayed in bed and I was left to take care of Amelia. Between feedings I took her out for walks, bathed her in the kitchen, and diapered her on the painted wooden desk which just weeks before had been my writing desk. Diaper covers, moist towelettes, and pastel-headed safety pins filled the drawers where I once stored typing paper, a stapler, erasers, and correction fluid.

The responsibility of caring for this helpless creature awed me, as did the confidence that crept up on me very quickly. Just the fact of my being bigger than she was, my ability to reach for jars and boxes and open them, to cross the room in four or five long strides, made me godlike in comparison with Amelia's utter inability to do anything.

Norma looked on and directed me as I gave Amelia her first full bath in the plastic tub we perched on the kitchen table. The baby books I had read made bath time seem more complicated than building a house. As prescribed by these authors, I had arranged in arms' reach Q-tips, clippers, petroleum jelly, three washcloths, baby powder, special soap, and mild shampoo. But still unsure what to do, I abandoned the instructions in the book and listened to Norma. "Just hold her head above the water and sponge her off," Norma said. It was that simple.

Waking every few hours when Amelia did wasn't helping my exhaustion, which by now could best be described as ever-present, rather than merely chronic. So I tried to take naps during the day when she did. On the advice of my doctor, who thought part of my illness had to do with stress, I also began attending a therapy group. Once, I took Amelia with me to a meeting. As I was leaving, an old friend gave me the slanted grin she usually reserved for an introduction to my newest lover. "Look at you," she said. "You're in love with that baby." It was true. One by one my fears about being a mother were falling away. In their place grew a bond which I had once thought I'd have to work to create, but which was creating itself from the inside out.

One warm fall afternoon shortly after her birth, Amelia and I set out for a walk to Marcia's house. Norma helped ease the baby

into the cloth carrier I had strapped to my chest. When we arrived, I placed Amelia on a cotton blanket on the lawn in front of
Marcia's duplex. We were admiring the baby when, out of nowhere, a Doberman pinscher came loping toward us. I gathered
Amelia into my arms while Marcia shooed the dog away. It took
me a minute to remember my phobia about large dogs. Time and
again in the months to come I would see my own fears dissolve
when I was with Amelia. Maybe this was what they called "maternal instinct." Maybe I had it.

Looking back, I am grateful for the fact that Amelia and I had
those first few weeks to ourselves while Norma recovered. Once
she was back on her feet it seemed a competition began between
us. What we were jousting for was the title of Mother. I knew that
I was being unreasonable when I insisted on holding Amelia on
my lap when someone was taking a family picture. I also knew
that the reason I wanted to hold Amelia in public was that I felt a
need to prove my relationship to her, whereas Norma's, I
thought, would be taken for granted. It wasn't until much later
that I realized Norma felt the need to prove herself, too; that I
wasn't the only one who worried about maintaining my connection to Amelia.

While we waged a quiet struggle in our home, debate was
raging within the lesbian community. Some women argued that
lesbians having babies was counterrevolutionary. Lesbians, they
argued, were trying on heterosexual privilege: Once they became pregnant, people stopped seeing them as lesbians and admitted them to the hallowed halls of Motherhood. This was all
laid out in, among other places, an opinion piece published in
the local feminist newspaper to which Norma and I subscribed.
The writer, who went by only a first name, added that staying
home and caring for babies drained energy from the women's
community.

I wrote an equally strident letter in response, insisting that lesbians who decided to have children were radicals, not sellouts.
Telling a pediatrician that you are a lesbian is a revolutionary act,
I insisted. Having a child who, once she reaches a certain age, can
and will come out for you at any time demands a new level of
lesbian visibility, I wrote.

When my letter was published in the paper, friends congratulated me on taking a firm stand. But if I pressed, I would have

had to admit that ever since Amelia was born I had begun skipping gay and lesbian pride marches, and lost interest in attending community meetings to discuss the latest threats by punks on local lesbians. Whereas in the past politics had consumed a large part of my free time, now changing diapers and grinding carrots and pears into baby food did. But I wasn't caving in, I told myself. After all, wasn't "the right to choose" something that we feminist lesbians believed in?

My unseen opponent wasn't as far off base as I wanted to believe on another point as well. For some reason, from the moment Norma's belly popped out far enough to announce her pregnant state, we were met with smiles instead of hostile stares when we walked arm in arm through the city. When the baby came, strangers complimented us on Amelia's dazzling eyes, and never hissed "dykes" as we passed by. And yes, we did bask in this new approval. We tried to puzzle out how people were interpreting our closeness. Maybe they thought I was proudly embracing my sister, or kindly taking the elbow of my unwed friend. Whatever they were thinking, the results were delightful.

Gradually we realized we had more in common with the straight couples we had met in childbirth class than with our lesbian buddies who were quickly bored by our musings about the merits of feeding on demand versus setting a schedule, and car seat safety standards.

When I took Amelia out for a walk people assumed I was just another young mother, and I didn't try to correct them. If another mother asked how the birth had been, I answered, "smooth as can be expected," not mentioning that I wasn't the one who had pushed for two hours to bring this child into the world. I didn't mind if they thought I had a husband at home preparing bottles of formula in anticipation of our return. In those moments I enjoyed blending into the easy current of the mainstream, always aware that any second my cover could be blown and the looks of sisterly understanding change to curious stares and hesitant remarks, feeble attempts to convey acceptance and not shock.

When Amelia was about two months old, Norma and I decided to enroll her in a baby swim class at the YMCA, and Norma suggested that I be the one to accompany her. We agreed that it would be a good way for me to build my confidence as a parent, and to have time alone with the baby, engaged in an activity that I enjoyed.

When I met my new classmates in the locker room, no one asked me my name; they simply referred to me as "Amelia's mother." For the first time in years, it seemed, a group of straight women instantly accepted me. Admission into this sorority was simple: A few theories about how to handle colic, reassurances that the sleepless nights can't possibly last forever, and a bragging remark about the baby's first signs of genius (she smiled before the books said it was possible, she reaches for her own bottle, has already tasted her first solids . . .), and voilà, you're in.

My classmates and I were undressing in the locker room. It must have been our second session together and already we were old friends. I noticed one of the women staring at my bare belly. "Would you look at her stomach!" she exclaimed. The other mothers looked up from their fidgeting babies or turned from their lockers, and gawked. Their hands seemed instinctively to grip the sagging flesh of their own abdomens, fingering the loose wrinkles where their skin had not yet retreated to its pre-pregnancy state. I imagined them returning home and doing sit-ups in front of the television set between feedings. But I didn't want to admit that I hadn't given birth. I didn't want to concede being *other* again.

"How did you do it?" the woman asked.

I tugged my suit up and wrapped myself in a bath towel. Our babies were nearly three months old. Had enough time passed to claim that I'd regained my prepregnancy shape? I tried to summon a picture of Norma's bare abdomen to my mind. Was it taut yet? "I didn't give birth to her," I admitted.

"So, she's adopted," the woman said.

"Well, not exactly." I wasn't practiced at this yet. It was harder than I'd expected. I picked Amelia up out of her car seat, ready to head to the pool.

"What then?" the woman pushed.

"She has two mothers. My partner gave birth."

There was silence for a moment while she digested this unwieldy chunk of information. "I see," she said, and the other mothers nodded behind her. The bonds between us were cracking. I could hear them.

It is no mystery to me why I wanted to preserve the charade. I was tired of being different. In my family normal had always been important but never clearly defined. Normal was what other people could see: Our white-pillared house was normal. The living room with a green velvet love seat, antique sofa, and spiraling staircase was better than normal. The living room was, in fact, a showpiece, displaying just how normal we were. It was a room for outsiders, just as the entire pretense of being the same as everyone else was built for external glances. The living room existed for visitors and in it we displayed exteriors, surfaces we wanted people to see. It was not a room for us at all. We three children were never allowed to walk across the oriental carpet, but were instructed to step around the narrow border of exposed floor. It seemed perfectly normal to me to trot along that band of floorboards on my way from kitchen to stairs, front door to den, countless times a day for the ten years we lived in that house.

Normal was my handsome father, six feet tall with wavy brown hair and blue eyes, and my slim dyed-blonde mother wearing clothes from Bendel's and Saks.

Normal was not the father who threw my brother's basketball against the wall when he got angry, letting it ricochet through the house, narrowly missing the piano, the antique clock hanging above the sofa, and the vase full of the spring's first lilacs. But no one saw that. No one saw the fights that my father came home from work at lunchtime to have with my mother, or the pains in my intestines that made it hard to sleep, and which the doctor said were the result of stress.

By the time I reached adulthood I knew perfectly well the dangers of succumbing to the desire to want to fit in. By then my parents had divorced, the first couple I knew personally who had done such a thing. But despite my initial horror at being different, I found life was happier this way. When I followed my heart into my first love affair with another young woman, I knew I had found peace I could never have again if I chose to deny this new understanding of myself. I knew when I decided to have a baby with Norma I was adding still another level of complication to my life story. Ultimately, my urge to be truthful always seemed to win the battle with my desire to be accepted.

I blew a light stream of air onto Amelia's cheek before I lowered her beneath the warm pool water. Just as the teacher had promised, Amelia copied me and blew bubbles as she paddled with her eyes wide open until I caught her in my hands again.

Like all the other mothers in the pool that afternoon, I laughed with pride as I pulled Amelia into the air after her first successful swim.

It was around this time that I stopped nursing Amelia. Although I had originally decided to breast-feed Amelia because Norma had threatened not to, that had long since ceased to be an issue. I could no longer justify continuing, and I had to admit that I didn't enjoy nursing her. The romantic descriptions of nursing I had heard from other mothers never fit my experience. My breasts ached, and having always been modest, I never felt comfortable feeding Amelia when other people were around. While at first I had thought nursing would be a good way to strengthen my bond with Amelia, now I was beginning to see that I had a unique relationship with her that didn't revolve around feeding time. Our ties weren't based on blood or milk, but on time, love, desire, and responsibility. More and more often, when Norma wasn't around and Amelia rooted for a breast, I'd offer her a bottle instead. Occasionally if she was fussing and I could see that all she wanted was comfort, not food, I would offer her my little finger to suck on, and sing her to sleep.

My mother visited us more frequently after Amelia was born. In the beginning it seemed as though she would have to compensate for all four grandparents. Norma didn't get along with her parents, so their visits were rare, and formal. My father had barely acknowledged Amelia's existence, and made clear his limited tolerance for our new family. On the other side, Norma's brother Eli worked extra hard, as he was the only one of the aunts and uncles who accepted Amelia fully and without reservation. My sister and brother sent Amelia gifts, and asked after her, but they seemed to be holding back. It was as though they felt or feared that their first niece wasn't really part of their family.

Amelia and my mother, however, fell easily in love with one another. By the time Amelia was four months old, she and Grandma Sue had evolved their own style of communication.

My mother would sit at the table with Amelia under the pretense of feeding her a bowl of applesauce. Amelia would start a conversation by making one of her unique sounds, like the one we called "elephant eating pig." My mother would break out laughing, while Amelia listened and watched as her grandmother's face shook with happiness. Just as Grandma Sue's chuckles began to subside, Amelia would respond by making another noise, or by laughing herself. Their cackling back and forth could easily last half an hour.

As one of these routines drew to a close, I started to pack a tote bag with extra diapers and a bottle for Amelia. "Come on, let's get ready to go," I said. My mother and I had promised Norma we would go downtown and buy Amelia some new undershirts.

As my mother wiped the mashed apples off Amelia's face she asked about the scratches on her cheek.

"I guess her nails are getting too long again." I was embarrassed that I'd avoided trimming them, but I dreaded taking the sharp clippers to those bird-delicate fingers.

"Get me the clippers," my mother said, taking one of Amelia's hands between her thumb and forefinger.

The next thing I knew I was leaning against the kitchen counter, watching as an experienced mother took action. She unstrapped Amelia from her highchair and took her into her lap. My mother cooed in Amelia's ear to distract her as she pinched each of Amelia's fingers between her own. Amelia barely struggled.

"Done." My mother ran her index finger along Amelia's now-smooth fingertips. I bent down to take Amelia, wondering if I could ever become a "Real Mother," the way my mother was.

"I used to avoid this when you kids were babies, too. The nails are so tiny."

"But look how fast you just did it. It takes me forever. Sometimes I just get a few fingers at a time before she starts crying."

As I lifted Amelia out of her lap I caught my mother staring. "Just then," she said, "you looked exactly like I did when I was your age."

II

"She's only four months old," Norma protested. "Doesn't that seem too young to be thinking about day care?" Norma pinned the corners of a clean diaper around Amelia's bottom and lifted her up.

"We've been through this a thousand times." I was impatient with Norma's resistance to enrolling Amelia. We couldn't afford to get by on just the check from her part-time job and the small income I was generating taking on word-processing and editing jobs at home. We had agreed to sign Amelia up for three mornings a week at a day care center so I could get more work done.

"We have to start being realistic," I told Norma, who was looping the knit straps of Amelia's hat into a wide bow beneath her chin.

"But the whole point of you working at home is so she can be with you, instead of some stranger."

"That's part of the point. The rest is that I have to earn some money."

Without discussing the subject further we drove to the day care center. Norma pulled into the parking lot behind a single-story brick building next to a bus terminal. "That's not much of a playground," she said.

"We're just looking. Try to have an open mind." But as soon as we stepped inside, my mind snapped shut. Right away I was irritated by every aspect of this child-centered paradise. The carpet squares scattered on the floor, the plastic indoor slide, and even the children dozing on nap mats while a lullaby played—everything seemed sinister instead of soothing. The director, who was describing the center's approach to discipline and learning, directed all of her comments to Norma, as though I wasn't present. I counted the seconds until we could march out of there, past the rows of bright jackets hung on low pegs and the tangle of winter boots beneath them.

As soon as we were out on the sidewalk, Norma demanded to know why I had been so sullen for the past half hour. Hadn't it been my idea, after all, to visit the center?

"Don't talk to me about rude. You didn't even acknowledge that I was part of the discussion."

"How could I have?" Norma asked, strapping Amelia into her car seat. "You didn't sit still for a minute, you kept pacing around like a lion in a cage."

As we drove home, I sat in silence, feeling the sting of Norma's anger. I wanted to be angry, too, but I knew she was right. I had stomped through the day care center as though it were enemy territory. I felt my anger soften, turning from frustration to sadness.

"Why are you crying?" Norma asked as we turned onto our street.

I didn't answer and made no move to open my door when we

stopped in front of our building. "I can just picture her first day at day care," I said, looking back at Amelia, who was asleep in her seat. "I'll come in to pick her up and she won't even recognize me anymore. She'll love her day care teacher more than me."

Norma laughed and reached over to wipe my tears away. "You're her Ima, silly, she can't forget that."

That night, for maybe the second time since Amelia's birth, my father called. "I want you to know I wish you my best. I don't approve, but it's your life."

"Thanks, Dad. But it's not something you need to approve or disapprove of."

"I didn't call to fight." he said. "So, how are you?"

"We're doing great." Norma walked by and handed the baby to me. Just out of her bath, Amelia was fresh scrubbed and wrapped in a towel. "Say hello to Grandpa," Norma whispered into Amelia's ear.

"How's little . . . what's her name again?" my father was asking.

"Come on, Dad, you have to be kidding."

"Something with an A, right?"

"Amelia. Maybe you should write it down."

"Don't get fresh," he said, in all seriousness.

"Anyway, it's her bedtime. I've got to go."

As I put Amelia into her pajamas I sang to her in nonsense rhymes. "Here's the caboose, sweet little goose," I said, slipping her top over her head. "Whaddya think, bottle of ink? What's the surprise, little blue eyes?"

Norma came into the room and tickled Amelia's belly. "How are you two doing?" she asked.

"Just winding down," I said. "So don't get her riled up again."

"Why not?" Norma tickled Amelia's belly again. "That old Ima's a stick in the mud sometimes, isn't she?" Amelia kicked her feet and giggled, so Norma lifted the baby's pajama top and blew onto her belly. When she pulled her head back, Amelia squealed, begging for another trick. Norma obliged, and I couldn't help laughing, too.

"Okay, now that you've got her ready for a night of carousing, you try putting her to sleep," I told Norma.

"No way, it's your night. Besides, *Roseanne* goes on in three minutes."

I didn't argue, but I was annoyed. I had a hard enough time putting Amelia to bed. Norma could just nurse her to sleep, but I had already given up trying. So I tried singing, rubbing her back, and holding her in my lap while I worked the rocking chair. But it was useless, Amelia wanted to play. Finally I decided I'd just leave her awake in her crib.

Roseanne was half over by the time I came out to the living room, and Amelia had already begun to cry.

"What's going on? Why isn't she asleep?" Norma asked

"Why don't you nurse her? She's too excited to sleep now."

"I'm just starting to relax. Can't you do anything around here?"

"If you hadn't gotten her all worked up, I could have put her to sleep easily."

"You started it."

Amelia's cries were building strength. "Go on, Norma, she'll be asleep in five minutes if you go in there and nurse her."

Norma stormed across the apartment. When she returned all was quiet in Amelia's room.

"Thanks," I said.

"If you don't mind, I'd like a little peace and quiet now."

" 'You're welcome,' would have been a nice response."

"Look, Nancy, I'm tired. I'd like to just watch some TV without any more interruptions."

I jumped up and turned the television off. "I'm sick and tired of your moods. One minute you're bright and happy and the next you're a raging bitch."

"Well, maybe if you'd be a little more helpful around here, I'd be happier. You don't lift a finger for this family."

"What are you talking about? I earn my share of the money. I take care of the baby at least half the time. I may not have as much energy as I used to, but I've been sick a lot."

"Sick? Try lazy."

"What's lazy? Trying to start a new business, which, by the way, was your idea? Taking care of a baby which you insisted on having?"

We had been warned that the stress of a new baby could challenge even the most stable couple. As it turned out, we were far from being an exception. Our fights had become so frequent that either one of us could have navigated blindfolded the course it would take. Norma would collect more and more complaints against me. I would become so tangled up trying to defend myself that I would be unable to figure out what had started the fight, whether I was in fact guilty as charged, and how to some-how end this tirade.

At some point, I would apologize for something and promise to be better, healthier, anything. Eventually, Norma would apolo-gize too, sounding sweet and convincing. But I was past believing that these reconciliations would mean that anything would change.

Amelia woke at four the next morning. Since Norma had to leave for work in three hours, I let her sleep and got the baby. "A little early for breakfast, little goose," I said, as I fed Amelia a bottle. After a few tugs at the bottle, her eyes slipped closed. Now that the house was peaceful again I didn't dare risk moving Amelia back to her crib. I put her in the carriage, which was parked in the kitchen, and I sat at the table with my journal. With one bare foot I rocked the carriage as I wrote:

Norma's moods are like the eye of a tornado. They pull me into their vacuum of negative space. Here, on my side of the storm the sky is blue. Here I'd like to stay.

III

"Why couldn't we have a normal baby who just eats oatmeal?" Norma asked as she put a pint of strawberries, Amelia's new fa-vorite food, into the grocery cart. Although we had planned to put off feeding Amelia solid foods for as long as possible, by six months she had already begun grabbing for anything Norma and I were eating, and seemed particularly fond of strawberries, pesto pizza, and shrimp.

The grocery cart was filling up with frozen pizzas, jars of strained peas and carrots, plastic tubs of vanilla yogurt, Pampers, and fruit juice. Amelia was fussing in her wire basket-seat. At eight months old, she had her own ideas about not only what to eat, but how to do just about everything, including how she wanted to sit in the cart. She rebelled against sitting with her feet through the spaces between the bars so she'd be facing forward. Instead she wanted to stretch out across the metal bench so she could watch the colorful rows of cereal and soups without turn-ing her head. For the first five aisles or so, Norma and I resisted her whining demands to be resituated. The reason we shopped at this supermarket to begin with was that it was one of the few stores that provided special carts with seat buckles for babies. But by the time we had worked our way through half the aisles, it no longer seemed worth the trouble. Norma unbuckled Amelia's straps and turned her in the seat. By now we were all getting cranky, so we split up for more efficient shopping. I raced ahead to the next aisle to pick up some pasta, while Norma and Amelia finished up in the cookie section. As I stood deciding between linguini and shells, I heard a thud, like the sound of a sack of flour hitting the ground. Then, from across the wall of food I heard a piercing scream. It was Norma's cry. I dropped the box of pasta I was holding, and ran to the aisle where I had left them.

There was Amelia, lying dazed on the hard floor. Norma was crouched above her, wailing. I begged her to calm down. Amelia was the one who was hurt; we had to stay composed so we could take care of her.

At the sound of Norma's anguish, Amelia began to bawl, too. A crowd formed. "She was craning around to see her mother," one woman explained to another. "It was horrible, she fell out head first." "Don't move her," the store manager was shouting. "An ambulance is on its way."

I held Norma with one arm and stroked Amelia with the other. Before we knew it, a paramedic had plowed through the crowd of shoppers and was checking Amelia's eyes, her pulses, her arms and legs. "Her spine is all right, but you were right to leave her where she was, as a precaution," he said as he lifted Amelia into his arms. "We'll have to take her to the hospital and run a few tests." Without discussion, Norma and I agreed that she would ride in the ambulance with Amelia, and I would follow in the car.

I instantly regretted letting myself be separated from Norma and Amelia. I'd had enough experience by then to know that I might not have any luck getting past the reception area at the hospital. I was entitled, by my power of attorney, to be admitted. But by now I knew all too well that it wasn't enough to say you possessed such a document at home, and once again I didn't have it with me. I sped through a yellow light to keep up with the ambulance. As I slipped past one red light and then the next, I prayed I wouldn't get pulled over. I didn't care about the ticket, I just didn't want to lose the ambulance. My only hope, I thought, was to walk through the doors at the same time as Norma and Amelia.

Finally, my luck ran out. A car turning right managed to get in front of me. Now what? I wondered. I decided to try a shortcut. I was terrible with directions, so I focused all my attention on navigating the curving side streets. My heart was pounding so hard I felt as if it would burst through my chest and the windshield both. As I pulled up to the hospital I saw an ambulance unloading at the closest emergency bay. I recognized the driver. Without taking the time to let out a sigh of relief, I parked in an unauthorized space and ran to the ambulance, just as the paramedic opened the backdoor and was carrying Amelia inside. For a split second I let myself feel furious that while my daughter's well-being hung in the balance, I was forced to wonder whether I would be barred from being by her side.

"It looks like she's going to be fine," the ambulance driver told me, as she motioned me to follow the procession inside. For the first time I took a good look at the woman who had been driving. From the creases around her lips and the efficient way she moved I could tell she was the no-nonsense type. She addressed her comments to Norma and me equally, a small gesture I had come to appreciate beyond measure. We followed her and the paramedic through the double doors into the same emergency room that had once been off-limits to me. Later we learned from a friend who worked at the hospital that this woman was a lesbian. Had we been paying a little more attention, we might have realized why no one needed to explain to her that I was family.

Amelia was unharmed by her tumble to the ground. The only reason the paramedic was so concerned, he explained later, was that Amelia hadn't made a sound when she hit the floor. To him this indicated the possibility of a concussion. Had anyone asked, I could have told him that was just Amelia's way: a new sensation was nothing but a new sensation to her, even a four-foot fall.

At home we nestled Amelia into her crib and did a lot of sighing at the kitchen table. We were relieved, to say the least. But Norma, who had worked with children for a living, explained that if we showed up at the emergency room one more time in the next six months because of an injury to Amelia, we could be investigated for child abuse. The statute was meant to protect children from abusive parents, but we feared the same rule could be used to take Amelia away from us. Although we were living in Massachusetts, a state with a reputation for liberal politics, it was 1989, and it would be another year yet before Dukakis' election-year ban on gay and lesbian foster parents would be reversed. With the precedent still in place that prohibited the Department of Social Services, the same agency that investigates child abuse claims, from placing children in gay and lesbian homes, we were more than just a little wary of calling attention to ourselves.

Norma and Amelia drove with me to my first appointment with the acupuncturist. A few weeks earlier I had had a full slate of blood tests to find out why I was always getting sick and feeling so tired. The tests showed I was anemic and that I had the Epstein-Barr virus. "Most doctors don't even believe this is truly an illness," my doctor explained. "Unfortunately, whether it is or not, there is nothing you can do about it. It will just have to run its course." Its course, she explained, could take anywhere from five to ten years. She suggested I try an alternative healer. "It can't hurt," she said.

I decided to see the acupuncturist who had treated Norma the day she went into labor. At the same time, we could introduce her to Amelia and thank her for her help bringing our child into the world.

I lay on a padded table looking up into a cloud of curly blonde hair that framed the acupuncturist's face. Although it was long, her hair never seemed to fall into her eyes. In fact everything about her, from her pressed cotton blouse to her black Chinese slippers, was just right. Even her movements, as she tapped needles into my wrists and ankles, were precise and focused.

I knew what to expect from the needles, having seen Norma go through this. As each fine point entered under my skin, I felt a dull electrical charge, which the acupuncturist explained was my *chi*, or energy.

"I don't have much of that these days," I said.

"You have it. You just don't know how to access it," she said, twisting gently on the last needle. "Recovery means to return what was lost," she explained. "You can't imagine right now how many wonderful changes this process is going to bring to you." With that she left me alone in the room while the needles did their work.

She was right about one thing. I couldn't imagine the wonderful changes this illness or recovering from it would bring. All I could see was the frustration of not being able to do what I wanted to. I hated having to give up karate and having to take more naps than the baby. I hated being weak. I was tired of fevers and bathrobes and tissues. As I lay on that table staring at a tree outside the window whose new white blossoms must have just unfurled, I tried to bury my fears, and believe that what the acupuncturist had said was true.

But that week it seemed that everything in my life was tinged with sickness of some sort. Norma had yet another confession to make. She told me that the poem she had given me for our first Valentine's Day together, the one she had said she stayed up all night to write, was actually something she'd found in an anthology.

I had loved that poem and had carried it in my wallet, believing that Norma had written it. This time I couldn't bear to listen to Norma's apologies and explanations. Instead, I observed her reactions and mine. I noticed that each time after Norma revealed another lie, she looked cleansed and at peace. Did she thrive on this cycle of sin and repenting?

"Are you angry?" she asked, as she always did. But I wasn't mad. I was ashamed to have been so gullible, to have hoped, and to have loved so uncritically. I was ashamed that I had forgiven so much so easily in the past. I felt guilty, too, as though I had somehow caused all of Norma's deceptions by believing her.

Who then did I fall in love with? I asked myself. And who was this woman with whom I had joined my life?

The next day I ignored Norma's plans for me, which included doing the laundry and taking Amelia to the park. I ignored my own plans for finishing the résumés and cover letters I was typing for newly graduated college students who were paying me twenty dollars an hour to make something out of their lack of experience. Instead I asked my friend Sam to watch Amelia, and I went to the library where I checked out armfuls of books by authors I used to love: Whitman, Blake, and E. B. White. At home I dug through old papers and scrapbooks I kept in my closet, and found articles I'd written for my high school newspaper. I sat at my computer and made my own résumé.

There was no need to delete words or tighten phrases to fit it all in. Everything I had done since graduating from college fit easily onto one page surrounded by plenty of white space. But I refused to be discouraged. I called a woman who used to work as a cashier at the health food store. She had gotten a job writing obituaries at a nearby suburban newspaper.

"Jolene? It's Nancy, from the health food store. Am I catching you at a bad time?"

She said I wasn't, and we caught up with each other's lives. "Guess what," Jolene said, "I've been promoted. I'm a city hall reporter now. How about you? How's the baby?"

Before we hung up, Jolene promised that if I applied for her old job she'd put in a good word for me with the editor. It had been years since I'd had something published, and that was in the *Blue and Gold,* my high school paper. Still, Jolene thought I had a shot at the position. I thanked her and hung up the phone. If it was true, as my acupuncturist had said, that recovery meant returning what had been lost, I had a lot of work to do. By her definition, recovery referred to more than just physical health. Physical illness, she said, reflected a problem on the emotional, spiritual, as well as material level. I was just beginning to realize how much I had to recover.

Two weeks later, the process had begun—on the material plane at least. That is, I got the job.

My new boss, Jerry, knew I had a daughter. At exactly four-thirty every afternoon I had to leave the office to pick Amelia up from day care. Once or twice I had to leave work early to take her home when she developed a fever or earache during the day. Although it seemed obvious that I was a mother, I was vague in conversations with co-workers about the rest of my family constellation. Jerry, a tall man with gray hair and a youthful gait, seemed to be an easygoing man. But I had grown careful about opening up about my personal life, first judging just how easygoing a person really was.

One afternoon when Norma, Amelia, and I were at the playground, I ran into my boss and his son. Jerry said hello and took a seat alongside me at the edge of the sandbox. Norma was sitting across the park on a bench near the seesaws, catching up on her reading. After engaging in conversation with Jery for some time—admiring each other's babies and avoiding talk of work—I had to tend to Amelia, who had just let out an impatient whine. No question about it, she was hungry. I excused myself, picked Amelia up, and returned to the bench where Norma sat.

I wished she didn't have to nurse Amelia right there and then, as I didn't feel ready to "come out" to my boss. But I had already learned that with a baby around, things don't always go as planned. As he left, Jerry waved to us. From the distance I couldn't get a clear reading on his reaction, but I took the lively salute as a sign of acceptance. Either way, I thought, now he knew I was a lesbian, and that our baby had two mothers.

But he didn't. At work he never asked about my partner. I assumed he was trying to be nonchalant about it. Then one day as we were discussing our respective day care setups, he said, "Looks like you've got a nice arrangement with that baby-sitter."

"Baby-sitter?"

"That woman in the park."

What did he think? That Norma was a wet nurse? I couldn't stand the thought of letting him think Norma wasn't part of my family, so I persisted. "Jerry, didn't you notice she was breast-feeding our baby?"

He hadn't. That situation stuck with me. It demonstrated how hard people try to fit what they observe into the corset of their rigid version of reality. Every child has one and only one mother, our mythology goes. The space for Mother had already been filled in my boss's mind. Therefore, even seeing Norma nursing Amelia didn't alter his picture. Instead, unconsciously I'm sure, he glossed over the piece that didn't fit.

This misunderstanding, and many more like it, taught me that if I wanted to be sure people understood who our family was, I had to be painstakingly diligent in my explanations. I also learned how strong was people's need to believe in One Mother, with the same fervor that they believe in One God, or One Nation.

IV

By the time we celebrated Amelia's first birthday our family seemed to have formed some kind of cohesion. My job at the newspaper didn't pay very well, but I was on a career path that could ultimately support us. When it came time to send out invitations to Amelia's birthday party, Norma and I felt we had survived something. And in a way, we had. Already one of the couples with whom we had attended childbirth classes had separated from the added stress of a new baby.

By now Amelia was walking. She was not a dainty child; in fact we'd dubbed her out little truck driver. Her legs were sturdy and powerful, propelling her from one end of the room to the other, a bit drunkenly, but effectively somehow. Her hair had grown in a rosy brown, like the color of polished wood. Her round chin and full cheeks made her look always ready to laugh. She like to play hard and preferred Norma's wild roughhousing to the gentle games I engaged her in. I refused to push her as high as she wanted to go on the playground swings, or to toss her as far above my head as Norma would. "You can play that game with your other mom," I'd say.

I was the mother who loved to give her a bath, read books to her, take her swimming, make up rhymes for her, and rock with her on the chair in front of the television set with *Cosby* on until she fell asleep.

In the snapshots from that birthday we all look happy, and I think we were. Norma is holding her head particularly high as she strides out of the kitchen carrying the birthday cake she had made from a mix and decorated with gumdrops. I am leaning forward on the chaise lounge, serious and dedicated as I help Amelia tear the wrapping from her presents. In one photo, my father balances Amelia on his hip, while he grips a large teddy bear he'd brought her with his free hand. He had driven up from New York for the occasion, offering his presence, it seemed to me, as a peace offering of sorts. He laughed nervously when we referred to him as Amelia's grandpa, but he was trying. My mother was there, of course, and Norma's brother Eli and his wife, Lindsay. Other babies Amelia's age had come too, but they paid little attention to each other. The balloons, the smiles, the children tired from too much cake and the effort of sharing someone else's toys, all seem to float dreamily past in the pictures.

But within six months of the day those photos were snapped, Norma and I had decided to split up.

After Norma and I broke up, my friends said they had seen it coming. But to me, the end of our relationship still seems to have burst out of nowhere, like a summer storm. While I can trace back to the beginnings of all of the problems, small and large, between us, it is harder to track the progression of the realizations that led me one day to know without question that I had to leave Norma.

A month or two before I admitted to myself just how bad the situation had become, my friend Sam broached the subject. She was tired of seeing my life completely run by Norma's demands, she told me. Whether it was that Norma wanted to have a baby, move to Canada, sell the car, or eat vegetarian, I was always just following along. "What about what's good for you?" she finally asked.

Instead of defending Norma, as I usually did, I asked Sam what else she had observed. She told me that Norma would be civil to her only when I was around. If I wasn't home and Norma answered the phone, she would be very short. This bothered me more than Sam's saying I subverted my will to Norma's. That was my problem. But my friends are family to me, and I wouldn't stand for having them treated this way. "That's why I don't drop by anymore if I'm not sure you'll be home. And honestly, I hesitate to call your house and run the risk of getting Norma on the other end of the line," she said.

That same week, my friend Veronica called. Although we used to be quite close, I hadn't heard from her in the past couple of years. "You know I saw Norma on the street and asked her to tell you I said hello," Veronica said. "But she said she was too busy to give you the message."

"Too busy? How much time does it take to say, 'Veronica says hi?' "

"Well, that's what I thought. I almost didn't call you at all because I thought maybe you were angry at me and that was why Norma said that."

"That's ridiculous. In fact I've been wondering why I haven't heard more from you and Grace."

"Which is why I'm calling. Grace and I are going to have a commitment ceremony and we wanted to invite you. But I felt awkward about it since we haven't spoken in so long."

Hearing Veronica's voice again made me realize how much I missed her. She had been a great companion over the years. We were both from Long Island and liked to reminisce about familiar malls and fresh bagels. When we got together we inevitably began speaking faster and louder than any of our New England friends could bear. I congratulated Veronica and silently thanked her. Her phone call confirmed for me what Sam had said. The fact that Norma wouldn't pass along a simple message infuriated me. And I got the impression from speaking to Veronica that her distance from me lately had something to do with my relationship with Norma.

These two conversations with Sam and Veronica woke me up

to the fact that the Norma I tried so hard to believe in was not the Norma the rest of the world knew. Throughout our relationship I had looked on as her friendships, one after the other, would crash and burn. One day someone was her best friend, the next they weren't on speaking terms. When I asked what had happened, Norma would give me some excuse about tensions that had been building. But once or twice when I came home earlier than I'd expected, I overheard her fighting with someone over the phone. Norma's cruelty in these instances shocked me. This was a side of her she kept hidden from me. I tried to talk to her about going easy on her friends. I seemed to always end up joking about it: "I'm sure glad *I'm* on your good side."

Slowly I was realizing that I might not always be safely ensconced on Norma's good side. If she had begun turning on my friends, it seemed to indicate that my immunity might be wearing off. When Norma came home that evening, I told her what I had heard, and asked what was going on. She apologized profusely, and promised to be more hospitable to my friends. And from all reports, she was. But the veil was lifting. I was beginning to see that there could not be two sides to a person.

Even this knowledge would not have caused me to walk out on Norma, not then anyway, with a new baby in the house. I clung to the old-fashioned notion that a family should stick together at any cost. In light of the fact that my own parents split up when I was in junior high, my stubborn persistence seemed out of place. It was even more inexplicable since I'd be the first to admit that divorcing was the best thing my parents could have done for one another, and for my sister, brother, and me. Or perhaps it was because of all that that I tried so desperately to protect my ideal of the intact family—until it was no longer possible.

Soon after Amelia's first birthday, Norma began talking seriously about wanting a second child. Our discussions sounded like repeats of the ones we had had before Norma became pregnant with Amelia. Except now it was more obvious than ever, I thought, that we were not prepared to add to our family. Norma was talking about quitting her latest job as a substitute teacher and collecting welfare as a single mother, so she could spend more time with Amelia.

Presenting Norma with the logical problems inherent in having a second child, given our circumstances, was no more successful this time around than it had been the first time. I began to fear that I was incapable of stopping Norma from doing what she wanted. My health, our finances, the ability of our relationship to sustain the strain of a second child—none of it seemed to matter.

When Norma told my mother she wanted to have another baby, my mother immediately voiced her objections. My mother was one of the few family members to offer her unconditional support when we told her Norma was trying to get pregnant the first time, but a second child at that point would have been ridiculous, and my mother felt she had to say so, both to Norma and to me.

"You have to say no to her," she told me later.

"I know."

"So, will you?"

I told my mother I was afraid to insist. She was baffled. She had been afraid to speak up to my father when they were married, but he was bigger than she was and he had all the money. What could I be afraid of, she wanted to know. "If I say no, that will be the end of our relationship," I told her. I really feared that it would mean the end of my relationship with Amelia, but I couldn't bear to put this possibility into words.

"That's not good enough," she said. "You'll have to risk it."

I knew I wouldn't speak up to Norma without a third party present, so I waited until we had an appointment with the couples counselor we began seeing again to work through this argument. Norma and I sat in matching chairs like guests on a talk show, while our therapist, like a TV host, looked on in silence. "We can't have a second baby right now," I said.

"Well, when can we?" Norma wanted to know.

"When I'm better, and when we can afford it."

"But that could be years."

"Exactly."

"But I want a baby sooner than that."

"Norma, we can't. It isn't reasonable."

"Give me a date at least. Maybe we can compromise."

"I can't tell you when I'll be healthy again, or when we'll be on our feet financially. But when we are, we can discuss it."

"That's not a compromise." Norma turned her pleading gaze to the therapist. I can't remember what the professional we'd hired to glue us back together had to say about all of this, only that I knew that my fears were justified. Norma said she was going to have a second child, with or without me. It was the same ultimatum she'd given me when we were contemplating having our first child. But that time we couldn't have imagined the stress a baby could put on our lives. This time we knew without question. Our bank balance and my failing health were two concrete arguments for the fact that we simply couldn't handle the enormous task of caring for yet another human being. But Norma was clearly more concerned with having another baby, and having it immediately, than she was about me, our relationship, or our ability to care for Amelia. I could see now that it was beyond me to interfere with whatever it was that was driving her. I also knew I wouldn't agree to another child now. And that meant it was over.

"I guess that's that," Norma said that afternoon. "We just have different priorities."

The end was sudden and clear in my mind, like walking out of a movie theater into a bright afternoon. It was a complete and jarring sensation, accompanied by a startling loneliness. The person I loved the most had become a total stranger. Or maybe I had finally let myself see who she had been all along.

That night, Amelia and I had a peaceful dinner hour alone while Norma was out with a friend. We chatted as we often did, I asking Amelia questions, or commenting about our day, and she spitting out syllables that sounded like sentences to me. It was hard for me to believe that other people thought she couldn't speak yet. I gleaned so much from what she said, and from the sparkle in her eyes.

As I rocked her to sleep in my lap that night, I noticed how huge my hands looked as they cradled her body. Her pulse beat visibly in her neck, like a beacon of vulnerability. It was my job to protect her. At that moment, leaving seemed impossible. But within days it seemed inevitable. Norma was combing ads for apartments and talking about breaking up as if it were the only logical step to take. We were oddly civil about all of this. There was no more fighting. We agreed that I would move out since it would be easier for me to find an apartment than it would be for Norma and the baby. Norma asked me to take the pets since she didn't think she could care for them alone. We agreed that I would live nearby and see Amelia often. "You're her other parent. I'd never keep her from you," Norma promised. We shed some tears, but there were no hysterics, no begging, no dramatic scenes. Each night we fell asleep holding hands.

Then, after a week and a half, the sugarcoating began to wear off. Norma decided we shouldn't break up after all and began a campaign for compromise and reconciliation. But by then I was certain that leaving was the answer.

Having no place else to go, I moved in temporarily with Sam. By the first of the month I found a one-bedroom studio apartment just a few blocks from Norma and Amelia.

As I threw my belongings into crates and boxes, I had the feeling that I was escaping.

Prisoner

Once, soon after the breakup, I woke after midnight, sure I had heard you cry. I sat straight up in bed, ready to go to your crib. But when my eyes adjusted to the darkness, I remembered I had moved; you weren't there. I went back to sleep and forgot about the dream until morning, when Norma dropped you off for a visit. "Amelia misses you," she told me. "She woke up calling for you last night." I looked at you in wonder. Had I really heard you? Was it just a coincidence? But it happened again and again. I dreamed you had a stomachache, and when Norma brought you for our visit she warned me to feed you only bland foods because you had indigestion. Much later, when you moved even farther away, I noticed that some days when I called you on the phone, you seemed distant, as though you would rather be watching a video or playing jump rope than talking on the phone with me. Other times, especially if I'd had a dream in which you had appeared the night before, I felt as though you were there in my kitchen with me, no matter how many miles were between us.

I still have dreams about you. They're always vivid and they feed all my senses. Sometimes in the dreams I cry. Sometimes we both do. Sometimes I try to tell you something important. Once in a dream I scolded you. Last night you wouldn't look at me. I told you how much I missed you. I said it again and again. Finally you looked up at me, and you asked, "Really?"

I want to tell you the answer so you never doubt it:

Yes. Really.

I

It's hard to believe now that at first Norma and I were grateful to be able to work out our "divorce" agreement on our own, without lawyers or written contracts. I was Amelia's parent because we said so. I could visit her because Norma agreed that I should.

Despite the fact that Amelia had not yet turned two, we decided I would have her overnight at my apartment every other week, and that I would pick her up from day care and keep her until after dinner three days a week. No judge had to instruct me to write Norma a check for ninety dollars every month for "child support." The amount, though small, covered the costs that weren't being paid by public assistance. By this time Norma was receiving welfare checks, day care vouchers, medical insurance, and food stamps. And with Amelia eating multiple meals and sustaining multiple diaper changes with me, and having a supply of toys and clothing at my apartment, the finances for the time being seemed fairly split.

No lawyer had to tell me to surrender our new color television or La-Z-Boy recliner to Norma. I took only what I needed from our apartment before Norma's new roommate moved in. I had no desire to bilk the person who had primary responsibility for our child. And Norma said she had no desire to keep me from Amelia, because Amelia needed my love. Besides, Norma was happy for the breaks that my time with Amelia allowed her.

The wrinkles in our plan were faint at first. Arguments erupted over who should pay for Amelia's new stroller (I didn't think she needed such a fancy contraption, and besides I had an umbrella model at my apartment), and who should take her to see the Fourth of July fireworks (it was my day on the visiting schedule, but Norma didn't want to miss spending a holiday with Amelia). Months into our separation, Norma started to claim my support check was too small, saying that if she and Amelia were ever going to be able to move into their own apartment she would need more money. I argued that even though I was working full-time now, my salary was still modest, and besides, I needed to save for a larger apartment with more room for Amelia, too.

Before we split up, Norma and I had once again been contemplating taking the next legal step to cement my place in our family. Now the idea of trying a second-parent adoption was more daunting than ever, because we feared that the publicity involved in being a test case could jeopardize my job as a reporter. Filing for co-guardianship status would be the simplest course of action, but everything else—from researching better day care options to figuring out how best to cure Amelia's recurring ear infections—seemed to come first on our lists of things to do. I didn't realize then that time was running out.

So, when I first visited Amelia after our breakup the only right I had to see her was the one Norma and I had tacitly agreed on.

I walked up the back steps to the apartment that had once been mine to enter freely, and rang the bell. Norma's new roommate came to the door and told me that Norma and Amelia had gone for a walk and should be back any minute. I hadn't seen Amelia for two or three days, a period that seemed like an eternity then.

Within moments I heard Amelia chirping my name. I turned to see her wobbling toward me, bundled in her snowsuit and school-bus-yellow boots. She tugged her mittens off and let them dangle by their strings at her sides. Norma shook her head.

"You have to put your mittens on if you want to play in the snow," I said, interpreting Norma's gesture. Norma folded her arms across her chest and nodded as Amelia wagged her hands in defiance. "Put on your mittens or we can't play outside together," I said. Amelia ran past me up the sidewalk. "Hey, Norma, give me a hand, will you. Get her to put on her mittens."

"No way! You two are on your own." Norma laughed as she chased Amelia and gave her a hug. "Have fun with Ima this afternoon," she said. "I'll see you at bedtime."

I picked Amelia up and forced her red hands into the mittens. We had only a couple of blocks to go to get to my apartment, but now I wished I had brought the car. All I wanted was to shower Amelia with kisses, to hold her on my lap and gather up as much of her warmth and weight as I could to make up for the days she would be away. But she was in a different kind of mood. Again, she threw her mittens off her hands.

Now this was becoming a matter of principle for me. I imagined that Amelia knew just what she was doing, that she was testing to see if she could use my guilt over leaving to her advantage. What is more likely is that I was used to having Norma step in when I couldn't get Amelia to behave.

I knelt down on the sidewalk and faced this toddler, whose impish grin told me who she thought was boss. "If you take these off again you'll have to take a time-out in your crib when we get inside." I pushed her hands back into the mittens and we continued on our way.

The mittens were off again after we'd trudged forward about three steps. "That's it," I said. "I'm going to carry you the rest of the way, and then you're going to have a time-out." Amelia wailed from that moment until I got her to my apartment. I was sure Norma could hear every high-pitched whine and protest, and wondered if she would find it funny or if she would use it as an excuse to cut my visits with Amelia short.

Back in my apartment, Amelia settled into the crib for her time-out without complaint, and we had no more disagreements for the rest of the afternoon. I am certain now that her tantrum that day was not a test for me; that it was just the random eruption of a toddler. Still, the mittens became symbolic. I would constantly be tempted to let Amelia have her way, not wanting to waste any of our precious time together on mundane haggles over rules and behavior. I can understand the divorced father's urge to "buy" his children's love with new toys and ice cream sundaes when he visits. I have felt that desperation, too—the desire to undo absences with treats and presents. But in the end I chose the opposite route. Eating dinner together, cleaning up together, and brushing our teeth together would be the things we would learn to treasure.

During another visit, Amelia spent the afternoon counting to eleven. I tried introducing numbers twelve and thirteen, but eleven was as far as she was interested in going. Tired of hearing the same numbers chanted again and again, I took out a stack of books, hoping to derail her train of thought. We read a favorite about a little girl named Jane, her mommy, and daddy. My ploy was a success: Amelia had forgotten about eleven. But now all she could talk about was "daddy."

"Daddy!" she said, as she pulled on my earring.

"No, Ima," I said, loosening her grip.

"Daddy!" she insisted.

"Amelia, who is your daddy?" I was curious what her answer would be.

"I have two mommies," she said.

"That's right. You sure do." I was relieved that at least she was clear on that.

The phone rang just as we were about to start making dinner. It was my boss, Jerry. I prayed he wasn't going to ask me to help cover a breaking story. I hated saying no; I wanted to appear ambitious and ready to work.

"How would you like to take over for Jolene? She's moving on to the arts desk."

"Really? You mean I'd be covering city government?" With the phone wedged between ear and shoulder, I settled Amelia at the table with a bowl of Cheerios, hoping that eating would keep her quiet for a few minutes.

"Well, in part. Your beat would be a little more limited. We're reorganizing the staff, and the way I have it figured you'd cover some council business, cops, and fire."

"Wow! I mean, great."

"So you'll give it a try?"

After I hung up the phone, Amelia and I danced around the apartment. That night we fell asleep on the couch with Chance and Ahab curled at our feet.

The fact that I was now single sunk in slowly. But little by little, on the days when Amelia was not with me, I began to take advantage of my new status. I drove off to visit friends in New York and went out dancing on weekends. I put on my black strapless dress for the first time since Amelia was born. When I was with her I was a mother. The rest of the week I was someone younger, less responsible, less worried. I liked being two people. But it wasn't always possible.

On one of my days off from motherhood, I was filling a canvas tote bag with a towel and sunscreen, preparing to spend the afternoon at the beach. Since I was on my own that day, I'd packed novels instead of a sand pail and shovel, and snacks with no redeeming nutritional value instead of sandwiches and fruit. Just as I was about to leave, the phone rang. On the other end, Norma's therapist was trying to enlist my help.

"I'm concerned about Norma," she said.

That's your job. Why are you bothering me about it? I wondered. But I said nothing.

"She's been talking about hurting herself. Has she said anything about this to you?"

"Norma and I don't talk very much anymore, except about Amelia."

"I understand, but maybe there's something you could say to her that would help."

This request seemed odd. I didn't think therapists usually solicited help, particularly not from the patient's most recent "ex." But maybe when a patient threatens to hurt herself the rules of professional conduct change.

"I don't think Norma and I are at a point right now where we can talk about something like this."

"I suppose you're right."

"Is there anything I can do that would help Amelia? I think that's how I could be most useful."

"No, I don't think that will be necessary," she said.

When I hung up the phone I felt confused. I knew Norma well enough to know that she wouldn't appreciate learning that her therapist had told me about her troubles. I was furious at the therapist for dropping this bomb in my lap and leaving it there. I tried to assess how serious Norma's problem might be, and what I could possibly do to help. What exactly did this therapist mean that Norma might hurt herself? Did she mean Norma might cut shallow scratches into her arms as she did when we first met? Or was she talking about Norma's quieter calls for help—showers that were too hot, meals that were too big or that were skipped altogether. Or was she reverting to the behavior her friends had once warned me about? Was she still the same young woman who had abused drugs and alcohol so badly that her college friends had worried she might one day die of an overdose? Those stories were from a long time ago. Surely Norma had changed.

For now, I reasoned, Norma was living with a friend, so maybe she would talk to her about what was going on. At least the presence of another adult in the house reassured me that Amelia would be all right. Maybe I should just go to the beach, I reasoned. Tomorrow, when Norma drops Amelia off for her visit, I could talk to her. I could offer to keep Amelia for a few days so she could get some rest, talk to friends, or do whatever she needed to feel better.

I was still thinking about leaving when the phone rang again. It was Marcia. "Norma just called us," Marcia said. "She asked John and me to watch Amelia for her. She sounded terrible. I'm really worried." Marcia said that Norma had threatened to drive herself into a wall or over a cliff or something, and that when Marcia had said she and John insisted she get some help, Norma just hung up. "Do you think she would really kill herself?" Marcia asked.

Kill herself? What was this? Maybe Norma wasn't just calling for attention. Maybe this was a serious plan. On the other hand, I knew Norma loved drama. She was always exaggerating.

Either way, going to the beach was out of the question. I kicked off my shoes, returned the chips and cookies I'd packed to the cupboards, and picked up the phone to call Norma. But as I began to dial her number, I reconsidered and called her friend Joan, instead. "Could you check on Norma and Amelia?" I asked. I explained what had happened, and Joan agreed that she would try to approach the subject without bringing up my name. "Call me if there's any news," I said.

I unfolded a lawn chair on the cement porch outside my ground-floor apartment and waited. The sky was a flawless blue and the sun on my face seemed to be reassuring me that everything would be all right. But just as I began to relax, I heard the phone ring inside. It was Norma.

"I don't appreciate your butting into my business," she said.

"Norma, I . . ." It was cool and dark in the apartment. The contrast was unsettling. I sank down onto the couch and tried to evaluate how best to proceed.

"If I had wanted your help I would have called you," Norma was saying.

"Listen, Norma, Marcia and John were worried. I just wanted to make sure that Amelia was safe and you were okay . . ."

"You only care about Amelia."

I took a deep breath. Conversations with Norma often took unexpected turns, and if I wasn't careful I knew I would become hopelessly lost. "Of course not. I was worried about both of you."

"You wouldn't have cared if it was just me."

"Oh, Norma, come on, I love you, I really do. Things have just been tense. That happens when two people break up."

"If you love me, why did you leave?"

"Norma, that's ridiculous! You wanted to split up, too."

"But then I changed my mind."

By now I was dizzy from trying to keep up with what was going on. It didn't seem like a good time to rehash our whole relationship just hours after Norma had threatened suicide. "Let's talk about all of this another time. Are you all right now? Would it help if I kept Amelia overnight so you can take care of yourself?"

"No. I don't need you anymore. I really don't."

"I know you don't *need* me. But this is a really stressful situation. Going through a breakup is hard enough. It's ten times harder when you have to take care of a baby."

I heard Norma start to sniffle. "It's really hard. I think she hates me. She throws tantrums over everything." Then she began to cry in earnest.

"Where's Amelia now?"

"Joan took her for a walk in the park."

"Okay, good."

"Is it hard for you, too?"

"Is what hard?"

"The breakup."

"Of course it is," I said without thinking. But the truth was, my life had gotten easier.

"That makes me feel better," Norma said. "I always think you're so strong. But you just don't show things the way I do."

"I show things in different ways," I said. But I was beginning to think that maybe I had been strong—too strong. I had propped Norma up for the four years we were together. Was she collapsing now because I had moved away? "Let me take Amelia overnight tomorrow. You probably just need a little rest."

"Okay," Norma said, sniffling quietly now. "I really appreciate this. Thank you so much."

I told her not to worry, to just take care of herself and Amelia. In the past my optimism had seemed to be contagious. If I could remain levelheaded and positive during a crisis with Norma, it seemed she could often stop slipping out of control. It felt as if there was still an invisible lifeline between us, and I had to stay on solid emotional ground or we would all—Amelia, Norma, and me—be pulled into oblivion.

In the weeks that followed, Norma confessed to me how fragile she felt her mental health was. She needed me to take more responsibility, she said. I was having my own problems with my physical health, but I was slowly improving. And besides, there was no question now that although I might be physically weak, I was on much more stable ground emotionally. We agreed that Amelia would spend more time with me, upping her overnight visits to one night every weekend instead of every other, and monthly weekend-long stays. Norma also decided to have a new power-of-attorney document drawn up, which in addition to giving me all of the standard rights (to make medical decisions for Amelia, to pick her up from day care, and so on), would also include a provision that I be Amelia's legal guardian if for any reason Norma could not make decisions on her own.

But what at first felt like a more equal sharing of responsibilities began to feel like a never-ending litany of demands. Months after the first big crisis, Norma asked me to promise that I would take Amelia anytime she was having trouble.

"That depends on what you define as trouble," I said. By this time there had been many occasions when Norma had asked me to change our schedule to accommodate her problems, large and very small. I began to feel like a baby-sitter, and "trouble" was becoming Norma's currency for buying my services. Meanwhile, I was beginning to worry again about my health. I hadn't been running fevers as often, and I could sometimes get through a day without having to take a nap after work. But I credited these improvements to the fact that I had become protective of my time, trying, in spite of everything, to keep my schedule manageable.

"I should never have let you help me," Norma was saying, alluding, I knew, to the first reluctant admission of defeat, after she'd threatened to drive off and kill herself.

No, I tried to explain. That was real trouble. But I started to feel out of control. If I didn't respond to each small request, did I forfeit my right to be depended upon in a large crisis? If she felt suicidal again, would she go back to calling Marcia and John? Did I actually want to keep propping her up?

"Of course, I'll try my best to be there if you're having trouble," I said.

II

Amelia, now a precocious two-and-a-half-year-old, had been driving her ride-on plastic fire engine across the floor of my studio apartment and kept finding herself nose to nose with the corner of the couch, the radiator, the handles of my bureau. "This house is too small for me," she whined. She was absolutely right. There was barely room for a double bed. I slept on a futon which I made up into a couch each morning so I would have enough room to move around in the apartment. On the nights when Amelia slept over, I unfolded a portable playpen in the hallway between the kitchenette and bathroom and used it as a crib. I kept the plastic dish drain in the kitchen sink because there was not enough counter space on which to put it. The possessions that I couldn't fit into my single closet, I stored in the trunk of my car. But I wasn't bothered the way Amelia was. Perhaps I didn't feel cramped because living on my own had been liberating; I was freer than I'd been in years.

After Amelia's outburst I began searching through classified ads for a more suitable apartment. Within a month I found one that I could afford, with a sunny back room that Amelia could sleep in on weekends and that I could use as a study during the week. The living room was large enough for the foldout futon and would make a comfortable bedroom for me.

The first time I'd moved I had hired a company to haul my belongings. This time, the first and last months' rent required for the apartment were more of a strain and I couldn't afford to pay a mover. I asked around among my friends, hoping someone would know someone with a truck I could borrow so I could do the job myself. I could certainly round up a few people who owed me favors and would help load the furniture in and out.

Veronica offered Whitney Sheppard's name. I was immediately suspicious of her true motive, because Veronica seemed to have appointed herself to the role of my personal matchmaker. Every time we met she dropped names of her single friends and asked which I found attractive. This time Veronica insisted she was only suggesting Whit because of her 4 x 4 pickup truck.

I had met Whitney a year before at a New Year's Eve party thrown by mutual friends. What I remembered most about her were her feet. That night Whit was wearing a tuxedo jacket, a white blouse, and tailored trousers. On her feet she wore a pair of black loafers, with no socks. I remembered staring at the bare arc of flesh visible between the cuff of her pants and the leather of her shoe, and wondering whether I admired her independent fashion statement or detested it.

I gave her a call and she said she wouldn't mind loaning her truck for the move. In fact, she'd give a hand with the boxes, too.

When she appeared at my house to help me move that day she was wearing jeans and workboots. I didn't ask if she was wearing socks. She joined my friends and me in packing and hauling boxes. She worked quietly, lifting the heaviest pieces of furniture, and seemed to appear out of nowhere whenever anyone else was swaying under too heavy a load. When it came time to drive to my new apartment she invited me to ride in her truck.

"I was glad you asked me to help," she said.

"I appreciate your being such a good sport. Especially since you hardly know me."

"Well, I liked you when we met at New Year's. But I was involved with someone then."

"Me too," I said.

There was an awkward silence, interrupted only when I had to tell Whit where to turn and which apartment was mine.

She helped unload the truck and stayed around until everyone else had gone.

"I'd like to do something to thank you for all your trouble," I said.

"No trouble." Whit settled into an armchair the previous tenants had left behind, as if she had no place else to go. "But I wouldn't turn you down if you asked me out to lunch," she said, her eyebrows arched expectantly.

When the day of our lunch date arrived, I spent an hour deciding what to wear. I hadn't been on a date in over five years, not since Norma and I had set off to go dancing and ended up stranded in a snowstorm. I should wear something casual this time, I decided. For one, it was just lunch. But more important, I was ambivalent about the idea of a real date, which implied the possibility of a real relationship, which for me at that moment meant the possibility of real heartbreak. I settled on a yellow sweater and a pair of print pants that I thought struck the right balance between casual and flattering.

For our date I had chosen a soup-and-sandwich shop in Central Square that was just on the verge of becoming trendy. When I entered the restaurant I saw Whit waiting for a table in a small crowd of students and shoppers. Her outfit didn't vary much from the one she had worn when she was helping me move, except that now she was wearing a button-down shirt with her clean blue jeans and workboots. The solid look of her stopped my breath.

"I hope you're not too hungry, they say it'll be ten minutes for a table." Whit's voice was cheerful and louder than I'd remembered it. As I struggled for things to say I began to feel depressed at the prospect of starting over, getting to know someone and trying her on for size as a potential love interest.

Finally, we were seated at a small round table along the rear wall, beneath a watercolor painting of a head of lettuce. Whit asked questions about my new apartment. She wanted to know how I'd decided to arrange my furniture, if the heavy antique sofa remained in the living room where she had left it, or if I'd moved it again. She said she'd noticed some of the windows in the bedroom and kitchen didn't have screens, and that there were some loose tiles in the bathroom.

"Do you always take such an interest in the details of other people's apartments?" I finally asked.

Whit's face reddened a shade. "No, just sometimes," she said, and looked back to her menu as the waitress approached.

After she ordered, Whit explained that she had bought a house in a small beach town near Hingham, and was in the process of renovating it. "I guess I'm a little preoccupied with home improvement these days," she explained.

By the time our food arrived I realized I had set up a mental scorecard on which to rate Whit. She would gain or lose points based on each new fact I learned about her. The way she leaned in to listen to what I had to say, her blue eyes seeming to widen with interest, impressed me. Her stories about her job as a wholesale sales manager at a local coffee roaster seemed to indicate that she worked hard at whatever she did, and I liked that, too. The location of her house, nearly an hour's commute from the city, was a negative. I liked being in the center of things, and was sorry to hear that she would avoid Boston altogether if it weren't for her work. She didn't think much of poetry, and preferred reading biographies of politicians and entrepreneurs, two groups of people about whom I wouldn't voluntarily read more than a thousand-word article at a time. By the time the meal had ended, Whit's plate was clean. Not an edge of crust nor a single forkful of coleslaw remained from her Reuben Special Lunch Platter. On my plate there was still a small pile of french fries, a pickle, and a handful of corned beef that I had pulled out of my overstuffed sandwich. Over Whit's protests, I insisted on paying the check. As I fished a ten and a few singles out of my wallet I decided that Whit and I weren't suited for one another. I wanted a partner who was interested in the arts. I was hoping for someone who loved sitting in city cafés, watching people pass by and imagining the stories of their lives. As for her desire to live closer to nature, a ride on the swan boats in the park was enough of a country getaway for me.

When I told Veronica what I had decided, she couldn't contain her impatience. "It was a date, not a marriage proposal," she said. "Give her another chance." I did. Over the next few weeks I went

with Whit to the movies, to dinner, and to a Red Sox game at
Fenway Park. Ater the game we walked through the Fens, admiring the different ways people had landscaped their small garden
plots. "Look there," Whit said, putting her arm around my waist
and pulling me close. Someone had made a Japanese garden with
rings of raked sand that looked like rippled water. I felt peaceful,
and suddenly I couldn't remember why I had been resisting this
closeness.

The next time Whit asked me out I told her it was my night
with Amelia. "Could I join the two of you for an ice cream cone or
something?" she asked. This was the kind of question my ideal
suitor would pose. I had told her about Amelia, of course, but
somehow I didn't expect her to care much for children, let alone
dates that involved a seven o'clock curfew. Nonetheless, Whit
rose to the occasion, and she and Amelia spent half the time in
the ice cream parlor playing a game that Whit invented, which
involved Amelia circling her chair trying not to get tagged. This
could really work out, I thought, as I watched them play. Then,
when I woke up one morning upstairs in the house Whit was
remodeling, and smelled bacon frying downstairs, and moments
later saw Whit coming through the bedroom door with a breakfast tray, I knew I was in heaven.

I thought it best not to say anything to Norma about Whit right
away. As for Amelia, I presented Whit as I would any other friend.
As much as possible I kept my time with Whit and my time with
Amelia separate. I knew what it was like to be a child witness to the
ups and downs of a parent's dating life. When my parents began
seeing other people after their divorce, they introduced us kids to
each of their new lovers. Besides the unavoidable awkwardness of
meeting the object of my parent's romantic interest, I never liked
the way these men and women came and went in our lives. It
seemed that just as we got attached to one of them, their relationship with my mother or father would end and there would be no
hope of ever seeing them again. I wanted to shield Amelia from
this kind of frustration. At the same time, I was trying to protect
Norma from feeling jealous and myself from Norma's reaction.

Maybe it was my insistence on erecting firm boundaries that
made my evenings and afternoons with Whit feel as though they
existed inside a soap bubble. The rest of my life was clouded with
concern over Amelia, who had been showing signs of distress.

She complained that she was too tired to build with her blocks, too tired to help in the kitchen, and too tired to bring her plate to the sink when she finished her supper. At first I had dismissed these moods as Amelia's way of adjusting to all of the changes in her life. But as these sullen spells grew more frequent, I could no longer deny that she was acting less like the toddler that she was, and more like a depressed adult.

One night I drew her a bath before bed, hoping that would brighten her mood. Amelia, like Norma, loved to soak in the tub. But on this night, Amelia just pushed a green plastic boat from one end of the bathtub to the other. Her mechanical motions reminded me of the polar bear we'd watched swimming at the zoo in New York. We had thought the bear looked graceful swimming back and forth from wall to wall with an unbroken rhythm. But later we learned from a friend who was studying animal psychology that the bear was acting out of intense frustration and boredom; it was lost in an insane dream.

Now Amelia was sending her toy boat from one wall to the other of the tub. The penny perched up front was the ship's captain, she told me. The hypnotic rhythm of her game was broken only when the boat capsized and the penny sank to the bottom of the tub. When Amelia reached down to retrieve it, she bumped her head on the faucet. Her cries sounded as panicked and inconsolable as if she had split her skull. Yet the accident was less serious than most of the dozens of mishaps that marked her days as a curious toddler.

Amelia's cries that night could have been my own. I was desperate to help her break out of the dense unhappiness that seemed to have buried her. As I rubbed her head where she had bumped it I felt as though I were sending a tendril of my spirit down to reach hers. I wanted to help pull her out of her sorrow.

I lifted Amelia out of the water and wrapped her in a Mickey Mouse bath towel. As she cried I rocked her and reassured her that she was okay. But I wondered whether I had misjudged the accident. I even hoped that this was the case. Any cut or bruise would be easier to heal than what I suspected was truly wrong. "Where does it hurt, little goose?" I asked, running my fingers through her fine hair once more.

"It doesn't," she cried, her sorrow so desperate, so complete.

I carried her into the living room. The change of scene had a calming effect. "I'm tired, Ima. Can I go to sleep now?"

In a reversal of roles, I suggested we read a book first. After getting into her pajamas, Amelia agreed. That night she didn't have to ask me to stay with her until she fell asleep.

As much as I tried to keep my worlds separate, it was inevitable that one day they would meet, and one bright blue afternoon in February, they did. Whit mistakenly came a half hour early to pick me up for a date, just as I was getting Amelia ready to return to Norma. I knew Norma would feel uncomfortable when she arrived to pick up Amelia if she met Whit unprepared. So I asked Whit to wait inside while Amelia and I went out to meet her. As if she suspected something, Norma asked to come inside to use the bathroom. I told her that Whit had arrived early to pick me up, and that it was up to her whether she wanted to go inside. "You're seeing Whitney?" she asked. "Whitney Sheppard?" I nodded. "For a couple of months, now," I said, sensing that Norma was building up to something.

"And does she spend the night here?"

"If you're concerned about Amelia, no, she doesn't spend the night here when Amelia's visiting."

"But she spends time with her?"

"A little. Sometimes."

Norma shot a look at Amelia who was climbing on a low pile of snow the plow had created at the edge of the parking lot. "Come on, pumpkin, let's go," she called, and loaded Amelia into her car seat without looking at me. After Norma went to the front of the car I opened the backdoor and gave Amelia a hug and a kiss good-bye. "I'll send you kisses tonight," I told her. "Don't forget to catch them." I reminded Norma that I would be picking Amelia up from day care on Wednesday.

"Fine," Norma said, as she shifted into reverse.

Wednesday was my birthday, and I was thrilled that my plans were to celebrate with Amelia. We would buy a mix and bake a cake. Given her age, this activity should consume the better part of the afternoon. First we would pick through boxes of cake mix at the grocery store, debating between chocolate or vanilla "outsides" and "insides" (frosting and cake). Then there was the joy of mixing. Amelia loved the wire whisk, the wooden spoon, the nested bowls. Making egg disappear into milk, and dry powder transform into batter, was a form of magic that mesmerized her. Then we would dump handfuls of colored sprinkles onto newly spread icing as if we were tossing stars onto the heavens. I couldn't imagine a better way to celebrate getting one year older.

But the night before my birthday, just as Whit and I were getting into bed, the phone rang. I picked it up in the living room. It was Norma. "You can't see Amelia tomorrow."

"What?" I turned my back to the open bedroom door where Whit was waiting.

"In fact, you are never going to see her again. I don't want you anywhere near her."

"Is this about Whit? Can we talk about it?"

"There's nothing to talk about. I'm her mother, and that's it."

I stood stunned in the living room, listening for a minute to the dead air after Norma had hung up the phone. I didn't want to go back to bed. I didn't want to tell Whit.

"I knew she'd do this," Whit said. "It's just jealousy because you're seeing someone and she's not. She'll get over it."

"You don't know her," I said. "She means it." All I remember about the rest of the night is how hard I cried. I had arranged to take the next day off as my birthday present to myself, but when I woke up, the idea of an empty house was appalling. Whit called in to work, saying she'd be late, and stayed around to listen to me cry until close to noon. "We're still going to celebrate your birthday, you know."

"But we don't have plans together. It was going to be my night with Amelia."

"Well, now we do have plans together. I'll pick you up at six-thirty, so dress up."

I did my best to enjoy the elegant dinner that Whit treated me to. The chicken bathed in cream sauce, asparagus out of season, and chocolate mousse for dessert distracted me enough that I didn't shed a tear through the entire meal. That night, Whit took me home and carried me into bed. She drew the covers up and held me until I fell asleep. I had never before felt so cared for. And yet I felt completely alone.

Each day that week when I pulled into the parking lot at work, I had to force myself to stop crying before I left my car. I considered calling a lawyer, but decided I should wait. Norma would change her mind, Whit reassured me. And while I suspected that she was probably right, the possibility of Norma's eventual change of heart provided little comfort. "How can I trust her again even if she does?" I asked.

Exactly five days later the phone rang. Norma apologized profusely. What she had done was wrong, she said. Why didn't I come by right away and take Amelia out for pizza or something? I wanted to scream at her for all that she had put me through, but I didn't want to waste the time, or take the chance that she'd change her mind. I should have known better than to believe that her apology meant she had truly had a change of heart. I should have known that this time was no different from all of the others. Since I had known Norma she had so often acted rashly, and later made up sweetly. Nonetheless, I was drawn as if by a magnet. The phone fell into its cradle, and I was jogging the three blocks to Norma's apartment. Before I could even come up with the words to express my anger I was gathering Amelia into my arms.

Norma didn't tell me until months later that during those five days she had gone to City Hall and changed Amelia's last name. I had called her during my lunch break to discuss my schedule with Amelia. For some reason she decided it was time to confess. "I took off Abrams," she said. "You did what?" I asked in horror and disbelief. "Didn't you need my consent? How could you?"

"I'm sorry," she said. "But I've never been happy with her name. You talked me into calling her Amelia. It was never my first choice. So I decided to give her a new middle name, and if I'd kept your last name it would have been too long."

Too long? When I returned to work I stormed over to my desk and called the probate court to find out what the procedure was for changing a child's name. "Are you the child's mother?" the clerk asked. "Yes," I said. All that was needed then was a copy of the birth certificate, she explained. "What about the child's father? Are you still married?" she asked. I told her I had never been. In that case the birth certificate should be enough. For a minor it wasn't even necessary to run a legal notice in the newspaper. I realized I was getting dizzy from holding my breath.

III

The only reason I tried the dress on was that it was June, the month of brides and weddings, and it was there in front of me, in my size. I was shopping with Sam for something she could wear to her cousin's wedding. She had in mind a dressy pantsuit, maybe some linen trousers with a matching jacket. She couldn't see herself in a dress. Neither could I. In fact, I hadn't seen her wear one in the six years I'd known her.

So it was that I was flipping through pants, blouses, and shirts on the discount rack when I found the wedding dress.

"Try it on," Sam said.

"Why? I'd never wear it."

"Why not? Go ahead."

I took the dress to the fitting room. It was white silk. The hemline was cut on a diagonal, giving the dress a playful look, as if it were winking at the chastity and purity it promised to represent.

The last time I'd put on a wedding dress, I was thirteen years old. It was my mother's and it smelled of mothballs and tired old wood. It had been stored in a box in the closet behind the washing machine, the same closet where she hid our Hanukkah presents each year—where we peeked into what wasn't yet ours. I lifted the dress out of its box. It was stiff and dry. It whispered to me of elegance.

Was I allowed? Without thinking, as if I were entitled, I stripped down, right there in the laundry room. The cement floor sent shivers through my knee socks. As I stepped into the dress, layers of lace and satin hugged me like a best girlfriend. At age thirteen my mother's wedding dress fit me. I remember thinking that I'd better not grow any bigger.

Once I had it on, I didn't worry anymore that I could get in trouble. I called my mother downstairs, pirouetted for her in the basement, then stood stiff as the old lace on my shoulders while she stared. It took her too long to smile.

Family legends keep their shape no matter how many years they are stored away. My mother was a beautiful bride. My father, glorious in his Navy whites, stood by her side in my grandfather's backyard. I've seen their wedding day click by in home movies. I've stared into the frame where they stand forever under a garden trellis, bride and groom. I still believed in this fairy tale then. It was then, perhaps, that I began to know that she no longer did.

A couple of years later, after my parents' divorce, and after my grandfather tore their wedding portrait down the center and left her half in the frame, my mother and I packed up our basement together. We sifted through cartons of old school assignments, canceled checks, ceramic ashtrays and glitter-dipped pinecones that my brother, sister, and I had given our parents as presents. But the dress was gone.

Did it disintegrate piece by piece? Did the fabric start to yellow and dry? Did it crumble away as the home movies clicked on, more and more slowly? When the film stopped, was the dress gone? Did she sell it at a tag sale? Was it donated to a thrift shop? She might have burned it.

When I asked, my mother said she didn't remember.

I think of the way bridesmaids dye pumps lavender to match their dresses. Trains that catch on the bottom step. Wedding dresses stitched from grandmothers' patterns. Antique lace. Mother of pearl. Father of the bride. Bridal fairs. Women who wear white the second time around. Women who wear cocktail dresses. Green velvet with valentine necklines. The bride and groom on top of a cardboard cake. Fairy tales dressed up like brides. Promises hidden under veils. I wonder what it means that some people believe them and some never will.

"Can I come in?" Sam asked from the other side of the dressing room curtain. I looked at myself in the mirror. Long, pointy sleeves tapped my wrists in just the right places. The skirt was tight with a long, easy slit down the side. I slid open the curtain and walked the floor in the dress. "It's perfect," Sam said.

"Perfect for what?"

"One day Whit might pop the question, and you always like to be prepared."

Norma and I had been engaged. We had exchanged rings while soaking in a bubble bath. I'd hidden hers in the bottom of a glass of champagne. Mine had been in one of those black velvet boxes. It was soon after that night that Norma became pregnant, and the baby took over our thoughts. The wedding never came to be.

Veronica and Grace had recently had their commitment ceremony. They made their vows in front of the Unitarian minister. It wasn't legal, of course, and neither set of parents attended the ceremony. Lesbians can't really get married, I thought. Not any more than we can really have children together. We can do it, as I had done, but without the protection or privileges afforded by society to straight people, we were really on our own, unprotected and unrecognized. I was tired of being different. Tired of inventing rituals and names for things and tired of trying to convince the world that I was just like them.

"How much?" Sam asked.

"I'm not buying it."

Sam shrugged and held up a silk jacket she'd picked out. I changed back into my jeans and helped her search for a pair of slacks to match.

That night Whit stopped by after work. "What did you do today?" she asked, stretching out on my couch.

"I think we should talk about something," I blurted out. Until I had said the words, I didn't realize how determined I was to end our relationship. I couldn't say why, but it just felt wrong. "I don't think this relationship is leading anywhere," I said.

"What are you talking about?"

"I really can't say. But I've made my decision."

Whit wanted to know what I meant, how long I'd been thinking about this, if there was someone else. But I couldn't answer her questions and I couldn't explain. All I knew, on some wordless level, was that I couldn't picture a future for us. Perhaps the problem was that I couldn't picture a future at all.

I didn't feel sad, but I did feel sorry as I watched Whit pull her fingers through her short blonde hair, as if the gesture could help her sort out my words.

After she left I broke the news to Veronica. "But everything seemed so good between you two," she said.

"Everything seemed good with Norma at first, too." I knew how cold I sounded. But I couldn't force regret. I had no reservations about what I had done. I didn't question my motives or my behavior. Hopelessness about human nature and human relationships seemed like a natural stance. In the meantime, I enjoyed how much simpler life seemed, pared back again to Norma, Amelia, and me.

Even though I didn't tell Norma that Whit and I had broken up, it seemed to have an effect. We began to get along better. By this time, she and Amelia had moved into their own apartment. Now that she didn't have a roommate, Norma seemed to call me more often. She confided in me about problems she was having. For starters, she was planning a vacation for Amelia and herself, and was worried that she couldn't drive to and from the Cape because the sleeping pills she'd begun taking again made her feel groggy. "Maybe you could come with us?" she suggested. I put off giving her an answer but I didn't mind considering the question. It meant I had my job back, I was taking care of Norma.

To this day I can't help wondering where my drive to nurture and protect Norma came from, but it was there, and it had been activated again. As the youngest of three children, the role of caretaker had never been mine to claim. As a child I didn't coo over dolls or push them in carriages. I preferred to play teacher, lining my stuffed animals up to be my students. It has always been disturbingly easy for me to pass by a stray, hungry cat without wanting to bring it home. Even in the coldest winters, I didn't feel compelled to fill the bird feeder a previous tenant had hung on my porch.

Norma was an exception for me. In previous relationships I had been the one who was coddled and cared for. Maybe I felt I had a karmic debt to pay. It was my turn to cater to someone else's needs. When I gave in to the urge to pamper and protect Norma, it felt good. I was surprised how glad I was to give. And give. It wasn't perfect but at least I was back in a role I'd grown used to. As if anesthetized, I continued forward without looking back. Then, two weeks after she had left my apartment, Whit called. She had some things I'd left at her house and wanted to know if she could come by to drop them off.

That night she climbed the stairs to my door carrying two shopping bags filled with some of my clothes and books that had accumulated at her house.

"Can you give me a better explanation about why you had to break up with me yet?" Whit didn't seem angry. Maybe hurt. Definitely very careful.

"I told you, I didn't think our relationship was going anywhere." I was standing in the front hallway, as though I were intentionally blocking Whit from stepping all the way inside.

"That doesn't make any sense. Where exactly did you want it to go?"

"Well, you know, we can't even get married. It's like we're faking it."

"Faking it?" Whit's round eyes narrowed into slits. Her mouth grew taut. "Because society won't let us get married, suddenly our love is fake? That's really fucked up."

"I can't help it. That's how I feel." I wanted to sit down. I backed up into the living room, but Whit made no move to follow.

"So what does this mean, you're not a lesbian anymore?"

"Maybe."

Whit reached behind for the doorknob. I couldn't tell if she was about to cry or scream. But then her hand fell to her side and her eyes relaxed into comfortable circles again. She looked straight at me, and stepped forward. All at once I couldn't believe what I had done. I felt as if I was waking from a dream. "You know, I don't believe you," Whit said. "This has nothing to do with marriage or being lesbian or anything else. You've cut off your emotions because they seem too difficult to deal with, and so it's too hard to have me around. When I'm here you have to feel something." I thought that in that moment Whit could walk away, and be at peace with losing me. She was confident that this had nothing to do with her. Her strength and calm impressed me. I had expected a scene—hurt feelings, angry words, slammed doors. Instead, I motioned Whit inside. She walked past me and took a seat on the couch as if to challenge me with her presence. Her shoulders were relaxed and round again. We both knew she was right.

I *had* turned off my feelings. But also, I felt I had lost the strength to live as a lesbian. I couldn't stand to have any more of my life denied to me. Already I wasn't being allowed to be Amelia's parent. I could never be Whit's wife. Not that I wanted to be a wife, exactly, but I wanted to be seen within my relationship. I wanted our love to exist not only in private, but outside, too. I wanted it to be there at the counter in the pizza place if I felt like holding Whit's hand while we waited for our order. I wanted it to be recognized at the YMCA so I could sign us up for a family membership. I wanted to lord it over the checkout girl in the grocery store when she complained that her husband never cooks. It would be nice to be able to tell anyone who would listen how lucky I was that my partner, Whitney (I could even use the feminine pronoun if I wanted), makes the world's best chicken enchiladas. If I were to turn my feelings on again, I would feel all of this; the losses and the longing and the love.

I opened my mouth to speak, but I could not. With words simultaneously forming and crumbling in the back of my throat I crossed the room and sat beside Whit. I pulled her into my arms and kissed her neck, her face, and her hair with an animal force, an urge to join, to survive, to have and to keep. Her arm wrapped around me, but cautiously. "What is this all about?"

"I was wrong," I said. "I'm sorry. I was wrong."

There had barely been time to heal the damage I had caused by my sudden need to break up with Whit, and my just as sudden change of heart, before the next crisis hit. An old friend of Norma's called me after spending the weekend visiting her and

Amelia. "Did you know that Norma takes handfuls of sleeping pills every night, and she's still nursing Amelia?" I knew that although Amelia was nearly three years old, Norma still nursed her before bedtime. I didn't approve, but I knew that in some circles it was considered good for the child to breast-feed for as long as she wanted. I also knew about the pills—more or less. Norma had begun taking them off and on after we broke up, and had occasionally, as far as I knew, used them when she was under a lot of stress. But handfuls? Surely this was an exaggeration. The last time we had spoken about it, Norma said she'd given them up. "I'm only telling you," my informant said, "because I'm worried about Amelia, and I think someone should do something."

Before I could decide what to do with this new information, I received a hysterical phone call from Norma herself. It was Saturday afternoon and she was saying that she couldn't cope anymore. "I'm going to put Amelia up for adoption," she said. I could hear Amelia in the background begging Norma for another cookie. My anger boiled over as I realized that Amelia was in the room listening to all of this. "I'm coming over," I said.

The first thing I did when I arrived at Norma's apartment was to call around to find a baby-sitter for Amelia. But having no success I worked on calming Norma down so that we wouldn't frighten Amelia any more than we already had. She wouldn't stay in front of the video I'd put on in the living room, so Norma and I took turns holding her in our laps. I got the phone number of Norma's therapist, and went into the other room to make some calls. Yes, the therapist knew Norma was taking too many sleeping pills, she said, but the addiction would just have to run its course. I didn't want to raise my voice because of Amelia and Norma in the next room, but that didn't stop me from seething. "What kind of a person are you? You know Norma lives alone with a three-year-old, and yet you think it's fine to let an addiction run its course? What if she went into a coma? How do you expect a three-year-old to take care of that situation? What if the building was on fire and Amelia couldn't wake her?"

"You're getting all excited about nothing," the therapist said.

"Well, perhaps you could at least help me get Norma checked into a rehabilitation center."

"She would never go."

"She just told me she would. I'm with her right now."

"No, I'm afraid I won't do that. I don't think it's necessary.

Norma has to learn to live within society." I crouched down on Norma's futon. The layers of tapestries and cushions made her world appear so inviting, so warm.

"Don't you understand what's happening here? She wants to go. She asked me to call you."

After going around with this woman for ten minutes I gave up. I called Emergency Services, and they said one of their therapists would meet us at an office nearby in half an hour. The news that help was on the way soothed Norma. I assured her that I would take care of Amelia while she was in rehabilitation, and that everything would be fine. I assured her that Amelia would visit, making no promises about myself. That afternoon, Norma was checked into a center for drug and alcohol addiction, and Amelia and I settled into our own routine.

I took Amelia swimming at the YMCA twice a week after work, and once a week we'd go for dinner at a nearby Burger King. Other nights we cooked dinners together, and I taught her how to set the table.

Like all children her age, Amelia was always asking questions. And like all parents, I suppose, I didn't always know the answers. But now, Amelia's questions, voiced and unvoiced, were even more difficult than such standards as, Why is the sky blue?

I decided that helping Amelia to develop a relationship with a caring, loving God might be the most substantial thing I could offer in the face of this latest crisis with her mother, and the latest round of unanswerable questions. I had been attending, off and on, a Reconstructionist synagogue which was led by a rabbi whose interpretation of Judaism seemed particularly compassionate and relevant. So on Saturday morning I told Amelia we were going to temple.

As we walked toward the T stop we noticed a swallow perched on the curb at the end of our block. I was in too much of a rush to wonder why it didn't fly off as we walked past. Having barely managed to transform Amelia, who had awakened weekday-early on a Saturday, into the bright-eyed, neatly combed child now clutching my hand, I was determined to carry on. By the time we turned the corner, I had forgotten the bird.

At synagogue I told Amelia that we'd have to be very quiet and listen carefully to the rabbi. But it was all I could do to keep her in her seat. I had brought along a bag of picture books for her just in case, and within fifteen minutes I'd resorted to letting Amelia page through her favorites. Within an hour we were out the door. If Amelia learned anything from the experience it was that the burnished wooden benches at synagogue are not cozy enough for snuggling up with a book, and that the rabbi speaks in a language not even Ima can understand. So much for answers.

As we climbed out of the T station and headed home, I noticed the same brown swallow still sitting on the curb. This time I stopped.

Having never touched a bird before, I hesitated before helping this one. But there were at least three cats on our block, and I knew if I didn't do something, the bird would soon be killed. A neighbor stepped out of his house and joined us as we hovered over the helpless creature. "Looks like he has a torn wing," the man offered.

"Where?" Amelia asked. "Who tore it?" More questions.

"I'd take it in," the man said, "but my cat . . ."

"Who tore it, Ima?" Amelia was asking.

"I don't know, sweetheart," I said, sinking down for a closer look.

"Can we fix it?" Amelia asked.

"You could try," the man said.

I had been hoping no one would suggest this. "I'm afraid we have a cat, too," I said.

"Ahab's at Whit's house,' Amelia offered.

She was right. Whit was taking care of our pets while Amelia was with me.

Minutes later, armed with a shoe box and towel, Amelia and I returned to the bird. I lifted it into the box and carried it home. We placed a saucer of cat food and another of water inside, as our neighbor had suggested, and set the box by the window, hoping the blue sky would inspire its recovery. "When it's all better can I play with it?' Amelia asked.

"When it gets better we'll let him go so he can find his family," I told her.

Peering into the box, Amelia dubbed our new pet "a Dalmatian bird," because of the spots on its breast. The bird tucked its head into its feathers and seemed to be resting, so Amelia and I went out to pick up some groceries.

When we returned the bird was lying in the box, legs at crazy angles. "It looks like the bird died," I said, feeling like a failure.

Norma, who was always so good with animals, would have been able to save it, I thought.

Amelia picked up the box. "Will its wing get better?"

I had expected Amelia to be devastated, but now I realized that she didn't know what death meant. I picked the bird up in the towel and showed its still head to Amelia. "See, he's not moving anymore. We'll bury him so God can take him back." Amelia looked puzzled. "Remember at synagogue today how we prayed to God?" Amelia nodded. "Well, God takes care of all the people and creatures on the Earth, when they are alive and after they die."

We took the bird out back to bury it. Amelia threw a handful of dirt into the grave as I explained is the Jewish custom. "Now will he go find his family?" she asked. I patted the last handful of dirt into place.

"No, sweetheart, death means now the bird can't fly anymore. We buried his body and now God will take care of his spirit."

That night at dinner Amelia said, "God will fix the bird's wing and then he'll fly home." She nodded, as if she were quite certain. This time I didn't try to argue. Our trip to synagogue seemed a long time ago, and now I knew what I had always known: There are no simple answers. And what Amelia would learn of God, she'd learn from all the looming questions.

One night a couple of weeks later, Amelia and I were returning from a block party in a friend's neighborhood when I heard a familiar voice calling my name. We were just about to get into the car when I looked up to see a man I knew well from my beat. He was the council president in a nearby district, and as such, he had served as a steady source of inside information. Just days before, as I sat opposite his massive mahogany desk which was crowded with models of warships, he'd asked if I were married. "No," I'd said.

"A girl as nice as you, I can't believe you've never gotten married."

"Never," I said.

Now, here I was with Amelia clutching my hand. He looked from me to her and back again. "And what have we here, a little friend to enjoy the festivities with?" The councilman's voice boomed through the night.

I imagined having to explain the situation on Monday when I

would show up in his office to find out whether the police chief was indeed under investigation for driving under the influence. I didn't want to lie about divorce or single parenthood, and I didn't want to come out to him either. It seemed easier to let him believe that Amelia was nothing more than my little buddy. "Yes," I said. "It's getting late, though. I'd better take her home."

Closed into the car I could scarcely stand the fit of my own skin. I felt like retching, as if that would purge me of my dishonesty and cowardice. What Amelia thought, I couldn't know; she fell asleep in her car seat almost instantly.

The next morning I explained to her over breakfast how some people have never met a family like ours, and how sorry I was that I hadn't taken the time to explain our family to the man we met after the party last night. Amelia, however, seemed far more interested in sifting through bits of her cereal, separating out the raisins. "Which man?" she asked.

During Norma's stay in the rehab, my mother called and suggested I speak with a lawyer. "Why?" I asked. "A lawyer can't do anything for me. I have no legal right to demand anything and if I tried to set some kind of a precedent I'd throw us all into a media circus. I can see the headlines now: Lesbians Fight in Bizarre Custody Case."

"But you don't know any of that for certain," my mother argued. "At least find out what your rights are. What if Norma doesn't get better, and you need to take care of Amelia full-time, on a long-term basis? You know how supportive of Norma I've always been, but if she's really this troubled, maybe you should consider getting custody."

"Okay, let's say I thought that was the best thing, and let's say I could fight for custody—where would I get the money to pay a lawyer?"

There was a long pause. I knew my mother wanted to offer to foot the bill, but she had been laid off from her teaching job and had been unemployed for nearly a year. My father wouldn't help. He didn't think I should have gotten involved with Norma to begin with, let alone have a child with her. "There are gay and lesbian advocacy groups. Maybe one of them would take the case pro bono."

"This isn't the kind of case they want. They want lesbians versus the system. Not lesbian versus lesbian."

"Why do you assume that? Why don't you find out?"

"Fine. Let's say I could find a lawyer to take the case, and who could get me temporary custody while Norma got better. You know Norma as well as I do, and I'd have to be dragging back to the judge every other month to fight her appeals or to try to make her keep to our agreement."

"Let's take this one step at a time," my mother said. "Just find out where you stand."

I knew this was nearly as hard on my mother as it was on me. Amelia was her only grandchild, and it never occurred to her to think of her as any less important because of our family structure. I wanted to do what she asked, if only to appease her, but it was all I could do to get my teeth brushed and my clothes on straight in those days, let alone find the time and focus to research my legal rights. "I'll do it, Mom, but just not right away, okay?"

"You know what kills me? If you were a man and had married Norma, this wouldn't be a question. Your rights would be guaranteed."

"I know, Mom," I said. But I was too overwhelmed to get angry over anything as abstract as that.

Still, that conversation made me realize that I should at least get some facts. First, I did some research to find out if Norma's behavior constituted neglect or incompetency of any kind, and if there was anything in my power to do. I visited a therapist, who listened to my tale about the pills, Norma's threats to put Amelia up for adoption, and Amelia's complaints of fatigue and her other signs of depression. Without registering any emotion on her face, the therapist instructed me to call the Department of Social Services and report Norma. "This sounds quite serious," she said. There was no question, in her mind at least, that there was trouble.

With a lurching stomach I went home and made an anonymous call to the Department of Social Services to feel out what course of action they might take. "Does the child have any visible cuts or bruises?" the man on the other end of the telephone asked. "She doesn't, but she has told me that her mother hits her sometimes." I explained quickly about the problem Norma had with prescription drugs and Amelia's emotional distress.

"To be honest, if there are no cuts or bruises we have no evidence of abuse. We're very backed up and we wouldn't get to a case like the one you're describing for quite a long time, if ever."

I wasn't altogether surprised that the outside world of professionals wasn't going to ride in on a team of white horses and save the day. I don't know what I expected them to do—agree that Norma was unstable and hand Amelia to me for good? I just wanted someone to help. This was becoming too much for me to shoulder alone.

Next I made a list of lesbian and gay advocacy groups. Those I contacted said they were quite sorry. They couldn't, or wouldn't, be able to offer legal representation. Instead, they sent pamphlets about lesbians and custody issues from which it was clear that they assumed custody battles would be waged against an ex-husband or boyfriend. Finally I visited a straight family lawyer whom a friend had recommended.

Attorney Barbara Kaplan's office was housed on the second floor of a professional building in Boston, along with a number of doctors' and dentists' suites. Sitting in the leather chair opposite her desk, I looked beyond her padded shoulders to the photographs displayed on a low counter. Two preschoolers frozen in Kodak time eyed me from within the borders of a green picture frame placed between vases of dried lavender and pink flowers. Their scrubbed faces, eager knees perched above tricycle pedals, and matching playsuits challenged me. Why did my daughter complain that she was too tired to play in the middle of a Saturday? Why did she say she was too tired to get out of the bathtub? Why did she shriek and insist I'd hurt her terribly when I had merely wrapped my hand around her arm?

I pried my eyes from the pictures of her children and listed my concerns: Amelia's mother had been overdosing on sleeping pills, and she even admitted to me that the reason Amelia had begun wetting her bed again was that she was too drugged to wake when Amelia asked to be taken to the bathroom. I described the breakfasts of cookies and doughnuts that Amelia reported eating at home. I emphasized the fact that I had a good job on a suburban newspaper. "I know I can take care of her," I said, adding quickly that I wasn't interested in taking her from Norma forever, just until she was well enough to take care of Amelia again. Looking back, I'm not sure who I was trying harder to convince of my optimism when I said that I was sure Norma would get better—that I just wanted to know what it was in my legal power to do, just in case when she returned from rehab Norma was no better off.

Barbara Kaplan's worried frown cemented for me the seriousness of my dilemma. I must have been hoping that an objective
professional would tell me that I was overreacting and my worries were all in my mind. I didn't want to face the fact that my
child was in serious trouble, and that I, with no legal standing,
was the one person who seemed willing to help. I remembered
my nightmares before Amelia was born that my arms weren't
strong enough to hold her. Now that fear was turning to reality.

"Normally I would recommend that you try to gain at least
temporary custody," Barbara explained. Normally being of
course if I had been the child's father; if I had been a man. While
it was rare, possibly even unprecedented, for a judge to give a
child to a lesbian co-parent, she went on, we could try. She didn't
think that my being a lesbian would be a detriment to the case per
se, but if a blood relative of Amelia's contested my claim, he or
she would have a far better chance than I to win custody. The
thought of Amelia being placed with Norma's parents terrified
me because Norma traced her own problems to her childhood.
Eli might take her, but I doubted that his wife Lindsay would go
along with it. The other possibility was that Amelia could become
a ward of the state and be placed in foster care. The judges in
Massachusetts had no track record with lesbian custody cases, she
explained. It was anybody's guess which way such a hearing
would go. The first step in the process, she said, was to prove that
Norma was an unfit mother. "I don't think we'll have any problem doing that," she added.

As I waited for the elevator to take me down, I felt horrified
that I was actually considering turning against Norma like this.
Maybe I was overreacting.

I thought back to our early days together, when Norma had a
cocker spaniel named Oliver. She had toted Oliver around in a
backpack when he was a puppy, and even when he became too
big too carry, she talked store owners into letting him accompany her through the aisles. She always fed him before she sat
down to eat herself. One day, as she was unloading groceries
from the back of her car, Oliver, who'd been sitting up front,
crawled between the seats and jumped out through the backdoor. Norma called to him, but he kept going. She put down the
bag of groceries in her hand and took off after him. She followed him through an alley between two rows of houses, but she
couldn't find where he went from there. This had happened

before, though, and he always came home. She didn't panic until evening.

"Why can't I ever keep anything I love?" she cried after we combed the neighborhood calling Oliver's name. "Why does everything I love get taken away from me?"

Recalling the depths of her utter despair, I decided to hold off on the idea of going to court. Despite everything, I loved Norma and I sympathized with her troubles. I couldn't bear the thought of causing her more pain. Balancing her needs against Amelia's seemed impossibly difficult. Amelia still needed Norma, after all. She missed her terribly while Norma was away and always wanted to go along when Joan offered to bring her on a visit to the rehab. And right now Norma was seeking the help she needed, wasn't she? There had to be some middle ground. Something we could do together without involving courts and judges and the possibility that the decision would be taken from us entirely. The threat of having Amelia land in the hands of the state and wind up in foster care stopped my blood.

Norma would be home soon. I would talk to her. I would suggest that she let me take a bigger role in Amelia's life. I could take her for entire weekends, or even weeks, instead of just one night at a time. We could plan longer visits at more frequent intervals so Norma could get more rest. I wanted her to agree that next time she would bring Amelia to me before a crisis built. If she wouldn't consent to some kind of dramatic change, I would raise the possibility of bringing our case before a judge. But I was sure that wouldn't be necessary. We'd work things out on our own, just as we had worked out all of our other problems. After all, it wasn't as if I *wanted* to become a full-time parent. Meanwhile, I secretly nursed the hope that Norma would return from the clinic cured. Maybe there would be no need for any major changes, after all.

But when Norma came home, six weeks after she'd been admitted, she announced a plan of her own: "We're moving to New Hampshire to be closer to my brother."

My grip tightened on the telephone receiver. She hadn't been home for twenty-four hours and already she was threatening to upend my life again. "Don't I get any say in this?"

"It's my decision."

"But it affects Amelia and me, too."

"I just can't make it here," Norma said. "Everywhere I turn I'm haunted by memories of hard times. Eli said he and Lindsay would help me out as much as I needed. You're always setting so many limits."

I wanted to say that I'd do anything she asked from now on, but I knew I couldn't stick to such a promise. I had a full-time job now and I wanted to succeed at it. I wanted things to work out with Whit, too. I was willing to help more, but how much more? Surely if they moved to New Hampshire Eli would feel the same way soon enough. Maybe they'd come back.

In the end I didn't argue too strenuously because I didn't believe Norma would really pull off such a big move anyway. Besides, I was so exhausted from the emotional upheaval of the past six weeks that I didn't mind entertaining the possibility that someone else was going to try to fix this mess. Why not let Eli and his wife try?

Then, two weeks later, I walked into Norma's apartment and saw large boxes from a moving company stacked against the living room wall. They were each labeled in thick black marker with an address I didn't recognize. My stomach sank. They were really going.

On our last afternoon together Amelia and I sat cross-legged on the carpet surrounded by an empire of peaked yellow and red rooftops and gumdrop-green trees. Under normal circumstances I would have told Amelia we had to clean up the block set because it was nearly time to go back to Norma's. But this time I preferred to leave the living room the way it was.

"Why don't you pick something special from here to bring to your new apartment in New Hampshire?" I offered. Amelia peered into the open toy cabinet where we kept her favorite books, the ones about Miss Rumphius who planted lupines everywhere, Maisy and her bedtime rituals, and the sheep beeping the horn of their Jeep. I started to pull out different toys she might like to take: her unicorn hand puppet, the play typewriter, her plastic doctor's bag. I wouldn't have minded if she took all the toys we could carry, but Norma had set a limit of one toy because there were already so many boxes. "Go ahead, little goose, what will it be?"

Amelia ignored the candidates I'd piled around us. "The lullaby," she said.

I knew what she meant. "The lullaby" was called "Berceuse," and was the only tune I could play half decently on the flute. It was the one I'd practiced when Norma was pregnant and had had little chance to play since Amelia was born. On the occasions when I did play the song, Amelia always lit up. I was sure it wasn't due to my talent as a musician. Instead, I attributed her attachment to the song to the fact that she'd heard it so often in utero that it had special meaning for her. "Are you sure that's what you want to pick to take to your new apartment?"

Amelia nodded, her bangs falling into her face. She looked very serious and grown up despite the plastic beads she had draped around her neck, and the fake red fingernails she was adjusting on the fingers of one hand.

"How about the wooden blocks or your baby doll?"

"The lullaby, Ima," Amelia insisted.

"Okay," I said. "I'll play my flute and record the lullaby on a tape. Then you can listen to it in your new house." Amelia was satisfied. And so was I.

I felt it was my job, as the adult in this situation, to reassure Amelia on the eve of her departure. I wanted her to know that I would always be her Ima, that I would always love her, and that just because she was moving it didn't really mean we were leaving one another. But three-year-olds have very little tolerance for lectures or serious discussions, and Amelia's request for the flute music should have told me that there was no need for wordy speeches. But I couldn't resist, and as I strapped her into her car seat and drove her back to Norma's I made several efforts to launch one. Amelia interrupted each time, by belting out a Raffi song, or letting loose a stream of nonsense chatter.

By the time we climbed the flight of stairs to Norma's apartment I had given up on waxing eloquent, and settled for a long hug while we waited for Norma to come to the door. I didn't want Amelia to see me cry so I kept our good-bye brief. "I'll come visit soon," I said. "And I'll call on Sunday."

"Thursday, Friday, Sunday," Amelia sang.

"Close," I said. I gave Norma a hug, wished her luck, and started down the stairs to the street. As I pushed the front door open I heard Amelia yell, "One more hug, Ima."

"All right," Norma said. She went inside and left the door to the apartment ajar so I could let Amelia in when we were through.

Amelia scurried down the stairs and wrapped her arms around my legs. "You're in prison, Ima, you can't get out."

I would have like to be in prison there; to have stayed forever. But it was my duty to escape.

"Oh, no," I said in mock horror. "What will I do?"

Amelia let out a self-satisfied laugh. "I caught you. I caught you."

"But if you don't let me go I won't be at work tomorrow and my boss will get mad and fire me."

"You can get a new boss."

"But if you don't let me go I'll have to sleep right here in the hallway."

"It's a prison, silly Ima."

"But if you don't let me go I'll get hungry and there's no food in this prison. You have to let me go so I can eat."

Amelia sprang her arms open. "Okay, you're free."

I lifted her up to give her a kiss. "You are such a kind warden," I said, and carried her back up the stairs.

In Loco Parentis

I heated up a pot of soup the night I said good-bye to you. But when I sat down on the couch with the warm bowl balanced on my knees, I knew I wasn't hungry. I heard footsteps on the stairs and Whit's voice at the door. "Are you all right?" she asked, striding into the living room. I nodded. "Would you like some help putting these things away?" She stooped down to clear away your books and blocks that were strewn across the floor.

"No!" I nearly shouted. "Just leave that." I didn't want to lose any trace of you.

All I had left of you: Your finger painting splashed with blue and purple tacked beneath the window in the hallway. The crayon drawings and collages on the refrigerator and two sides of the stove. The kitchen drawers filled with your plastic lunch box, your gnome doll with tangled black hair, wooden puzzles. On the couch, the inflatable teddy bear we bought at the holiday fair at the YMCA, and the chocolate-colored teddy bear with one eye missing. Your blue horsey cup on the bathroom sink, your red toothbrush. In my car, pages from forgotten coloring books rustling beneath the driver's seat like another season's leaves.

I

For the first time in my life I was having trouble sleeping. My friend Sam said she had a cure. She came over on a Saturday and suggested we go for a long bike ride. "You have to physically exhaust yourself," she said. "Then you'll sleep like a log."

She pulled her ten-speed off the bike rack on her car. I wheeled mine out of the building's basement.

"Time to take the baby seat off it, don't you think?"

Norma had put the seat on the back of the bike when we still lived together. She used to ride along the river with Amelia on back. I, on the other hand, lacked the confidence necessary to weave through traffic on two wheels by myself, let alone with my daughter in tow. But I kept thinking I'd get over my fear and give it a try. Sam was right, though; even if I overcame my jitters, and even if Amelia lived right next door, the truth was that she rode her own tricycle now, and was too big for the baby seat.

"All right," I said.

Sam pulled a set of tools out of her trunk and began to disassemble the seat. As she loosened each bolt she talked on about her graduate school classes, and how much work was involved in getting a master's degree. I was hardly listening. Instead, I was watching intently as the seat loosened from the rear fender.

I said very little that afternoon, as we pedaled up and down side streets. Sam didn't ask how I was feeling about Amelia being gone. It wasn't until months later that I told her how angry that made me. "But I knew how you felt," she said. "I thought you wanted to be distracted."

Work was about the only thing that could truly distract me. But even in the office, there were land mines. I had recently been promoted from a satellite bureau to the main newsroom. For most of that time, Amelia had been staying with me because Norma had been in the rehab center, so my new co-workers knew I had a child. I think they just assumed I was a divorced single mother, since I never talked about a husband.

One morning Richard, one of the copy editors, sauntered up to my desk carrying a cup of coffee. Richard looked to me like a marionette whose strings had been cut. He folded slightly at his neck, solar plexus, and abdomen, as if he were trying to collapse his tall skinny frame. He was balding, but continued to grow his remaining blonde hair and pulled it into a ponytail. He was dedicated to being a radical and crowned himself the most politically astute member of the newsroom. On our first meeting he decided that I was leaning to the right of himself and in need of lectures on the realities of oppression because I did not agree with him on some issue about race and class in the inner city. To make his point he pulled a pen out of his breast pocket and proceeded to draw me a little diagram on the back of a reporter's notebook. This collision of lines and arrows was somehow meant to compare the levels of oppression suffered by various minority groups including African-Americans and poor people.

But on this day Richard had yet to begin pontificating, and I was praying that he wouldn't. I didn't have the stomach for it.

"Will you be taking your daughter trick-or-treating next week?" Richard asked me, as he peeled the lid off his coffee cup.

"No, I won't. She's moved to New Hampshire."

Richard blew a clumsy stream of air across the coffee. "Ahh, is this a custody thing, or did she just go by herself?" His attempt at humor didn't grab me.

"Just got on the bus," I said, deadpan, staring into my computer screen in an attempt to look busy.

He sipped his coffee. "Lukewarm," he complained.

"Oh, well."

"So, you're divorced."

"More or less."

"Separated then."

"That's more like it."

"And Amanda's father . . ."

"Amelia."

"Amelia's father has custody?"

Being in an office full of reporters, who basically make a career of being nosy, is not particularly comfortable when you feel like keeping something to yourself. I knew better than to try and wriggle out of this one. "Amelia's other mother has custody. I'm a lesbian."

Richard's coffee sloshed against the side of his cup and dribbled down the front of his white shirt. "Ahh, I see." He tried to make his voice so nonchalant that it would cover up for the coffee stain expanding across his chest.

My phone rang, so I left Richard to mop up his mess. When I hung up he was gone. I would have to wait for another day to ask him if he'd like me to explain a little about oppression to him. I could draw him a chart comparing family rights for straights and gays.

I called Norma and Amelia on Sunday but there was no answer, so I left a message. When I returned home on Monday the phone was ringing. It was Norma. I asked her how the move had gone, and she told me that she was very happy in her new place. "Amelia really misses you," she said. "She kissed the answering machine when your message was playing."

"Is she there? Can I talk to her?"

"Actually she's at Eli's house. We'll call you tomorrow. But I had some things I wanted to discuss." Norma told me that she was going to have me taken out of her will as Amelia's guardian in the case of her death. It would be more practical for Eli to take her, she explained.

"What is this about?" I sputtered. "I'm her other parent. Why would you do that?"

"It's not something I need to discuss with you," she said coolly. "I was only telling you to be nice."

"Have you done it yet?"

"No. But I'm going to. I'm going to change the power of attorney, too. It doesn't make sense to have your name on it now that you live so far away."

"It's not like it was my idea for you to leave . . ."

"I really don't want to get into this. I was just telling you."

My mind was racing. I didn't want to fight with Norma. If I did and lost I would have no link at all to Amelia. Besides, she was just threatening. She'd change her mind. She often did.

"Let's discuss this another time, then," I tried.

"I told you, there's nothing to discuss."

"But I'd really like to talk about it. Another time. It doesn't have to be now."

"Okay, maybe. But I've already decided."

"Are we still on for the fifth?"

"The fifth?"

"The day I was coming to visit Amelia."

"Oh, yeah. Of course. She'll like that."

I was about to hang up when I thought of one more question. "What is Amelia going to be for Halloween?"

"A fairy princess. She's going to wear the tutu you gave her for her birthday."

That made me smile, and I hung up the phone. But then I felt the anger thud against the inside of my chest. At every turn, it seemed, Norma was taking something else from me. Doing whatever it took to compose myself after each new slight was becoming an all too familiar process.

Maybe that's why keeping something of Amelia had become so important to me. It had been two weeks since she'd moved, but my small apartment was still cluttered with the plastic yellow chair she used at her painting easel, the wooden step stool at the sink, and her doll bed on the living room floor. Finally, I decided it was time to put her things away. I tucked her toys onto shelves and into cabinets, and looked forlornly at all the space that was left without her.

My sister Julia had been visiting China for several weeks. When she came home she announced she wanted to go to a psychic who lived about an hour outside of Boston.

"Since when do you believe in that stuff?" I asked over the phone.

"The Chinese people are very superstitious."

"But you're not." Julia had a business degree from Wharton. Her husband was an art dealer and she had been keeping his books.

"Well, I got interested in it. Do you want to come along or don't you?"

I agreed. It would be a distraction if nothing else.

The next week, as we drove into the countryside, I gave Julia a blow-by-blow account of what had happened between Norma and me while she had been overseas. When I was done, she said, "Well, you know, this is probably all for the best."

"What are you talking about?"

"Norma was going to take Amelia from you eventually. Now you can get on with your life."

"But this *is* my life."

I stole a glance at Julia who was refolding a map of New England. Her efficient hands sank into the creases, easily bending the puzzle of paper back into a neat rectangle. I drove in silence for a long time. What my sister had said didn't come as a shock to me. I had thought the same thing from time to time. Norma was never going to let me have a normal, happy relationship with Amelia. Maybe it was better to make a clean break. But I also knew there is no such thing as a clean break once you've joined yourself to a child.

One day, I told myself, Julia will have a baby. And when the baby becomes a toddler she'll wonder how she could ever stand to lose this child. Then when her baby turns three she'll realize how absurd it was to think that a person could just forget a child and go on with her life the way she was telling me to do.

I steered the car up the long driveway to the psychic's house. I was surprised how ordinary it looked. I think I expected a creaking iron gate and a thundercloud overhead. "I'm going to ask if Gerald and I should open that gallery in Soho," Julia said.

"Does he know this is how you're making your business decisions?"

"As a matter of fact, he approves." Julia wrapped her crocheted scarf around her neck. Bundled up like that she looked like a little girl again. Even her voice sounded thinly defiant, the way it used to when, as a child, she would make pronouncements about rules for games she was inventing as she went along.

I turned the engine off and we ventured to the door. "You should ask her something too," Julia said.

"No," I said. "I'm just along for the ride."

The door opened, and a woman with a head full of disorderly hair invited us in. The psychic could have been any of the mildly unkempt middle-aged women I passed each week in the grocery store. She wore loose-fitting jeans and a white sweatshirt with calico cats appliquéed across the front. Julia and I followed her into her kitchen and took seats at the table, which like the counters and every other other horizontal surface in the room was cluttered with cookbooks, papers, and utensils. The prisms hanging in the windows and throwing shaky rainbows across the chaos in the room were the only New Age touch.

Julia began right away. "I want to know if my husband and I should open a gallery," she said.

The woman cleared a space in front of her, shuffled a deck of tarot cards, and laid them out on the table. Peering into them she told Julia that indeed she would open the gallery, and it would be a great success. She went on to make suggestions about every aspect of the business from where it should be located to which direction the front door should face. She proceeded to comment on Julia's past lives, her relationship to our parents, and the two children she predicted that Julia would one day bear.

"Now what about you?" the psychic asked me. "Why don't you think of a question."

"Go ahead," Julia prompted.

I took the deck of colorful cards the psychic offered, shuffled them, and watched as she laid them out.

"Hmm, I see you're testing me, you're not telling what the

question is. All right." She looked into the cards. "I'm seeing you on the prow of a ship. Yes, this is a past lifetime. You were a great man—a sea captain."

I rolled my eyes at Julia. Why were people always captains, queens, or generals in their previous incarnations, according to these psychics? Why wasn't anyone ever a bookkeeper or a dentist in a past life? Finally the psychic came up to date. "I see you in the present with a small child," she said, lifting her hand to her side. Her palm bobbed up and down until it settled at about the height Amelia's head would have been if she were standing there. Julia gasped. "It's about Amelia, isn't it?"

I shot Julia a look of annoyance. I hadn't planned to tell the psychic my question, and I didn't expect her to answer it. "Your child?" the psychic asked.

"Yes," I said. "But she doesn't live with me anymore."

"Her mother loves her, but she can't express that love properly," she said. She looked at me, confused.

Julia jumped in again. "That's her other mother. She has two mothers."

"I see," the psychic said. "You really were testing me." She looked into the cards and began to ramble on about how she saw Amelia buoyed by a cushion of light and that there was a beam of energy connecting us, even when we were apart. She was telling me these things to make me feel better, I thought. People don't pay return visits to fortune-tellers who predict their business will fail, their marriage will end in an ugly alimony dispute, or they'll be mugged at Christmas time. "She will definitely be back in your life," she said. "In the meantime you must do whatever you can to keep your connection. She needs you. There will be a time when you cannot see one another at all. Still, you must find ways to stay connected. She will feel it." Tears slid down my cheeks in spite of myself. I wanted to believe there was an unbreakable bond between us.

As we drove home Julia apologized for what she had said on the way up. "I don't know why, but after hearing the psychic talk about Amelia and you—well, I think I understand now. You can't just turn your back on her."

The sun was setting and the world was reduced to shadows. Trees on either side of the highway were black barriers, and the open sky in front of us seemed to lead us on, in the only direction.

II

I drove out to Whit's house in Hull for dinner. The next day she would come with me to New Hampshire for my first visit with Amelia.

Whit had bought this house when she was twenty-two years old. She fell in love with Hull and its long, slinky beaches that look over Massachusetts Harbor. It is an old-fashioned New England village in some respects, with its own barbershop chorus and a proud historical society that boasts of the town's three-plus centuries, starting when outcasts from Plymouth settled its shores. For years after, it was a place of purpose, serving as a lifesaving station for the Coast Guard. Nowadays its beach dwellers find work in Boston, leaving each morning from Long Wharf on the commuter boat, while artists make do in run-down cottages, selling seascapes to tourists in galleries cramped beside the old arcade.

Whit's house, several blocks in from the harborside, had been on the verge of collapse when she bought it for twenty thousand dollars. The first years she lived here, Whit spent the winters in a rented attic room. Her own house had no insulation, no inside walls, and wasn't hooked up to the town's septic system. Treks to the condemned outhouse were inconvenient past November, and the dangers of frostbite indoors grew increasingly real. The house became her weekends and summers project. It was primarily a single-handed effort, but there had been help from family and friends along the way. By the time I became a regular visitor there was pink insulation tacked up behind a clear plastic barrier in all of the rooms. The upstairs had been Sheetrocked, taped, and painted, and the indoor plumbing had been installed.

If you weren't used to seeing a kitchen counter and stove in the living room while the kitchen floor was being tiled, or if having a workbench set up across from the sofa was not your idea of fashionable decorating, then you might have called the house a bit odd. That's what Veronica seemed to think on her first visit. She came up for brunch one Sunday and let out a laugh when she walked through the door. I think the sight of insulation instead of wallpaper unnerved her. Whit was unusually quiet for the rest of the visit. She told me later that she was insulted by Veronica's initial reaction to her house, and all of the subsequent "oohs" and "aahs" over the solar-heated bathroom, three-tiered deck, and octagonal kitchen window didn't make up for it.

For Whit the house has never been anything but an object of awe-inspiring beauty. Like a mother, she overlooked all of its flaws in every step of its development. Once, when I marveled at how she could live a life with no creative outlet such as painting or poetry, or even gourmet cooking, she waved her arms at the walls around her. "This is my art," she said.

Of course, she finally forgave Veronica. And after that, I began to warn people about the state of the house before they pulled into the sandy driveway for the first time.

Amelia was nearly three years old when she came out for her first visit, and I didn't want her to unintentionally offend Whit, either. So I tried to prepare her. "The house might look a little odd to you," I explained on the car ride up. "You see, Whit is building it herself, and there are tools inside, and some of the walls aren't quite finished yet." I had reminded Whit to put away the saw blades, stray nails, and plugged-in power tools, both for safety's sake and to make the house appear a little more conventional for Amelia's visit.

But from the outside there was no inkling that the house was a work in progress, unless of course you observed the stacks of two-by-fours and scraps of floor molding in the side yard. The shingles were painted a peachy pink. The windows to the small front porch were etched with frosted vine leaves, and the flower beds beneath the living room window bloomed with tulips in spring and tiger lilies in summer.

Whit was outside pushing the power mower across the lawn when Amelia and I arrived for that first joint visit. She cut the machine's engine and opened my car door. I picked Amelia up out of her car seat and set her on the ground. "You're right, Ima, it is funny looking," Amelia blurted out.

"Not the outside, silly, the inside is the funny-looking part," I said, realizing only after the words had tumbled out that I was making the situation worse, not better. Whit gave me a piercing look. The same way, I suppose, I looked at her when she said that Amelia's short haircut wasn't flattering, or that she had acted too bossy during her last visit. "I was trying to tell her about the construction going on inside," I said, attempting to squeeze the words Amelia had parroted into some kind of context. "But the outside is just beautiful, isn't it, sweetheart?" I said, turning to Amelia.

"A funny-looking house," she repeated, as she crossed the threshold.

I was remembering Amelia's first reaction to Whit's house when I pulled into the driveway that night, so I couldn't help but think the words *funny looking* as I approached the door. Inside, the unsanded floors would be crisscrossed with orange extension cords, and there would be power tools stacked in the corners where furniture should be. What I didn't expect was to see, in the middle of this work site, a table set with elegant stemware and china plates. Candles provided the only light.

Whit was in the kitchen checking on the salmon she was cooking. "Just right," she said when I walked in.

"This is beautiful! What are we celebrating?"

"The eve of your first visit to Amelia, the fact that you're coming over for dinner and things like that."

"You're just trying to cheer me up, aren't you?"

"That too," Whit said. "Sit down. Dinner's ready."

"Well, it's working. I'm really happy." For the moment I was. I knew, and Whit knew, that these days my happiness was like a small break between clouds. Still it was there, and however fleeting it might be, we could soak it in.

Whit brought the fish to the table and took a seat. "I've been thinking," she said, "now that Amelia and Norma have gone, maybe we should consider having you move in here." I looked around at the metal toolbox sitting on the workbench that was set up under the windows. "When it's finished," Whit added, following my gaze.

I smiled and nodded.

"What's that look supposed to mean?"

"Well, it's a long way from finished."

"But when it is, how about it?"

"When it is, I think I'd like that." Talking like this was making me feel hopeful. It seemed like a long while since I'd thought about my own life moving forward. But in the next instant I felt guilty, as though by venturing out toward my happiness, independent of Amelia, I was leaving my child behind. "But we need a room for Amelia when she visits," I said quickly.

Whit dropped her chin into her hand, and frowned. "Let's just talk about us for a minute, okay?"

"But for me, us includes Amelia."

"But tonight, us just includes you and me. That doesn't mean we're banishing her forever."

I reached for Whit's hand. "You know, when Amelia was here I had all this love to give her. It was the most amazing thing—this unconditional love I had never felt before. I never considered that I could feel that kind of love if she wasn't around."

"But do you?" Whit asked. "Now?"

My eyes swept around the unfinished room and rested on Whit's expectant smile. I nodded.

Before the alarm went off I woke Whit and insisted we get started. The drive seemed endless from the moment it began. Every car, every mile, every minute seemed like an obstacle standing between Amelia and me. It had been three long weeks since I had last seen her, and suddenly I couldn't stand another second of separation. "She probably doesn't even miss me," I complained to Whit.

"I'm sure she's completely forgotten who you are," Whit teased. "She'll probably say, 'Ima who?' "

We arrived early and there was no answer at Norma's door, so Whit and I took a walk around the block. We were turning the corner, cutting through a vacant lot, when we saw Norma, laden with grocery bags, and Amelia at her side, coming toward us. Amelia, wearing the pink snowsuit my mother had bought her, hurled herself at top speed across the snowy ground. She nearly knocked me down with her hug. "Ima!" she cried. Whit laughed. "Still think she didn't miss you?"

Whit went to visit some friends she had in the area, and Norma went to Eli's house so Amelia and I could have some time alone together. The rooms already looked clean and cozy. In the kitchen Norma had hung Amelia's finger paintings on the cabinet doors and refrigerator. She had laminated some of Amelia's drawings and used them as place mats on the table. The living room, which doubled as Norma's bedroom, had a futon couch covered with Amelia's stuffed animals and Norma's pillows. A set of wooden boards stacked between cinder blocks formed a shelf unit along one wall. It was filled with cassette tapes, some books, and photographs in frames. Norma had made a curtain for the window, which she tied in the center with a thick hair ribbon. Amelia had the single bedroom, with a bed in one corner and a bureau on the opposite wall. Her toys were kept in bright plastic laundry baskets and the clothes that didn't fit in the bureau were folded into a stack of milk crates which had a piece of print cloth hanging in front of them to serve as a curtained door. As always, Norma had managed, with very little money, to make her home cheerful and cozy.

"Look, Ima," Amelia said, pulling a shoe box out from under her bed. I opened the box and saw stacks of letters and pictures I had sent her. The lullaby tape was there, too. "Do you ever listen to this?" I asked. Amelia shot across the room and pulled a Playskool tape deck out of one of the baskets. She wrestled the tape out of its case and popped it into the machine. After a quick survey of the controls, she pushed down on the green button with an arrow pointing to the right. "See?" she said, as the music started to play.

Amelia and I spent the afternoon playing Candy Land, drawing pictures, and looking through her baby album. When Norma returned and it was time for me to go, Amelia asked if she could come home with me. "No, you stay here with Mommy. I'll come visit again soon." I had brought her baby doll from my apartment and gave it to her then. "If you miss me you can hug your doll and tell her about it," I said.

"What will you do?"

"If I miss you, you mean?"

Amelia nodded.

"I'm not sure. What should I do?"

"You can write me a letter."

"That's a good idea."

"Or you can buy me a present."

"Ooh, aren't you getting smart?"

Whit tapped the horn outside, letting me know it was time to leave. I gave Amelia a hug good-bye.

"Here," Norma said, taking the baby album off the couch where Amelia and I had been looking through it. "Keep this at your place for a while."

I took the book, and left them there, feeling like maybe this could all work out.

I read somewhere that it's common for a couple whose child dies to divorce within a year or so of the death. They secretly blame one another for the tragedy, and the stress suffocates them.

In the months after Amelia and Norma left, Whit and I began

to bicker and fight. She said I wasn't affectionate with her. I blew up at small problems. If she picked me up fifteen minutes late to go out to dinner, or if she left the paper bag her coffee came in on the floor of my car, I would explode. I resented the fact that she didn't know my pain. I hated her for not missing Amelia the way I did. And I was waiting for her to disappoint me.

We began to notice a cycle. The week after I saw Amelia I was cheerful. Then my mood slid during the next weeks, until I was toxic to be around just before our next visit. I noticed something else, too. Instead of picking a fight with Whit, if I sat quietly for a few minutes and allowed my feelings to surface, I would begin to cry.

The loss settled in slowly. The distance, the stretch of emptiness, the square footage of air between us, became more and more real. The baby I chose to have. The one whose kicking I felt through Norma's belly. The baby who I held on my lap while I made phone calls and chopped vegetables. She was far away. I missed her racket. Her mess. Her sweet observations. Her constant chatter. I missed being her Ima, day to day. I kept thinking, I had this baby. And now I'm losing her. I couldn't seem to get past that.

To suddenly be a childless mother is so strange, I told Whit. "It's like I was in the middle of this peak experience that the whole world is always talking about, and then, boom, it's gone."

I visited Amelia for one weekend every month. Sometimes I went straight to her new day care center and took her back to Norma's apartment where we would stay while Norma took the weekend off to visit her parents, or friends out of town. Other times, Eli and Lindsay let us stay in their house. In the spring, Norma agreed to let me bring Amelia to my house for a week.

I decided to take the bus since my car was unreliable for long trips. Besides, I didn't want to have to focus on the road in my first few hours with Amelia, when instead I could be reading books to her, or playing a game.

I had no trouble finding my way to Amelia's day care, where I was to pick her up. I climbed the winding wooden stairs to the classroom, and immediately spotted her in the center of the carpeted floor. While the other children looked relatively neat and trimmed, Amelia had the look of perpetual motion, even when she was standing still. She was dressed in a blue jumper decorated with gold sunflowers, with a purple turtleneck underneath. Her flyaway hair was loosely anchored with two barrettes, one at each temple. Her haphazard style might have passed for a kind of cosmopolitan chic, except for the bold black line of dirt beneath her fingernails.

When she saw me, Amelia raced over to give me a staggeringly enthusiastic hug, then raced around the room saying good-bye to her friends and teachers, gathering up her lunch bag and the paintings she'd made that day. "Let's leave those here for Mommy," I said, because I was unsure how we would manage the large crackling pictures on the bus. Amelia pouted, but agreed. On the way out she pointed up to the bulletin board in the hallway. "Look, Ima, it's a family tree." The bulletin board was decorated with green leaf-shaped name tags. Brown yarn, representing branches, ran between them, making the whole thing look more like a forest of little shrubs than a single tree. I didn't say that to Amelia, instead I searched for her name, my heart racing. I was afraid, I think, to see how she had depicted her lineage—afraid that my side of the family would be missing. But when I found Amelia's tag it had two lines streaming off at wide angles like all the rest. One was labeled with Norma's name, and from there the yarn branches spread into a web of her parents and grandparents. The other one had my name, and a corresponding web with the names of my parents and grandparents. "How did you know all those names?" I asked. "Mommy told me," Amelia said.

We walked to the bus station, with Amelia shouting directions to me at every turn. "This way," she'd day when we reached a corner. "No, cross there," she instructed when I started to cross the street a block earlier than she and Norma usually would. Wait a minute, I wanted to say, I'm the grown-up, you just relax and follow along. But it was clear to me that this was a stage of innocence that had already passed for her. The faith in grown-ups most children seemed to hold was a luxury Amelia already seemed to know wasn't hers to enjoy.

On the bus Amelia and I took seats across the aisle from a middle-aged woman who was sitting straight and proper in her navy blue skirt suit. Amelia sat cross-legged on her seat flipping through the pages of books I had brought her. From time to time she squirmed around to get a look out the window.

"My, isn't she a well-behaved little lady?" the woman said, with an indulgent smile.

"Thank you," I replied.

But Amelia wasn't content to leave it at that. "Grown-up girls are women," she began. "Little kids are girls. Right, Ima?"

"Some women prefer to be called ladies. And sometimes people think it's nice to call little girls ladies, too," I said, smiling at our new friend.

"How old?" she asked.

"Three," I said.

"Three and a half and three-quarters," Amelia corrected.

"Three and a half and three-quarters," the woman repeated, pursing her pale lips. "Your daughter is very bright."

Amelia scrambled onto my lap and pushed her book into my hands. "You read," she said. Grateful to be released from the conversation with this stranger, I agreed.

Amelia turned to look out the window as we passed a river which looked gray under the cloudy sky. "The river is so polluted that the fish can't swim there. Isn't that sad?" Amelia bent across the aisle to ask the lady.

"I suppose it is." I noticed the lady was looking at Amelia with a changed expression, as if "cute" were wearing off and being replaced by something more real and, to her, less appealing.

"That's why we recycle," Amelia continued.

That stopped the conversation for a while. I suspected our friend didn't sort paper and plastic, let alone give much thought to people's responsibility to rivers. But then she made one last attempt. "On your way home, are you?" she asked.

"Yes," I said, folding Amelia's book open.

"I have two houses," Amelia said.

"Oh, I see," our new friend replied. "That's tough," she said, giving me a sympathetic look.

"I have too mommies, too," Amelia added.

Our new friend was quiet for a moment. "Is that so?"

I decided to let Amelia field this one for herself. She craned around to look out the window again, then turned back to give her answer. "I have a bunny named Ariel, too."

At home in Cambridge, Amelia walked through the house as if in a dream. She opened each cabinet and drawer and exclaimed each time: "Ima, my books are still here!" "Ima, my bowl is still here!" "Look, Ima, my pajamas!"

We visited all of her favorite places: the swimming pool at the

YMCA, Burger King, the swan boats, and the mechanical horse outside the supermarket which offers bucking rides in exchange for two quarters. We made dates with her friends from her old day care, and I brought her to my friends' houses, too. From time to time a vague look would come over Amelia's eyes, as if she were holding pictures at a distance so she could see everything at once.

"It's funny to come back someplace after you've been gone, isn't it?" I asked. "When I go away from someplace and then come back, everything looks almost the same but a little different."

Amelia nodded.

That night I cooked a dinner of macaroni and cheese.

Amelia stood on the stool to watch my progress. "What's that?" she asked, as I poured the noodles into the pot.

"The macaroni."

"Not that kind! It's the wrong color!" Amelia was shrieking her protest.

"What kind did you want?"

"Macaroni-an-cheese."

"That's what I'm making. See, there's the cheese," I said pointing to the plate of grated cheese I had just prepared. Amelia studied the ingredients carefully.

"Real cheese?"

"Yes, of course."

"Mommy uses the orange cheese in the macaroni box," she said.

"Should we get that kind next time?"

Amelia shook her head.

When Whit called, Amelia bragged: "Guess what, Whit, Ima makes special macaroni-an-cheese with *real* cheese."

At the dinner table Amelia clutched her soldier doll in her hand, and tapped him on the edge of the table. Thump. Thump. Thump-thump. Thump. Thump. Thump-thump. She repeated the rhythm again and again. I was about to interrupt and tell her to be quiet, when she said, "That sounds like 'I love I-ma.' " She repeated the chant a few times, then varied the rhythm. "That's 'macaroni-an-cheese, please,' " she said, labeling the next string of staccato. The game grew until we were having a little jam session at the table, me rapping out fork rhythms, and Amelia playing songs with the doll.

By the time I rode the bus back to Portsmouth with Amelia, I felt sated. I was tired and happy and willing to say good-bye until the next visit. Norma met us at the station, and Amelia launched herself into her arms. I sat with them on one of the wooden benches and told Norma a little about our visit, then gave Amelia a hug and kiss good-bye. "I'll see you next month," I told her. "And I'll call you soon."

When I turned to go I heard Amelia wailing, "One more hug, Ima!"

"Why don't you walk us to the car?" Norma offered. I picked Amelia up and carried her out of the station. Her weight strained the sling my arms made with a pleasant heaviness, like ripe fruit on a tree. "Here it is," Norma said when we reached her car. I loosened my hands to let Amelia slide to the sidewalk. But she tightened her grip around my neck.

"It's hard to say good-bye to Ima, isn't it?" Norma asked, lifting Amelia away.

A black border took shape around my moods. When I was very depressed the border would thicken, and only a small window of light and color could get through. Gradually, the border had begun shrinking back. I was adjusting to being a long-distance parent. I reworked my budget to allow for frequent travel expenses and long-distance phone calls. I set more ambitious goals for my writing, realizing that I had more time to myself now than I had had since Amelia was born. I could make the best of this situation if I tried.

In addition to working full-time, I set myself a schedule in which I devoted five hours a week to creative writing. I found myself cleaning my car and my apartment with an overzealous vigor, until everything was empty and shining.

Doing is one of the watchwords of my family's faith. Whenever I'd complain I had too much to do, my grandmother or my father would chime in, "Better too much than too little." Although in the past I'd roll my eyes and wax eloquent on the merits of having time to contemplate and relax, now I was finding value in their creed. I was beginning to feel a soothing sense of control, and the constant movement kept my sadness at bay.

But even as day by day I began to feel more comfortable, Norma seemed to grow more agitated. She had moved away, in part, because she thought a change of scenery would allow her to leave her problems behind. But the problems seemed to be catching up with her. The revolving door of Norma's breakdowns, which started turning just months after we split up, was beginning to spin faster and faster out of control. It got to the point where hardly a month would go by without some type of crisis, usually small, usually something I could talk Norma through over the phone. "Amelia won't listen to me," she once cried. "She says she wants to run away and live with you." Other times she'd say she just couldn't cope, or that she didn't like Eli's ways of dealing with Amelia, or that she worried she would never get through her emotional problems and be better. "You're trying your best," I'd assure her. "It'll get easier. The move is still new, you need time to adjust." The best I could do was hope my reassurances were true.

Anyway, I had my own changes to be concerned about. Whit's house was finally finished, more or less. The living room windows still needed trim, and the French doors hadn't been hung between the living room and the backroom, but the cottage was fast becoming a charming and habitable place. We shopped together for light fixtures and I helped pick out the carpet for the bedroom. I couldn't help but entertain worries about making a commitment again, and I cross-examined every hope before I allowed it to lodge anywhere near my heart. But I could find no argument against moving forward, so I prepared in earnest to settle in.

Then, one night, shortly after moving in with Whit, I found myself knee-deep in wrapping paper, preparing gifts for Whit's family. We were getting ready to head to the Berkshires for her family's annual Christmas reunion. It would be my first holiday with her clan, since before this I had always stayed close to home to be with Amelia. I was fastening a gold bow to a package for Whit's mother when the phone rang. It was Eli. Immediately I knew there was bad news.

Norma had tried to kill herself, he told me. She had taken an overdose of her sleeping medication, and was in the intensive care unit at the hospital where she had just regained consciousness. She had been found on her living room floor by the landlord who had come by to fix a leaking pipe. He let himself into the apartment when no one answered the door and came upon Norma robed in her favorite nightgown, sprawled across the floor. She had lost consciousness eleven hours earlier. If it wasn't for the leaking pipe, who knows if Norma would be alive, Eli was saying. Amelia, who had turned four by then, had been at a friend's house on a sleep-over when it happened.

I told Eli that I wanted Amelia to come stay with me while Norma recuperated and got some psychiatric help.

"I don't think that would be a good idea," he said. "She's already pretty shaken up."

"Of course it's a good idea. She has a home here. And it will be good for her to be away from the crisis."

"I'm sure Norma will want her to be close by. Besides, it wouldn't be good for Amelia to break her routine."

"Eli," I said, trying to stay calm, "she has a routine here, too. When Norma's in better shape we'll come visit her."

"I really don't agree. You're thinking about what's best for you, not what's best for Amelia."

I considered that for a moment. Maybe Eli was right. "So you and Lindsay don't mind having her there with you?"

"Actually we've decided to have her stay with Jared's parents."

"Who?"

"He's her best friend. She's really excited about it."

I was furious now. "But I'm her mother. She'd be excited about staying here, too."

"No one's arguing with that, Nancy." Eli's voice softened. "This isn't a fight. It's not about the adults at all. It's about what's best for Amie."

"Someone could have consulted me . . ."

"Everything happened so quickly," Eli said. "No one's shutting you out." I said nothing. "You can call her any time," Eli added. "It's just that she's really happy about spending time with her friend. This way she has something positive to focus on out of this whole experience."

How had he defeated me so easily? I wondered, even as I heard myself starting to make compromises. We decided I would take Amelia for a few days over the New Year. Eli assured me I would feel better once I saw that she was really doing all right.

"I guess you won't be coming to the Berkshires," Whit said when I hung up the phone. I shook my head. "Damn it," Whit said, and slammed her hand down on the table. "I'm so sick of this shit."

I was caught in a swirl of emotion. Terrified by the implications of Norma's act. Furious at her for doing this to herself, and to Amelia and to me. What if the landlord had not let himself in, and instead Amelia had come home from her sleep-over and found her mother there? And confused: What was really best for Amelia right now? Should I have argued more with Eli? And I resented Whit just then for being angry, for being one more person for me to have to try and console. And in the midst of all of this I was disappointed not to be going to the Berkshires. Like Whit, I was sick of all this, too.

The next morning I called Amelia at Jared's house and concluded that she sounded pretty much the way she usually did, except that she was a little more distracted. Then, I called my lawyer.

"Is Amelia safe?" she asked.

"Yes."

"Are you worried that her physical needs aren't being taken care of?"

"No," I said. I'd spoken to Jared's parents on the phone and they sounded like very nice people and devoted parents.

"You could try to get a lawyer in New Hampshire and make a motion for guardianship, but I'll warn you, your chances wouldn't be good. The courts are very conservative there, and judges are hesitant about custody cases that straddle state lines even in the best of circumstances. I'd say your best bet for now is to visit Amelia. Keep building a track record of being a responsible parent. If you can get the child to Massachusetts for a number of months at some point, with the mother's permission, we can try to get the case heard here."

"So for now, there's nothing more I should be doing?"

"That's right. But if anything changes, and you fear for Amelia's physical well-being or safety, call again."

A week later I picked Amelia up and took her down to Massachusetts by bus. On the way she pretended she was a girl named Rachel. "Rachel" told me that Amelia had gotten lost. For the entire trip I helped "Rachel" search under, around, and behind our seats for Amelia. As the game progressed, "Rachel" would have more and more trouble finding Amelia, until finally she said Amelia was very sick and would probably die. Again and again I tried to rescue the invisible Amelia with the help of the quite serious "Rachel." Again and again we saved her.

Whit was off with her family, and my sister, Julia, didn't want us to be alone on New Year's Eve. Her husband, who observed the Jewish New Year and never had much use for celebrating the start of a new calendar, preferred to work that night anyway, Julia said. So she canceled their plans in New York and drove up to spend the evening with us. She treated us to supper in Boston, and we stopped in a five-and-dime and bought confetti and noise-makers. Just before putting Amelia to bed at nine o'clock we threw the confetti around and yelled "Happy New Year." By mid-night, we had all been asleep for hours.

The next day, Amelia and I sat at the low coffee table in the living room writing a letter to Norma. I penned the words as Amelia dictated: "I hope your arms are all better so you can come home."

I hadn't heard this part, I only knew about the pills. Why was I being shielded from information, instead of Amelia, who was much too young to be carrying all of this knowledge? I called Eli after Amelia went to sleep that night and asked him about it. "Oh yes," he said, "Norma slit her wrists, too."

After I hung up the phone I looked in on Amelia. It is a cliché, that image of a sleeping child, features in perfect repose, conjur-ing all that is innocent and pure and good. What is beyond cliché, what is perhaps its opposite, is that even in this moment, even carrying all that she knew, Amelia, sleeping on her back, one arm thrown casually over her head, could evoke the same responses. Her slumbering face promised me that all was well in our world. That anything can be healed.

For me, just having Amelia within arm's length—seeing that by day she seemed upset, but not traumatized, and that she was cuddly and loving, and maybe even a little bit clingy, but not desperate—was reassuring. But I needed more. I needed to know I could protect her from deep pain. I needed to learn how to undo all of the damages. I needed a promise that her strong, happy spirit would never be broken. Every mother learns that she can't deflect trouble from her child's path. I didn't want to learn this so soon, and with such great sorrows at stake.

Five days later, I took Amelia back to Jared's house in New Hampshire.

Norma was now checked into a private psychiatric institute. The first time I spoke to her on the phone she told me she was disappointed that her suicide attempt had failed. Then she com-plained that the ambulance driver had ripped her best night-gown and ruined it in his attempt to save her.

I called Norma often and tried to convince her to let Amelia stay with me while she got better. But she refused, saying she wanted Amelia close to her now. I decided not to push it. I could tell from her tone that an argument would be senseless. Instead, I suggested that we schedule more time for me to spend with Amelia in the months to come, so Norma could focus on her recovery. She agreed to this and even suggested we look into making me Amelia's legal co-guardian. Although I should have been thrilled by this proclamation, I couldn't help worrying that she would change her mind before we had time to take any action. But for the time being at least, she seemed sincere.

"I really appreciate how you've hung in there with us," Norma said. I could hear in her voice how she was gathering up her strength, trying with all her might to pull herself past her worst instincts, to somehow push back the forces within her that kept happiness so far out of her reach. It wasn't just misguided optimism that let me believe the best of her. I'd cradled her when she cried through the four years we were involved. She'd held me like that, too. We'd been so young and broken together. Somehow I'd been able to gather in my pieces and make them something like whole. It was harder for her, and I was coming to see by how much. But I couldn't believe anything was impossible. And just then I hoped for the best.

III

The sun streamed through the window, spreading over my books and pads like a cat so at ease she could just sprawl wherever she liked. After a particularly harsh winter, the last patches of snow outside were finally submitting to the new warmth. Watching the ice soften into puddles, I luxuriated in the peace of April, knowing the cold had finally lost.

But then the phone's jangling ring broke my afternoon calm. Looking back, I believe that even before I heard Norma's voice, I knew something big was coming.

She told me she was back in the psychiatric hospital. It had been less than four months since her last stay there.

"Amelia's here, too," she said.

"What do you mean?" I was trying to keep my voice calm.

"In the children's unit. I checked her in." This pronouncement thudded somewhere above me, like the noises of upstairs neighbors fighting, furniture crashing on the carpet.

Norma has never figured out that the more disturbed I become, the quieter my voice gets. I was practically whispering then. "Why did you do that?"

"Eli wouldn't take her. And she's been kicking and biting me. I think she needs help."

Losing my temper wouldn't do any good. In my mind I was already calling Whit at work and begging her to come home. While I tried to keep the conversation calm and practical, my thoughts raced off in different directions. How am I going to get Amelia out of there? I wondered. What will it take to fix this mess? And what about Amelia? What explanation had she been given? How was she being treated, and how could I undo what Norma had done to our child? Now, forever, Amelia will know she has been in a psychiatric hospital and wonder if she really needed to be there. In my most measured voice I got all the information I could: the name of the psychiatrist in charge of the children's unit, the name of Norma's doctor, the name of the town the institute was in.

"You should probably come visit her," Norma was saying.

"Of course," I said, thinking that was the least of it.

"I think if you want to maintain a relationship with Amelia, you should come." These words echoed in my mind as I tried to understand what was happening. Looking back, I wonder if Norma's words had, after all, been meant to prod me to do all that I was about to attempt.

When I hung up the phone the world was normal again. My half-finished cup of tea squatted solidly among my papers which were scattered on the table where I'd left them. I could convince myself that the disembodied words that had floated through my ear were from a dream. Then it wouldn't have happened. I remembered a day when Amelia was just learning to walk. We were in a basement-level Laundromat, and I left her on the floor for a minute while I pulled clothes from the dryer. Her piercing cry spun me around. There she was, lifting herself from the second cement step, climbing up to the rear door, her face full of blood. In just one moment I had let this happen. I picked her up and hugged her to me as I ran next door to a beauty shop where I hoped to find a sink so I could wash her. A woman who was giving a shampoo pointed me toward the bathroom. Closed into the cramped room I assessed the damage. Just a split lip. It healed in a few days. We were lucky that time.

Maybe, I thought, I could rinse the red out of my mind as easily now and see that this wasn't as bad as it looked. I dialed Whit at work. She needed no convincing that this was serious. "I'm coming with you," she said. "We'll go up first thing tomorrow." Although she was the type to go to work even if she was suffering from the nastiest flu, she didn't hesitate to walk out in the middle of the afternoon, telling her boss that there had been a family crisis and she'd explain as soon as she had a chance.

Meanwhile, I called the children's psychiatrist at the institute where Norma and Amelia now were. When I introduced myself as Amelia's co-parent, Dr. Marjorie Childers didn't miss a beat. "Norma told us you might be calling." She assured me that Amelia was adjusting well, considering the circumstances. "We want to evaluate her to see if there is any need for continued hospitalization."

"Of course there's no need for hospitalization," I said.

"That may be, but her mother checked her in with certain complaints, and we have to make an evaluation."

"How long will that take?" I asked.

"I'd say we can do it in a week."

"A week? But she doesn't even need to be there. Can't you speed things up?"

The doctor said she'd do what she could.

"I'll be there tomorrow. Can I speak to you then?"

"Absolutely," said Dr. Childers. "In the meantime, don't worry. Amelia is doing just fine."

It was already evening, so I called my lawyer at her home. I could hear the noises of tired children in the background. Attorney Kaplan spoke over the noise, sounding like a harried housewife instead of a composed lawyer. She mulled over the situation I laid out for her. If I couldn't get Norma to voluntarily release Amelia to me, I would have to let a judge decide what to do. Again, she reminded me that if the case was heard in New Hampshire I had little chance of success. Also, if I pushed Norma too hard to let me take Amelia, she could turn around and accuse me of kidnapping. Since I would be crossing state lines with Amelia, that would be a serious charge. "Try to get the child down here, preferably with the mother's consent. Preferably with her signature. Preferably without lying," she said.

Whit walked through the door and suitcases appeared on the bed, their covers unzipped and flung open. She ironed my skirts and blouses so I would look crisp and maternal when we arrived. I was throwing evidence into manila envelopes: a copy of the will we signed before Norma took my name out as Amelia's guardian in the case of Norma's death; letters to me from Norma and her mother; Amelia's original birth certificate which gave her last name as mine and Norma's joined with a hyphen, and most important, the power of attorney, which clearly stated I was to make decisions on behalf of Amelia if Norma was unable to do so. I even took the baby book I had made for Amelia, which Norma had recently let me have.

I knew I was going on trial. I was about to have to prove my claim to motherhood.

In the morning, Whit and I drove through the last of winter's ice storms. It was as though an invisible hand was scattering crystals of slick rain along our path, like bread crumbs we would have to follow back. Except these crumbs would melt long before we would find our way home. For some reason we were talking about how we could save money and make our paychecks go farther, as if nothing was going to change that day; as if we would be able to buy fewer groceries, and carpool to work more often; as if we'd be returning soon to life the way we had left it.

What had been ice a hundred miles south fell as snow on the lawn of the Holiday Inn where we stopped to get a room. This far north the promise of spring was dying.

I usually love staying in motels. But this time I didn't enter the room, latch the door behind me, take in a lungful of stale, sweet air, and collapse on the bed. Instead, I dropped my suitcase in the closet-alcove, washed my face, unpacked the bundle of papers and notebooks I had brought with me, and said: "Let's get started."

Whit didn't even bother trying to convince me of the merits of taking a little rest. She didn't insist I have a sandwich or unpack first, the way she usually would. Instead we made a list of people to call and steps to take.

First I dialed the institute and found out visiting hours didn't start until two o'clock. In the meantime I sorted through my papers and pulled out a list of gay and lesbian advocacy groups I had compiled. I called them first to see about the possibility of pro bono representation. As I suspected, none was forthcoming. Then I called the state's bar association, and a friend of the family who worked as a lawyer in New York but who had grown up in New Hampshire and would still have connections. By the time I hung up the phone I had gathered the names of a half dozen lawyers in the area who specialized in family issues. I left messages with secretaries stressing the urgency of the situation, and hoped for the best.

Next I phoned the hospital and asked to speak with the administrator. He took my call and apologized for not being able to give me any firm answers about when Amelia could be released. "We all want to see this resolved," he said. "We've already reported the case to the state."

"The state?" I asked.

"I'm afraid so, Department of Social Services," he said. "We're all quite concerned."

I told him I would like to take Amelia home with me, that there was no reason for the state to get involved. "Look," he said, "I know you have a special relationship with Amelia, but we can't just let her go home with anybody."

My temper flared. "I'm her parent."

"We're concerned with legalities."

"I have a power of attorney."

"Yes, Dr. Childers mentioned that to me. And we will certainly have our legal board review this case."

I put in a call to Dr. Childers and requested a meeting at the institute that afternoon. Feeling I'd accomplished all I could just then, I hung up the phone and looked over to Whit who was unpacking our bags. Whatever I might have thought this mission would entail, now I saw it would not be quick or easy. I remembered that we had invited friends to our house for the Passover seder which was just two days away. "I think I should call and cancel. It looks like we'll be here awhile," I said. It was to have been the first holiday Whit and I would host since we began living together.

When Whit finished calling our friends, I called my boss, Jerry, and told him that I probably wouldn't be back to work that week. I explained that Norma had to be hospitalized but didn't mention what kind of hospital she was in, or why. I told him that I had to take care of Amelia but that I hoped I would be able to bring her home with me soon. I didn't mention that I was about to hire a lawyer to help me do so. I was anxious over the amount of money I was losing during this time because only sick days, and not personal days, were paid for at our paper. This was especially alarming given that I was about to incur yet more legal fees, not to mention the cost of the hotel room and other expenses that would be involved in getting Amelia out. "Let's see," Jerry said, as if he were reading my mind, "you are out of work and it has to do with hospitals. Let's call these sick days." I thanked him and promised I'd make up the time somehow. "You just take care of Amelia. Don't worry about the rest."

Whit's boss had been nearly as generous. All she asked was that Whit try to be back later in the week for an important sales meeting.

A half hour before it was time, Whit drove me the few miles to the Eastern Institute, which was located just one exit south on the highway. In my state of mind, we tacitly agreed, I should not get behind the wheel myself. Between us there was a silent pact of efficiency and importance. We were driven by the image of four-year-old Amelia stuck in a psychiatric hospital, and the knowledge that if I couldn't get Norma to voluntarily surrender Amelia to me, we would be lost in a legal maze. I felt as if I were on my way to deactivate a bomb. I had to move quickly, with extreme care and precision. I had to remain calm. Someone else's life was at stake.

Eastern Institute: The name sounded elegant and formal, a name suitable for a pillared institution of learning. Instead, the hospital was a low-slung, modern building with few flourishes, surrounded by gently sloping, snow-swept lawns. Whit drove around the circular driveway and reminded me to call her at the hotel when I was ready to leave. I walked through two sets of glass doors that led from the parking lot into the lobby. The receptionist had rosy brown skin and wore hoop earrings that grazed her cheek. She kept poking buttons on the switchboard, and maintained a constant patter into her telephone headset.

I was fifteen minutes early for visiting hours on the children's floor, but even so, I was afraid that the receptionist wouldn't have time to direct me there until after my two hours of visiting time were up. The receptionist spoke to me between demands from the buzzers at her fingertips. "I'm here to see Amelia Friedman," I said.

"Relation?" she asked.

"I'm her mother."

I was sure she would doubt me. For one thing, Amelia's mother was already checked into Unit A, the women's unlocked hall. Or else she'd recognize my green and pink print skirt and blazer as a costume; a cover-up hiding a girl in jeans and a second-hand sweatshirt, the girl I really was. I suddenly felt that everything about me was strange. No color-coordinated getup could ever erase it all. I'm the other mother. She has two, you see.

The receptionist looked up at the clock. "Visiting hour starts at two. Have a seat."

From where I sat I could see a web of hallways connecting the various sections of the hospital. The institute was clean, sunny, and new, a pristine place for so much pain. I wanted Amelia out of there.

I didn't doubt that some of what Norma told me on the phone the previous night was true. Maybe Amelia had kicked her, bitten her, and cursed at her. She wasn't an easy child. But she was only four years old, and besides, she hadn't had an easy life. But a psychiatric hospital? It was worse than wrong. It was indelible. A child can't just enter a mental hospital and come out the same kid. She'd been stamped with the word "patient." "Problem." Now she would have a history. A record.

Other things Norma had done to her didn't seem as bad. The pierced ears at two months I consented to because the holes could heal over and close. The extreme haircuts with half-inch spikes on top and shoulder length locks in back would grow out. But what she'd done now I was afraid I couldn't undo. All I had was my resolve to get Amelia out.

I picked up one of the brochures stacked on the glass-topped table in front of me. On the front cover was a glossy picture of the collegiate green lawns of Eastern Institute. Inside, it explained that the children's program was for six- to twelve-year-olds who suffered from hyperactivity, depression, or psychosis, among other things. Amelia was having normal reactions to a stressful home life, not to mention the fact that she was two years too young for admittance according to the brochure's stated age range. I gritted my teeth and read on. Therapies, the pamphlet said, included art, music, and pet play. "*Separation from the family can be traumatic . . . the children's program keeps that trauma to a minimum by creating a warm community environment and a daily routine . . .*" Yes, Amelia needed consistent care and love. I wanted to bolt through the doors and take her home where I could give her all of that. The hell with my lawyer's warnings.

At a minute before two o'clock, the receptionist nodded in my direction, indicating that I could proceed. I didn't dare ask where the children's unit was for fear she'd reconsider. I chose a direction and wandered down the hallway past the bathrooms and soda machine, to another set of double doors. They were locked. Miraculously, there were children on the other side. I'd stumbled through the labyrinth in the right direction. I tapped the thick glass square set at eye level on the solid, bolted door. A doctor, a psychiatrist probably, wearing the requisite white jacket and carrying a clipboard, came through the door. "I'm looking for Amelia Friedman," I said. "Through there," she answered, pointing to a second set of locked double doors, which she buzzed open for me.

My eyes fumbled through a group of children sprawled on couches in front of the television set. For a moment I worried that I wouldn't recognize Amelia. This was an old habit of fear that began when she was an infant and I would pick her up from day care. What if I mistakenly greeted another baby instead of mine? There was no rational reason for me to think I would forget my own child. I was bad with faces, and am the kind of person who often must apologize for not recognizing an acquaintance out of context. But my own daughter? I knew it was ridiculous. Nonetheless I would stand for an instant, breathless in the doorway, then laugh out a sigh when my eyes found her. Only then would I realize my fear was unfounded. It was one more way of testing myself: A real mother would know her child blind.

Then, before I had a chance to take another breath, she was there, standing beside a row of white cabinets where a young woman in a hospital smock was unwrapping a blood pressure gauge from her upper arm. As the doctor jotted something on her clipboard, Amelia turned and saw me watching. She jumped up and down as I approached, chanting: "Ima! Ima! Ima!"

As I lifted Amelia into my arms, the woman introduced herself. She was one of the nurses on the unit, and she'd be happy to answer any questions, she said.

I began with the obvious: "Why are you doing that?" I asked, looking at the chart of Amelia's blood pressure and temperature.

"It's just part of our routine. We check all of the children every day," the nurse answered.

"But she's not sick," I said, gently swinging Amelia on my hip.

"Come look," Amelia said, wriggling out of my arms. I let her down, and without waiting for the nurse's response, I followed Amelia to the bunny cage where she introduced me to Rocky the Rabbit. "See, Ima, he's just like Ariel, but he's white." So this was pet therapy, I thought, as she unlatched the bunny's door and reached inside.

I looked Amelia over. She appeared healthy and well cared for. Her hair was brushed behind her ears and held in place with matching barrettes. Her red-checked shirt and red jumper looked clean and neat. As she turned to hand me the bunny I saw her eyes light up, but that was just the surface. Underneath I could see her fears, as if she were swimming under a sea of questions—not just about why she was there but bigger ones, too. And smaller. Like about the rules for when to eat, when to go outside, whether to lock the bathroom door, and where to put her dirty clothes. There were rules for everything here: who could leave the unit, when to speak and when not to, when to close the door to your room and when to leave it open. There were charts on the walls with the children's names and their "marks" for the day. There were tallies of how many infractions each had committed, such as talking during silent time. According to the chart, Amelia had a clean record.

She led me to the room she shared with two other girls. Trying to help her straighten up, I put a shirt on the wrong shelf in her closet. "No, Ima," she shrieked, and broke into tears. That was the shelf for dirty laundry. The shirt was clean.

Visiting hours came and went and no one asked me to leave. One of the nurses told me that Dr. Childers had been detained, but she'd be available after dinner.

While I waited, I talked to the young social worker who was in charge of the floor. He led me into his office where he shuffled through files looking for Amelia's. "Ahh, here it is," he said, and read off the list of complaints Norma had dictated for the admitting psychiatrist. "It says here she kicks, curses, and bites," he said. "But I haven't seen her do any of those things."

"Me, neither. Occasionally she does have a tantrum though."

"That's normal," he said. "She's only four."

"So what's she doing here?"

"I don't know," he answered.

Dr. Childers arrived on the unit after Amelia had eaten and we were sitting on the couch with the other children watching a video. "Mind if I speak to your Ima for a few moments?" she asked Amelia.

I felt reassured by how she spoke to Amelia, and by the way she validated our relationship. She led me to a small office decorated with framed watercolors of southwestern landscapes. Dr. Childers didn't look anything like what I'd expected. Her stern deep voice on the phone didn't match with the whisper of blonde hair surrounding her wide forehead, nor with her pale pink pants suit. As she lowered herself into her cushioned chair, she seemed to become a part of it. It was as though she and her role and the furniture of this room were one eternal entity.

She explained that she would need to spend some more time with Amelia to make a complete evaluation. "At present there don't seem to be any major problems," she said. "There are some signs of hyperactivity, but that might just be a reaction to the current circumstances."

"That doesn't seem like enough reason to keep her here," I said.

"Maybe not," Dr. Childers agreed. "But I can't discharge her to you just like that. We have to go through certain procedures."

I could have told her what I thought of her procedures, but I kept myself in check.

She said she would speak to the director and we could talk more the next day. It was getting late now, she reminded me. Nothing more could be accomplished that night.

I went down the hall to say good-bye to Amelia, promising to be back the next day. Then I made my way to Norma's floor.

Norma was staying on Women's Unit A, an unlocked hall. That meant she was allowed to move around the grounds during certain hours and also to have visitors.

My goal for my first visit with Norma was to determine how she was feeling about her situation and what we should do about Amelia. Maybe she was ready to allow me to take her, and all my preparations and worries were for nothing. Maybe she'd come up with the idea of my taking temporary guardianship herself.

I walked to the end of a corridor lined with windows and through a set of swinging doors. At the end of that hallway I turned right. The desk nurse, who barely looked up from a chart she was filling out, directed me to Norma's room. Along the white corridor some doors were open and I could see into what looked

like undecorated college dorm rooms. Women lay belly down on
their beds reading, or sat knees to chest, staring intently into the
hallway as if the view framed by their open door was a television
screen.

Norma was not in her room. Now what? I looked around.
There were two beds in the room and I could tell which was
Norma's immediately. Someone, probably Eli, had brought the
purple pillow she had embroidered with gold string and which
she considered lucky. Taped to the wall were some index cards,
like the ones she'd had in her apartment, with positive affirma-
tions written on them. They told Norma that she looked beautiful, was filled with power, and was loved by God.

I felt like an intruder and was about to leave the room when
Norma appeared in the doorway. She was wearing black leggings
and a long, almost sheer, lavender blouse that flowed to her
knees. Her hair fell in soft waves around her face. Her arms,
which looked unbearably thin, were extended toward me as if she
were offering me a hug. Instead, I grabbed her hands and held
them.

There were light scratches on her forearms and on her face.
Her neck seemed too fragile to be holding her head up. She
looked as vacant as the rooms up and down the corridor. According to her psychiatrist she wasn't taking any drugs, so this was a
mood state Norma had chosen. For some reason she was showing
me her weak and helpless side. I knew from experience that any
moment her spine could stiffen, her eyes burst into fury, and her
arms close like steel bars across her chest.

She led me to her bed, like a gracious hostess seating me on an
antique sofa. The intimacy implicit in sitting there didn't appeal
to me, but there was no other choice besides her roommate's bed
across the room.

I didn't ask about Amelia right away. First I had to let Norma
know I cared about her. And I did. Part of me wanted to hug her,
to let her cry in my arms. I would have liked to check her out of
there and take her home, tuck her into her own bed, fix her a
mug of hot chocolate, and tell her everything would be all right.
But I had already done all of that and more. In the years since I
had known Norma I had tried everything from late-night doses
of warm milk with honey to appointments with therapists recommended by friends. I had tried pep talks, yelling matches, and
twelve-step meetings. I had even tried pretending nothing was

wrong. And all the while I had watched her life churn like a raging storm, pulling more and more lives into its vortex. Now my daughter, her daughter, was caught, too.

"What do you think?" Norma asked, motioning to her surroundings.

"What do *you* think?" I asked.

"I don't like it. I don't think it's helping."

"But you've just been here a couple of days. You have to give it a chance."

"No, I don't want to. I want to go home."

"Norma, you know better. You know what happens."

"What about my Amie? I just want to go home and be with my daughter."

"We need to find a way to take care of Amelia. But first you need to take care of yourself."

"Eli won't do it anymore. He won't take care of her. God, I hate him."

"Eli has tried. He and Lindsay need to . . ."

"And you can't have her. She'd never want to come back to me if you took her."

"That's ridiculous, Norma. Of course she'd come back. I'd bring her back."

"No, she likes you better. I know I should let her go live with you, but I'm too jealous."

Norma's honesty was always startling. In less than five minutes we'd already landed at the bottom line. The starkness of her statement almost impressed me. But anger was begging for top billing. My intent, though, was to avoid fighting and to convince Norma to agree on a course of action.

"Look, I know how upsetting this is for you. It is for me, too. But we have to do something."

"Maybe you could move closer to us. I could use the help."

"I've been thinking about applying for jobs in the area. But we both know that's not the answer. This happened when I lived across town, too."

Norma flopped back against the headboard and started to sob. Her cries rose and rose until they were wails. I could hear her manufacturing more misery, and I could feel myself being pulled toward her, toward my old habit of consoling her. But I reminded myself that I had been dealing with this dramatic pitch for two years now, and moreover, there was a child who was stuck in a psychiatric hospital, and who was in danger of becoming a ward of the state. And here was Norma, still plotting what was best for herself. Then my fury rose to meet her cries. I knew I should hug her or at least put an arm around her shoulders. But I couldn't. Nor could I bring myself to raise my voice over her cries and tell her to cut it out, to think of her daughter and not herself. Finally, I took her hand so as not to seem cruel. "We'll work this out," I said.

That night I called Eli from my hotel room. He was taking a hands-off approach to this whole disaster. "My whole life is falling apart," Eli said. "I can't keep taking care of my sister's shit."

"I had hoped we could work together on this to make Norma see the light," I told him. "Without Norma's written consent the hospital won't release Amelia."

"I'm sorry," Eli said. "Those are my limits."

I spent the next morning calling back the lawyers whom I'd contacted the day before. Finally, a secretary put me through to one who would help me, and who, miraculously, could meet me that very day. I should be prepared to give her a fifteen-hundred-dollar retainer, she said. She suggested we meet at the hotel at three o'clock. "Could you make it four?" I asked. I didn't want to miss any of my time with Amelia.

I visited with Amelia that afternoon, and played games with her in the small playground outside her unit. Then I went to Dr. Childers' office to check on the progress she was making.

She agreed that the best solution would be for me to take Amelia home, at least temporarily. But Norma was checked in on a voluntary basis, and she would surely check herself and Amelia out if I made any move to take her just now. The hospital would try to stop Norma if she were to attempt that, Dr. Childers assured me. But for now the best solution seemed to be to try to get Norma to voluntarily release Amelia into my care.

"But we don't have all the time in the world here," I said. "This whole thing could be turned over to the state, and Amelia could wind up in foster care."

"Hopefully that won't be necessary," she said. "Let's see what we can do."

"I'm not feeling particularly patient," I said.

Dr. Childers leaned forward in her chair and looked at me as if she were seeing me for the first time. "I know this is frustrating,"

she said. "But if we release Amelia to you without Norma's ex-
plicit consent, the hospital could be subject to a lawsuit. We want
to avoid that." She reassured me that in the meantime Amelia
was faring well. Another day or two on the unit wouldn't hurt her.

I returned to our hotel room to find our new lawyer leaning
against the bureau, talking to Whit. She was in her mid-thirties,
conservatively dressed, slim and serious looking. There was
something slightly off about the way she wore her stockings and
suit jacket, and the way her cotton dress hung on her angular
frame. It was the look, Whit and I later agreed, of a butch in
corporate drag. I imagined her on weekends wearing clothes that
suited her: an Izod shirt, collar up, khaki pants, and Reebock
sneakers. Our suspicions turned out to be correct. Attorney
Eileen Lewis didn't rush over to our hotel room because she had
nothing better to do. As it turned out, she and her life partner
hoped to have a child themselves someday. She had a personal
stake in my right to be recognized.

Rather than hold a conference sitting on the edges of the two
double beds in our room, Whit, our new lawyer, and I walked to a
diner a half block away. In an attempt to brief Attorney Lewis on
our case I pulled out my manila folder full of letters and legal
documents. I was so unnerved I couldn't seem to explain what
was happening. Instead I began showing our new lawyer pictures
Amelia had drawn, and letters she had written me. I skipped
right past the legal papers, and broke out the baby book. As diplo-
matically as she could, Whit suggested she do the talking. I
sipped my Seven-up and listened again to the whole horrible tale.

Unfortunately, Eileen Lewis explained, the power of attorney I
held, which Norma had never gotten around to dissolving, would
not carry enough clout to convince the hospital's counsel that
they wouldn't risk being sued by Norma if they honored it. "In
New Hampshire, the nonbiological parent has absolutely no cus-
todial rights," she explained. We would continue to pursue the
route of getting Norma to voluntarily release Amelia to my care.
Meanwhile, Attorney Lewis would try to negotiate with the institute's lawyers, and would contact the local court about setting up
an emergency guardianship hearing. "Unfortunately," she explained, "because of the Jewish holiday, a lot of the key players
won't be doing business for the next couple of days."

Whit was right. This was going to take time. But I wanted it to
be as little time as possible. Each minute that ticked by was intol-

erable to me, because I knew that Amelia was spending it inside a psychiatric hospital.

In an effort to keep track of what was happening in case there would be a court hearing, Whit and I kept a record of all of the phone calls we made to lawyers and administrators and what they said. At first I jotted down information while I was on the phone or immediately after. But as I became increasingly upset my handwriting degenerated until it was nearly illegible. So we changed our routine and after I hung up the phone I would dictate to Whit, who recorded the conversations on a pad of stationery with the motel's name stamped across the top.

But dictating to Whit was difficult, too. Even repeating conversations was painful, as it forced me to relive another moment of agony. My summaries of the conversations grew briefer, so Whit coaxed the details from me.

"So, she talked to the hospital guy," I said after one phone call with my lawyer.

"Which hospital guy?" Whit held aloft a black pen printed with the motel's name.

"The head one."

"The director?"

"Right."

"About what?"

"What do you think?"

Whit stopped writing. "Don't take this out on me," she warned.

"About when Amelia can leave," I said, falling onto the double bed.

"And?"

"And they can't discharge her without her mother's permission." I fixed my eyes on the stuccoed ceiling.

"But you *are* her mother!" Whit dropped the pen.

"You know what they mean," I said, ignoring her burst of temper. "Anyway, Norma won't give her permission."

"So, we're waiting for a mentally ill woman to act sanely?" Whit began pacing the room, I sat up, took the pad, and noted at the bottom that the lawyer had agreed to call me in the morning. With that I put the day's notes away in the desk drawer, beside the souvenir postcards and laminated room service menus.

"How can you stand this?" Whit was storming back and forth across the room now, pacing from the window's empty view on one end to the door at the other. "I want to go over there in the morning and just take her. Just walk out."

When she's angry, Whit's face flushes until it can get no brighter. Then she slumps into a chair or onto the bed, as if her inner fire has defeated her. "I don't see how you can just sit here every day making these calls and talking calmly to all these idiots!"

"Look, Whitney," I said, hissing out the words. "My getting mad won't do a damned thing. Amelia already has one mother who can't hold it together, she can't have two. Besides, the hospital doesn't want to release her to an unrelated lesbian to begin with. They certainly won't want to deal with an incensed, ranting, unrelated lesbian."

Whit had heard this speech before. She shook her head, unconvinced. I sat next to her and stroked her hair back from her forehead. "Before, when things got bad you could just watch me deal with Norma and go on with your life. Now you're in it with me, so you have to keep cool, too. We can fall apart when it's all over."

Whit sat up, brushing my hand aside. "You *can* get angry now. It doesn't mean you'll go crazy. You won't become like Norma."

I felt myself about to cry. "No. I can't," I said. From the framed mirror across the room, my reflection stared back at me. I saw myself leaning against the headboard, my arms wrapped around my knees which were tangled in a print cotton skirt. If I had met this woman on the street, I wouldn't have known her. For one thing, she was sad. Serious and sad.

Whit watched me watching myself. "I think you're getting more beautiful," she said.

"Really?" I asked, watching my face ease into a half smile. "Does that mean misery becomes me?"

Whit patted her shoulder, inviting me to rest my head there. I turned away from the mirror and into her arms.

That night Whit and I ate dinner at a nearby Friendly's, then drove to a department store so I could buy Amelia some more socks and underwear, and a lighter jacket. I picked up some books and games, too, since the toys on the unit were all meant for older children.

On the third morning of our vigil, Whit and I took a walk through the shabby neighborhoods around the hotel. As we turned corners that brought us from one row of weather-worn front porches to the next, we discussed what gains we had made and what we should do next. I told Whit I thought she should go home. I was afraid her boss would run out of patience with this extended absence, and I didn't want her to miss the sales meeting. Besides, we were both concerned about our pets, who had been left with one of our friends for what we had thought would be just a night or two. We decided to call my mother, who agreed to come up right away.

That day as I pushed through the doors to the children's unit, I realized that I was the only adult who was making regular visits. Of the other children's parents I had seen only one set, and to my knowledge they had visited only once. As for Amelia, my mother was on her way up from New York and Eli visited once or twice. Neither of Norma's parents had come, nor had Lindsay, or anyone else. Usually I was the only one arriving the moment visits began, and leaving reluctantly, only after being reminded my time was up. Sometimes no one asked me to leave, and I would sit on the couch and watch videos with the children, accompany them to the playground just outside of the unit, or invite one or two to join Amelia and me for games of "Where's Waldo."

I wondered what Amelia was making of all of this, so I asked. "Why are you here?" I said, as we hunted through a busy illustration looking for Waldo's telltale striped shirt.

"So I can be close to Mommy," she answered. Amelia was allowed a visit with Norma once a day, usually after dinner.

"Why are the other children here?" I asked.

Amelia thought about that for a while. "I don't know," she said. I was relieved at her ignorance, happy to let her believe she was in some sort of day care situation while her mother recuperated.

In honor of Passover, Norma had instructed the hospital to provide Amelia with matzo instead of bread. When I arrived for a visit just before dinnertime, I asked Amelia if she wanted to observe Passover—that is, abstain from all foods containing leavening—since all the other children would be eating bread and cakes and it might be difficult for her. "Mommy will understand, I will understand, and so will God," I assured her.

Amelia insisted that she wanted to try it. We agreed that since this year was different she could eat cake and cookies, and only forgo bread. "But you don't have to do it for all eight days," I said. "We'll just do it for as long as you want."

"I want to do it for eight days," Amelia insisted.

"Okay," I said. "Let's try."

I pulled a chair up next to Amelia's. Plastic platters of food were wheeled in by a young uniformed woman who set one in front of each child. Amelia protested when she saw the water roll on her plate. "Then you must be Amelia," the woman said, and pulled a special plate from the bottom of the cart. Amelia smiled when she saw the matzo in the spot where the other children had rolls. I improvised a mini seder for Amelia, reconstructing from memory, as best I could, the story of the Jews' flight from slavery in Egypt. One or two of the other children listened and asked some questions. The others just gobbled down the slabs of pale turkey, piles of green peas, and mashed potatoes. Liberation was certainly a fitting theme that week, as we sat behind locked doors on the children's unit.

"Moses led the Jews away from the Pharaoh, but they had to move very quickly in order to escape," I told Amelia and her friends. "We eat matzo to remember how they fled through the desert in such a rush that they didn't have time to let their bread dough rise."

I helped Amelia remember the prayer over the food and the prayer for the wine which we recited before she drank her grape juice. There were no candles to bless as there would have been at home, but Amelia didn't seem to notice. At least she didn't complain.

I had been proceeding gently with Norma during our daily visits. I didn't want to upset the gains I felt I was making in winning her trust and confidence, as ultimately I was dependent on her goodwill to get Amelia out of there. But besides the fact that Norma was speaking freely and openly with me, we had made no real progress. After a few days of this, I decided it was time to press my point. I found her in her room reading, and took a seat at the foot of the bed. This time I wasted little time on small talk.

"The hospital won't keep Amelia here indefinitely," I told her. "and if we don't work something out, the state will decide. Then we all lose," I said.

"What are you saying?"

"The hospital has reported your case to the Department of Social Services. If we don't do something, Amelia could wind up in foster care."

Norma thought about that. "Shannon said she'd take her," she said. "I'll talk to her tonight."

"Who's Shannon?"

"She's my roommate. She's being released tomorrow. She said she'd take Amelia."

At that moment the storm I had managed to keep in check up until this point broke loose. "If you don't let me, or even Eli, take her out, I am no longer going to work side by side with you on this. I've had it with your games."

In less than an instant Norma's skinny body sprang to attention. She was all steel and sinew now. "I'm leaving this place right now and I'm taking Amelia with me." She ran down the hall to the nurse's station and I followed.

"I want to sign myself out," she announced.

The nurse looked up from her paperwork, but didn't appear to be alarmed.

"Are you sure? Wouldn't you like to speak to your doctor about this first?" I couldn't believe the desk nurse was treating this as a reasonable request.

"I want to leave now! You can't stop me."

The nurse began pulling out forms. "What are you doing?" I asked. "You'll just let her go like that? She's going to take her four-year-old child with her. Do you think this is safe?"

"You get out of here!" Norma screamed at me. "Get her off this unit," she told the nurse.

"I will have to ask you to leave," the nurse said.

"I won't leave. This is ridiculous. Can you get her doctor up here?"

Another nurse came up to the station. "You can't raise your voices like this," she said. "You'll have to speak calmly or you'll have to leave," she told me.

"Can we get some help here?" I asked. "I'm happy to speak calmly but we really need some help."

Just then we were approached by a woman dressed in crisp jeans and a turtleneck, whose mane of curly hair was pulled back in a full ponytail. Only a white smock jacket emblazoned with a pale blue name tag distinguished her as a person with authority here. She introduced herself as a counselor and led us to a corner of the visiting lounge where we took seats on the modern cubes of furniture. Norma began to sob. "She never loved me," she said, motioning toward me as if I were a pile of crumbs to be wiped from a table. "She only wants to hurt me." The counselor talked to Norma, never once asking me for any input, I sat back and watched, wishing I could be anywhere else. Finally the counselor asked me to leave. "Are you going to let her check herself out?" I asked.

"That shouldn't concern you," she said quietly. "Let me see you out."

I felt as though I'd been trapped in a horror movie where sanity and insanity were reversed. My mind was racing through different ways to fight my way back to solid ground. But as she escorted me away from Norma and toward the door, the counselor assured me that Norma would not leave that night and that she certainly wouldn't be allowed to take Amelia with her. I thanked her, and felt foolish for the way I had behaved. What had I been thinking to try to argue with Norma like that?

The next morning my lawyer called and told me she'd been informed that Norma had become very upset and cut herself again that night after I left. "She's on a locked unit for now," she explained. I thought that was it, that I would never succeed now.

But by this time it seemed that the hospital administration was growing as uncomfortable about keeping Amelia as they were about letting her go. There was uncertainty about who would be paying for Amelia's stay, and the possibility that the state would become involved was becoming increasingly likely. The hospital's lawyers were arguing the validity of my power of attorney, and whether Norma was of sound mind enough to make a decision on her own.

Whit hesitated to leave given all of this, but I assured her that my mother and I would do fine. At noon I saw Whit off on one bus, and my mother arrived on another.

We got in my car and drove over to visit Amelia. As soon as we arrived on the unit, Amelia took Grandma Sue by the hand and began to play the "Rachel" game again, in which she pretended to look for "Amelia" who had disappeared. When she caught on to the fantasy Amelia was creating, my mother turned to me, and I saw anguish in her eyes.

The game was interrupted by Dr. Childers, who asked to see me. My mother insisted on joining us, and we reassured Amelia that we'd be back very soon. Before she even took a seat in Dr. Childers' office, my mother launched into a speech. "Excuse me for butting in like this, but I'm Amelia's grandmother and I demand that this hospital . . ."

"Mrs. Abrams, if you'll allow me to speak." Dr. Childers waved my mother into a seat. I sat, too, feeling suddenly inadequate with all of my politeness and patience. "I have some news that I think will make everyone very happy. Norma has agreed to let Nancy take Amelia home."

My mother cocked her head to one side, as if waiting for the catch. But I wasn't waiting. "She did?" I asked, and I felt myself hit by opposing waves of relief and anxiety. I didn't know if I should say what I was thinking—that surely Norma would change her mind unless we packed Amelia's things and fled that very moment.

"We're moving as quickly as possible to prepare the paperwork. In the meantime, you might want to avoid visiting Norma this afternoon. I think we should leave well enough alone."

To celebrate that night, my mother and I went out to a movie and ate dinner in a Chinese restaurant. We tried to piece together the events of the past twenty-four hours, and guessed at what could have happened to make Norma change her mind so abruptly. That night I could hardly sleep.

"She'd better not back down now," my mother said the next morning, as we checked out of the hotel.

"It'll be all right, Mom," I said, not believing my own words.

While I went to meet Norma for the official signing of the papers, my mother received special permission to stay with Amelia before visiting hours.

Norma agreed to sign the papers prepared by the hospital administrators and approved by my lawyer and the hospital's lawyers. The documents simply stated that I would be taking Amelia with Norma's consent. I was led to a tiny room on the women's unit where Norma and a notary public from the institute were waiting. Norma's doctor stood just outside the door. "The lawyers have just finished with the forms. They'll be brought up any moment."

I took a seat across from Norma, but in that small space our knees were nearly touching. I couldn't figure out what purpose this room had originally been meant for. Maybe storage.

"I know this is hard for you," I said, looking into Norma's tear-swollen eyes. We were crammed so tight in that room that I felt as if we were breathing each other's air.

"I'll wait outside," the woman who was the notary public offered. I wished I could sneak out as easily. We were seated on
chairs that had little desks for arms, like the kind you'd find in a
high school. I reached across and patted Norma's shoulder. The
gesture felt forced and wooden, but in such close quarters I could
hardly ignore her misery.

"You promise I can have her when I'm well?" Tears poured
down Norma's cheeks.

I remembered my lawyer's instructions about not lying.
"When you're well, I promise."

The notary public came in with the papers. Norma stared at
the writing for a long time before signing her name. The document said she was releasing Amelia to me, "in loco parentis," in
the place of a parent, and that Norma would not sue the hospital
for allowing Amelia to leave with me. Norma's hand shook as she
signed her name. I scrawled mine quickly. The notary public wit-
nessed the documents and took them from us to copy.

I stayed long enough to give Norma a hug and a kiss good-bye,
but my heart was already racing out the door.

In loco parentis: The phrase from the release papers worked itself around in my mind. Legally, I knew the words meant I was
taking temporary guardianship "instead of the parent." But I understood the phrase differently. I imagined it as a locale. The
Place of the Parent. The Land of Parenthood. It was that green
field of emotion, response, love, hope, attachment. Like an exile
returning, I felt I'd been offered a home, a safe harbor in which
to care for this child. To see this thing through.

I found my mother seated on Amelia's bed where she was helping her put together a puzzle. Over Amelia's head I gave her a
smile that said, "We did it!"

"Guess what, little goose, we're going to Massachusetts today,"
I told Amelia.

Amelia scanned my face as if to see if this was good news or not.
I must have looked elated because she bounced up and yelled,
"Yippee!" My mother wasted no time. She fished Amelia's quilt
duffel bag out from the closet and began packing her clothes

"Will Mommy come?" Amelia asked.

"No, Mommy's still not better yet," I said. "She'll stay here until
the doctors say she's all better."

Dr. Childers appeared in the doorway. "I see you're getting

ready to go," she said. Looking at me, she added, "Mommy just wants a few minutes with Amelia before she leaves. We'll be right back."

"I hope there won't be a scene," my mother said as Amelia reached for Dr. Childers' waiting hand.

"I'll stay with them," Dr. Childers assured us.

When they left, my mother sat back down on Amelia's bed. "I don't know how you've done it. I can't stand this place another minute," she said.

If I had known how long we'd all be camped here, maybe I couldn't have tolerated the wait either. But in the end, I felt the victory more than the frustration. Throughout the ordeal I'd feared that I wouldn't succeed in getting Amelia released into my care, and that the worst could happen—she could end up in foster care. Just the day before, I'd been certain that Norma would check them both out and refuse to let Amelia ever see me again. By comparison, this purgatory had its merits. Anyway, now we were leaving, and I had it in writing: I was Amelia's de facto parent.

My mother and I sat with Amelia's packed duffel bag at our feet for another fifteen minutes. While we waited we made our plans. I would drop my mother off at the bus station. In a week or two, after we were all settled in, she would come up to Massachusetts to visit. That settled, there was nothing else to distract us.

"I can't stand this. How long can they take?" my mother asked.

"It'll be soon," I said. But the minutes dragged, and there was no way to hurry them on.

Finally, Dr. Childers returned. "Mrs. Abrams, why don't you and Amelia check with the nurse to make sure she hasn't left any other belongings with us while Nancy and I have a quick chat," she said. As soon as my mother left the room, Dr. Childers told me there was a problem.

Tears filled my eyes. "No," I said, "we're going."

"Yes, yes, don't worry. It just might be a little longer."

"How could she!" I blurted out. Then, immediately, I tried to pull myself together. I didn't want this psychiatrist to think I couldn't handle stress. I didn't want her to decide I wasn't competent to take care of Amelia.

"She's just upset. She said she wants to talk to her therapist first. I promise you he will see to it that she lets Amelia go. But it won't do anyone any good if you take the child under duress."

The door opened, and my mother poked her head inside. "Ready?" she asked. I could hear the impatience in her voice.

"There's been a little delay. Norma wants to talk to her doctor first."

Amelia squeezed past my mother into the room. "We're going to Massachusetts," she sang.

"Soon, honey," I said.

"I won't let her do this," my mother muttered.

"Just a minute, Ma," I whispered. I sent Amelia to find a video for us to watch while we waited. When Amelia had reached the lounge, out of earshot, I told my mother we would give Norma a half hour. "Let's give her the benefit of the doubt."

My mother turned to Dr. Childers. "But she signed the paper."

"Still, if you leave with Norma upset like this she could try to make a case that she was pushed to sign under duress. Then we'd all be in trouble. I suspect she just wants to feel in control of the situation." Dr. Childers left us alone then. I looked out to where Amelia was watching her videotape. Two more children and one of the social workers had joined her.

"Norma shouldn't be allowed to do this," my mother said. "Enough is enough already." For a moment I thought she was going to cry. But she didn't and I was relieved. I didn't feel I could comfort anyone else just then. "You know I love Norma," my mother began. "But now she's gone too far. I can't abide this."

We walked into the lounge and sat on either side of Amelia, who was engrossed in a Pippi Longstocking tape. We stared blankly at the characters on the large television screen as the rest of the children from the unit filed in from the gym.

"I'm going home today," Amelia sang out as her new friends gathered around her.

A few minutes later, Dr. Childers returned and put a hand on my mother's shoulder. "You can go now," she said. "Just let me have a word with Nancy while I check Amelia's chart."

I followed her into the nurses' station. "We didn't find anything clinically wrong with Amelia," she explained. "Nonetheless, this has been a very stressful time for her, and I would recommend that you find a therapist for her when you return to Massachusetts." I didn't think Amelia needed therapy. I thought what she needed was to be away from doctors and diagnoses. But I would have agreed to anything right then. I told Dr. Childers that I had a friend who was a therapist who could surely recommend a doctor for Amelia.

"I'm sorry this all took so long," she said. "Amelia is really a lovely girl."

I nodded, anxious to leave.

"She might act out when you get her home, but just try to listen to her. She'll need a lot of love."

"Thank you," I said, looking toward the door.

When my mother, Amelia, and I stepped out of the building together I let go a whoop of delight. "We're out," I sang.

"We're out," Amelia yelled, as we skipped to the car, where my mother was already locking Amelia's bag into the trunk.

Losing

In the rearview mirror I see you carefully sucking your strawberry milkshake through a straw. You appear content, having charmed the waitress and the retired couple who sat at the booth behind us. But you also know that this trip is serious, and you are quiet and obedient for the occasion. You are happy, too. I imagine you share my exhilaration at having just escaped. For the time being, the safety of the cushioned arm of your car seat convinces you, and the simple pink of your lips puckered on the sweet straw convinces me that all is well. I can relax my vigilance. I can let you out of my sight long enough to look ahead at the easy black highway that will take us home.

Home. My home which I want to call yours, too. Sometimes you say home and mean our house in Massachusetts. But only when you have been there for many days. Usually you mean the apartment where Norma lay bleeding in her best pink nightgown that evening while you were sleeping at your friend's house.

I want to tell you that home can be a relative term. It can be any place where you are loved; you will be at home in my house.

The one home we shared—you, Norma, and I—was so many houses ago. One day you were in the backseat of the car, just as you are now, and I drove past the house where you were conceived. It sits on a sloping side street. In the yard, a tree that blossoms white gave us an awning against summer sun. "That's where Mommy and I lived when you started to grow in her belly," I told you. "Stop, stop," you cried. I kept driving slowly up the hill. At the stop sign on the corner I asked what was wrong. "I want to touch it," you said.

"Touch what?"

"The house."

"You want to touch the house?" I circled the block and parked. This was where we lived when we got Chance, the first bit of living glue that

joined us. Then we made you, laughing and daring the fates to give us
what we asked for.

I unbuckled you from your seat and you marched, pulling me behind,
across the street, up the driveway, to the white clapboard house. We lived
in the second-floor apartment, but I didn't mention this, for fear you'd
demand a ladder. The rooms were full of sun and Norma made things cozy
with pillows and throw rugs everywhere. She liked to rearrange the few
pieces of furniture we had, and I liked things to stay the way they were.

"Where was I?" you asked, your hand plastered to the house's cold
outer skin.

"You were inside Mommy's belly."

"Was I sleeping?"

"Yes, I think you were."

Satisfied, you traipsed back to the car.

Now I drive you home, leaving Mommy farther and farther behind.

I

Since I had moved into Whit's house, Amelia had visited only a
few times. But already we had a routine. Before each visit I would
adapt the backroom into Amelia's bedroom. Then, when she
went back to New Hampshire, I would put her toys away in the
wooden chest that Whit picked up at a tag sale, and I'd put her
clothes in the closet. Her larger dolls and stuffed animals were
stowed beneath the single bed which I covered with large cushions and used as a sofa. Then, in her absence, Amelia's room was
once again my study, our laundry room, a storage area, and a
guest room when we needed it.

Downstairs, the kitchen, living room, bathroom, and Amelia's
room huddle together, wall to wall, with no hallways between
them. A steep set of stairs leads to our bedroom, which is nestled
beneath the eaves of the house. The house itself perches on stilts;
the three feet or so between the living room floor and the rocky
New England soil is as close as we get to a basement. Whit stores
scrap lumber and leftover rolls of insulation in that little space
where the dog and cat take turns hiding.

"We're here," I announced, as I pulled into the driveway and
shifted into park. I opened the backdoor and unbuckled the
straps of Amelia's car seat. I loved watching her eyes open slowly,

first looking half annoyed to have her sleep disturbed, then quickly sharpening, taking on the challenge of the new scene that she was waking up to.

"We're in Massachusetts already, Ima?"

"Already for you, sleepyhead. You've been napping for more than an hour."

Whit came out and pulled Amelia's duffel bag from the trunk. I gathered up the empty milkshake cup, storybooks, and the Where's Waldo game, which were strewn across the backseat.

When I stepped over the threshold, my exhaustion caught up with me. But I was too happy to lie down. Instead I took Amelia into her room, which Whit had transformed perfectly, and listened as she exclaimed at the precise placement of all her toys. "My dolls are tucked into bed, just how I left them," she beamed. I put my arm around Whit and whispered, "Thanks."

In the days that followed, Whit and I would discuss how long we thought Amelia might be with us. My plan was to wait for Norma to leave the hospital, declare herself well, then ask for Amelia's return. At that point I would try to convince her to leave Amelia with us for the summer at least, to be sure that she would be well enough to resume parenting again without another incident. She had never had a significant span of time alone to get her bearings, a pattern I blamed in part for this cycle of self-abuse and hospitalization. I truly believed that if she would just let herself rest and rehabilitate, this trail of crises might end.

"I think after a few months Norma will be well enough to take her back," I would say to Whit on my more optimistic days.

"It wouldn't hurt to check out the elementary school just in case, though," she would answer.

In the meantime, I had to give up the idea of having my own study. There'd be no time for writing now anyway, so it hardly seemed to matter. We moved my desk and computer out of Amelia's room and into our bedroom. Amelia quickly filled up the empty space, setting up her dollhouse where my desk had been, and filling my emptied bookshelves with her toy doctor kit, the fifty-cent handbags we picked up at church bazaars, dolls, balls, and stuffed creatures of all shapes and sizes. Though she settled in easily, nights were still hard. Amelia was, after all, used to the creaks and groans of another house settling into sleep, another neighborhood's whispers as it tucked itself into night. The blackness against her bedroom window frightened Amelia. I plugged in her Cinderella night-light at bedtime, but still there would be a period of debugging her imagination. "What are you afraid of?" I asked one night, curled up at the edge of her bed.

"The monsters outside."

"Did you see any monsters when you were hunting for treasures in the flower beds today?"

"They're nighttime monsters," she said, incredulous at my ignorance.

"Oh, no. Do you know what's really out there at night? The grass, the birds, the squirrels, Rico, the dog from next door, the woodpile, your bicycle . . ."

"My sled?" she asked.

"Yes, of course."

"And the plastic pool?"

"Yes, that too."

"And no monsters?"

"Not a one. Just the things we see in the daylight. And it's all waiting to see you again tomorrow. But first you have to go to sleep." Amelia relaxed enough to sleep, and I went upstairs, exhausted.

"What are you going to do if Norma just decides to take Amelia back?" Whit asked as I settled into bed.

"Do I have to think about this now?" I asked.

"When do you want to think about it?"

"When I'm not so tired," I said.

"That may be awhile."

So I propped myself up on one elbow and looked down at Whit, whose serious eyes were achingly handsome even as she was pushing me toward conclusions I didn't want to reach. I'd come a long way in the past two weeks, Whit was saying. Now what was I going to do? What was my goal in all of this? "You have to be clear because the minute Norma gets on the phone you're just going to want to do what she says again," Whit warned.

I remembered a day a year or so before Amelia was born. Norma and I were walking home from the Museum of Art when we turned onto a run-down street where a woman was dragging her son by the arm. As we got closer we could hear her cursing him. He was protesting, and finally she threw him to the ground. I was appalled, but I didn't say a word. Norma meanwhile rushed ahead of me toward the woman. As I caught up to her I could hear Norma saying in a kind voice, "I just thought you might need some help. Some days we all do." Norma stooped down to give the boy a hand up, and patted the dust off his trousers as if he'd just had a tumble on the playground. The woman shook her head. "Jesus knows we all need help and I need it more than most today." We walked with her and her son for a block or two, Norma keeping up the conversation. When we turned and went on our way I marveled at what Norma had accomplished. "You were amazing," I said. "You really diffused that whole situation. I wanted to say something myself, but thought she'd haul off and hit me if I tried to interfere." Norma shrugged it off at the time. But now I realized she'd taught me a lesson that day. Maybe one she'd have wished she hadn't. Because now I couldn't just walk past and pretend I didn't see what was happening in my own family. Jesus knows we all need help, and Norma needed it more than most now.

I went to sleep that night knowing what I had to do. I knew that I had to keep Amelia with me until Norma was fit to take her back. That could be three months. It could be three years. That was all I knew. And this: It wouldn't be easy for me to steer my course; sometimes I knew I'd just want to stand on that curb and keep my opinions to myself.

In the days that followed there were times when my resolve felt cool and steely. Unshakable. Other nights I found myself lying face down on my bed after Amelia had gone to sleep, crying into my pillow, muttering, "I can't do it, I can't do it." I was afraid of hurting Norma, worried about standing up to Eli and their parents. I was afraid of hurting Amelia, too, even though I knew that the pain of missing Norma in the short term would easily be outweighed by the gains of her mother really having a chance to heal, to create a workable life. And I feared the courts. I feared losing everything, and I knew that that was a very real possibility. When I tried to fall asleep these thoughts would jolt me awake.

Then morning would come, and I would wake to a household that bustled with a new level of energy and purpose. Amelia and I would have tea parties in the backyard with her stuffed animals. In the mornings we'd take walks to the shore and collect shells that we'd bring home and plant in mosaic lines along the flower beds. I arranged for Amelia to return to the day care she'd attended before she moved, and sometimes when I picked her up at the end of the day we'd treat ourselves to a dip in the children's pool at the same YMCA where she'd had her first swim. Some days we'd take the ferry to Boston together, and the familiar commute would become an adventure with Amelia on board calling out the sights and throwing bits of pretzels to the seagulls who'd greet us on the dock.

At work, I called my lawyer and interviewed therapists for Amelia. I spoke to Norma's psychiatrist who said that the time away from full-time parenting would certainly do Norma good, although now she was still struggling daily. I drafted an affidavit that would outline my story to a judge, should we end up in court, and in between all of this, I tried to keep up with my reporting assignments.

I spoke to Norma once or twice a week. She said she felt okay about having Amelia stay with me for a while, although precisely how long a while remained undefined. Sometimes she'd say things that made me think she agreed that a few months would be a good length of time. Other times, she seemed to think she'd recover from her emotional problems as quickly as she might get over a cold or flu. But even when our conversations went well, there would be so many odd moments when her seemingly random contradictions, denials, and refusals would make me want to scream. One day she said that the doctor recommended she take a six-month break from major responsibilities, including parenting, in order to recover. Then, in the same breath she said that she was going to check herself out of the hospital the next day and get on with her life. Once she announced that when she left the hospital she would move overseas; another time that she didn't want Amelia eating hot dogs because she and Amelia were going to keep kosher now.

I'd hang up the phone feeling as if I'd just endured some force of nature. I felt trapped in Norma's circular thinking and ceaseless demands, and I knew the only way out of the trap was to let go of Amelia. I also knew that that was how the trap was meant to work.

One morning when I was in the bathroom drying my hair, Amelia pushed the door open. "Good morning, little goose," I said. Amelia reached across the sink on tiptoes, stretching for her toothbrush. I gave her a boost and she pulled it free.

"Ima, are we going to have cake today?"

"You mean for dessert? After dinner?" I put a dab of Crest on Amelia's toothbrush.

"Not dessert, cake," Amelia insisted.

"Well, cake is a dessert. Anyway, I haven't thought about that yet. Why?"

Amelia busied herself with her toothbrush before she answered. "We don't eat dessert in New Hampshire. We just have cake."

I tried to puzzle out what Amelia was getting at.

"I like to eat cereal like you and Whit do." She took a gulp of water. "Jared eats cereal instead of cake, too."

Now I knew what she was trying to tell me. Norma let Amelia eat cake and pie for breakfast sometimes. Or was Amelia informing me that this was a daily ritual? A set meal plan. If so, it wasn't nutritionally sound, but it wouldn't necessarily be horrible. That is, if I had any reason to believe that meals the rest of the day were more balanced. I remembered looking into Norma's refrigerator the few times I'd been in their apartment. There was rarely a vegetable or a piece of fruit. But the cabinets were filled with cookies, and the freezer with Tater Tots and easy-to-heat snacks. "Do you mean that you like to have cereal instead of cake for breakfast?" I asked, rinsing Amelia's toothbrush for her.

She nodded.

"You can just tell Mommy that. Maybe she thinks you like cake better." I squirted some mousse into my palm and swiped it through my hair. I could think of nothing more useful to say.

"Mommy yells much louder than you do," Amelia said, by way of explaining her acquiescence, I suppose.

"How do I yell?" I asked.

Amelia squared her shoulders, took in a deep breath, and made her voice as low as it would go. Even in her nightgown and bare feet she looked suddenly more grown up. "I'm going to count to three and then you're getting a timeout," she huffed.

I laughed. It was a good imitation. "How 'bout Mommy? How does she sound?"

Amelia took in another breath. "You're in big trouble!" she boomed. Even I was a little scared.

Driving Amelia to day care that morning, I looked down at my hands on the steering wheel and saw my mother's: the same long fingers, the same raised veins and pronounced knuckles. They looked adult and sure, the way hers always did when as a child I glanced at them from the backseat of our car.

I used to admire the unconscious things grown-ups did, like the way my mother turned the steering wheel, making slight adjustments for small dips and turns in the road. I always envied the way parents talked to one another, indifferent, while their children played. At school I studied the way my first-grade teacher made stars on top of our homework assignments, how with one blithe stroke she could shape all of those points. I liked how people could take things for granted, could fit so easily into their own lives. Their unself-conscious competence and confidence seemed unattainable to me.

For me, life seemed an awkward proposal. A foreign language to be lived in broken phrases. A stranger's suit that would just have to do.

First comes love, then comes marriage . . . It was supposed to be so simple. My own song started over and over in the middle, with no repeating choruses. There'd been sex and then love, and solo trips to explore the world while others were making out résumés. I'd been focused on girlfriends and rebellion in the years reserved for engagement showers and china patterns. A child came without mating, before and outside of marriage. Now there was Norma in a psychiatric hospital, lawyers hovering in the background, and a house without enough room for a family we weren't counting on housing. And at the end of each day there was a very conscious kiss on my daughter's forehead.

I was very aware of the steering wheel, my foot on the gas pedal, how I was working to make things smooth.

Amelia loved to draw and paint, so after day care one day I took her to an art museum. I thought she might like the pale green canvas filled with the featureless figure of a man fishing from a beach, painted by Milton Avery; or she might be drawn to the flowers by Georgia O'Keeffe; or to one of my favorites, Degas' sculpture of a young dancer. Just across from the pedestal of the bronze ballerina, a six-foot canvas caught Amelia's eye. It was a nineteenth-century painting called *Charity*. Despite its size I had never really noticed it before, maybe because it was hung on a narrow partitioning wall, facing into the long rectangular gallery.

"Look, Ima," Amelia said. I turned to examine the painting she was studying. In it, a woman wearing nothing but burgundy cloths draped across her shoulder was seated on a marble ledge with her four children clinging to her. An urn was tipped at her feet, spilling the coins passersby had tossed for the hungry family. Two of the babies were cradled in the mother's arms, hiding her bare breasts. At Amelia's eye level was a nearly life-sized boy, naked and huddled against his mother's knee. "Ima, why are they naked?" she asked, without taking her eyes from those of the child.

"What do you think?"

"Are they homeless?"

"It looks like that's what the painting is about," I said, making a move to continue through the gallery. Amelia remained planted. "Why are they homeless?" she asked.

"Well, I don't know exactly. That was painted a long time ago."

"They didn't have enough money and they couldn't pay for their apartment," she said. I flinched at the candor with which she revealed her worries, and at their scope.

After we finished looking through the rest of the gallery, Amelia circled back once more to look at the painting. She stood face to face with the naked boy for a long moment, as if she were going to speak to him. But she said nothing.

On the way home, Amelia flopped into her car seat. "I'm so tired, Ima," she kept mumbling, as she let her eyes close.

Norma called a few days later to tell me she had left the institute. It had been about three weeks since she'd checked herself in, and two weeks since Amelia had come home with me. "Did your doctors agree that it was time?" I asked, settling down at the kitchen table. Through the window I could see Whit and Amelia on the lawn, teasing Chance with a stick.

"No," she answered. "It was my decision. I grew up with crazy parents. Amelia will have to, as well."

"It doesn't have to be that way. You can get better." I could hear my voice turning frantic.

"Getting better takes too long. My doctor said I would need six months of rehabilitation."

I steadied myself with a deep breath. "Norma, you almost died this winter. Then you would have never seen Amelia again. Why not take your time and recover? We can work out a visiting schedule. Give yourself a chance to really get better this time." The dog yelped outside. I watched as Amelia shot across the yard, waving the stick over her head.

"I am not leaving Amelia there for six months. I can't be away from her for that long."

"It might not have to be six months. But it will take some time. You can do it."

My insistence pushed Norma to rage. "I'll take her home as soon as I'm ready. You have no say in this. I'm her mother and I decide!"

"But I'm her parent, too. I take my responsibility seriously." Amelia was calling my name. I wondered if Norma could hear her.

"She's not your responsibility," Norma shouted, and hung up the phone.

The next morning Eli called me at work to ask what had happened between Norma and me that might have upset her. Norma had been staying with him and Lindsay after returning from the hospital, but after our phone call the day before, she had disappeared, he said. She hadn't come home for dinner, and none of her friends seemed to know where she was, he told me. I recounted our conversation and heard Eli let out a disheartened sigh. "She'll turn up," I said, only half believing it. "Call me as soon as you hear from her."

I tried not to worry about what had happened; tried not to feel guilty for being firm with her. Sure enough, when I got home that evening there was a message from Eli. Norma was home. She'd spent the night at a friend's house.

A few days later two letters arrived in the mail, both from Norma. One was addressed to me. In it, Norma apologized for yelling at me over the phone. "Mother's Day is still a few weeks off, but I wanted to thank you for being such a great parent to Amelia, especially when I have made it difficult for you to do so." The other letter was for Amelia, and in it Norma apologized for not being able to control her temper with her, for spanking her, and for yelling at her.

Norma's apologies had so often had the power to soften me and convince me of her good intentions. But this pair together had the opposite influence. Succinctly they laid out the problem, the fact that Norma could barely keep herself from warring with me, making it as difficult as possible for me to be a caring, responsible parent to Amelia. Her apology to the daughter she'd wanted more than anything else in the world was little more than an admission of guilt in my eyes. She was sorry she had lost her temper. The phrase made it sound like a simple accident, like Little Bo Peep losing her sheep. But I knew firsthand what it was like to grow up with a parent who "lost his temper" time and again, then apologized as if it were so easy to erase the marks of rage. My father's irrational outbursts resulted in torn-up schoolbooks, ruined meals, shouted threats and insults that echoed through our house and through the years. Each of us, my siblings and I, have had to fight this legacy of fear and insecurity through adulthood. Norma's outbursts were no less terrifying to Amelia. Her letters told me that she, the head of our fractured household, was truly out of control, cut off from her ideals and intentions. She would always be Amelia's mother, but she didn't have to be the one Amelia lived with every day.

Whit and I met with Attorney Kaplan to discuss what steps I would take to file for temporary custody in the event that Norma insisted on taking Amelia back before I agreed that it was time.

One night, just as I was about to get into bed, the phone rang.

"It's your father," announced the voice on the other end of the line.

"Hi, Dad." Whit, listening now, sat up in bed. From across the room I could see her eyes roll back into her head. "Of all people," she muttered.

"Your mother told me what's happening."

"You mean that I'm thinking of suing for temporary custody?"

"Whatever. The point is, I think you should just forget this whole episode and get on with your life."

"Dad, I'm really tired."

"How much is this costing you anyway?"

"I don't actually want to talk about money right now."

"A lawyer is, minimum, seventy dollars an hour. Minimum. And whether or not you're right, you won't win. You have no legal standing."

"Well, I have to try." While reality ticked on, a fantasy ran through my head. I wanted him to say he would help me, that he was writing out the check as we spoke. I wanted him to say that while he had never approved of my having a child, now that Amelia was here he respected my commitment to take care of her. But I knew better. He had threatened to withhold my college tuition after he found out that more than half my courses had something to do with feminism. He changed his mind only after my mother intervened, but the lesson had been learned. His support, financial and emotional, was conditional.

Across the room, Whit was slicing her hands across the air as if it were a substance she could mangle or destroy. *Hang up,* her lips were saying.

"I know she means a lot to you," my father was saying.

"Of course she does. She's my daughter."

"Whatever. But you have to think about yourself. Norma's parents will fight you on this."

"They haven't yet."

"But when they see that their daughter is in court they are going to fight, and they have a lot of money."

"Dad, that's enough. This is my responsibility."

"Norma is the one who wanted a child. You didn't."

"That was before she was born. Now she's my child."

Whit jumped off the bed, slapping her hands on her thighs. "I'm going to take that phone and hang it up for you," she hissed. I waved her away.

"Dad," I said. "You'd do the same thing. You wouldn't let a child end up in foster care. You'd do the same as me."

"No, I wouldn't," he said. "And I think you're making a big mistake."

"Dad, I've got to go." Whit had already left the room. I knew she was probably sitting on the steps just beyond the doorway, still listening.

"I'm not telling you what to do. I just think you're making a mistake."

"It's late, Dad. I'll talk to you another time." I hung up the phone and went to the doorway.

"Don't come in here if you're going to get angry at me," I told Whit, whispering so as not to wake Amelia.

"Why do you take that from him?"

"He's my father."

"He should be proud of you. He should be offering to help with the lawyer's bills."

"He's my father."

Whit came back in, but I could tell she was still furious; angry at my father, and at me for listening to him. I was angry too, but mostly I was sad. I wanted to be the child for a moment. I wanted him to help me. I wanted to believe he would do the same thing I was doing. And I feared that he wouldn't.

I remembered the summer day when my father gave me swimming lessons in Bear Lake. I was twelve years old, and it was visiting day at Camp Shawnee. It was my father's idea that he and I should go swimming together. I didn't have to ask, beg, whine, or be let down. We were in the part of the lake enclosed on three sides by floating docks and on the fourth by a string of buoys. I was trying to pretend we always got along this way, as if he always wanted to teach me and to be with me, as if he always made time for me like this.

He was showing me how to breathe when swimming the crawl. His mouth tightened into a small *o*, then slid across his face toward his ear so he barely had to turn his head to get air. His face looked contorted, unspeakably ugly, and he was clearly unaware of this as he skimmed through the water.

"You see?" he asked when he reached the metal ladder and rested on its red rungs. He was perfectly solid and handsome again. As I churned my feet underwater to stay afloat, I wondered what to make of the contorted face I had just discovered by accident. It was the way another child might react to catching a glimpse of her father undressed, or her parents making love. In that instant he was neither god nor monster, nor even father: just a man, gaping for a mouthful of air.

I didn't know yet that he and my mother had decided to get a divorce.

Nothing was said until camp was over and we kids came home. One late-summer afternoon we were gathered on the back porch, my father sitting on one cushioned cedar lounge chair, my mother on another. My sister, brother, and I sat in a row, stiff as the stems of the geraniums planted in the flower box at our backs.

After he told us he was leaving, we each went to our own room and closed the door, as though these exits had been choreographed. There was a knock and he appeared in my room, still in his Brooks Brothers shirt and trousers. He must have come home from work early for this. He hugged me. It was the only time I remember feeling peaceful and precious in his arms.

On the Rosh Hashanah after he left, my father took us to synagogue in town where he now lived. Somehow he didn't realize we would need tickets, or if he realized, he hadn't managed to buy them in advance. Or maybe he just couldn't face the task, knowing with certainty that taking care of the business his wife had once tended to meant it was really over.

This new temple had an unfamiliar wooden door and a strange blue carpet in the foyer. No one knew us there and they wouldn't let us in without tickets. My father talked and talked to the man at the door, and finally we were led to a Hebrew school classroom in the basement where people who came late, or who didn't have tickets, could hear the rabbi over the sound system. Before we could even sit down on the small chairs, my father motioned us back out.

Standing in the crisp autumn air I knew he was disgusted and disappointed and that we were all seeing how our lives were changed, and that he would never say so. I also knew that my father believed every word in the Torah and that synagogue was where he belonged that day. But he seemed to take heart from the sunshine and the fact that things could be different. He drove us in his new Trans Am to the beach, and we took off our good shoes, tights, socks, and walked along the water's edge. "See," he said, "this is nice." And it was.

When people talk about what they learned from their parents, they often recall a skill, a set of aphorisms, a moral code. I like to think I learned from mine how to divorce amicably. My father never said a bad word about my mother in my presence, before or after they split up. My parents worked their divorce out with their two lawyers and without custody battles. There were no dramatic days in court fighting over alimony, possessions, or anything else. My parents spent holidays together so we wouldn't have to choose between them. They sat together at our school assemblies and graduations. They had a hard time being with one another on these occasions at first, but they made it as easy as possible on us kids.

It wasn't until Norma and I split up that I appreciated how hard a time this must have been for my father. I imagine he regretted his absences finally, and tried to make up for them after he was gone for real. It was more and more difficult for us to understand one another, but we didn't stop trying. I attempted to tell my father some of this once, but we didn't communicate very well anymore.

For all of these reasons and more, I had been avoiding the seemingly inevitable conclusion that Norma and I would have to take our differences before a judge. I was clinging to the hope that we'd be able to work things out together as my parents had, to spare Amelia the spectacle of a court battle. But Norma seemed intent on having her way at any cost, I was done conforming to her way, and my lawyer was proceeding as though a hearing were imminent. She began to make me see my actions as they would appear to a judge. For example, I had been planning to take Amelia to a child psychologist because Dr. Childers at the institute recommended it. When I mentioned this to my lawyer, she lit up. A psychologist's evaluation of the situation would be helpful in court, she said. She even suggested a few names of psychologists I could call. "How do you know these people?" I asked.

"I've worked with them, and they are very good in front of a judge."

But we're not going to court, I wanted to tell her. Norma and I can work this out on our own.

I explained to Amelia that Dr. Thompkins, the psychologist my lawyer had recommended, was a talking doctor, and that he helped children understand their feelings. I picked her up early from day care on a Friday afternoon and brought her to his office where I had already had a consultation with him a few days before.

Dr. Henry Thompkins was a bear of a man, big and lumbering, but friendly looking. He had come to psychology as a second career some five years earlier. Before he began spending his days playing dolls with small children and looking for clues to their emotional lives in how they stacked building blocks, he had worked for fifteen years as a business consultant.

"You can't just sit and talk to a four-year-old and expect to understand what's going on," Dr. Thompkins told me during our interview. "What I do is bring the child into the playroom, and let her choose what toys we will engage with. We might play with dolls, or trucks, or whatever. Children's play reveals a lot about what is on their mind. I don't force discussions about the heavy stuff, like abuse. If it is there, it generally comes out on its own."

"Knock, knock," I said to Amelia, as we waited for our first appointment with Dr. Thompkins.

"Who's there?"

Amelia squirmed a little in my lap. We were paging through a book of jokes and she knew the punch line would be coming soon.

"Amos," I say.

"Amos who?"

"A mosquito bit me." Amelia let out a raucous laugh, which I was quite sure was because she was learning what a joke is and how to respond. The humor of the wordplay, I was certain, was beyond her. Still, I giggled along with her because I was glad that she was laughing, for whatever reason.

Dr. Thompkins appeared in the waiting room and invited us inside. Since it was the first session, I would participate too. In the therapy room, Dr. Thompkins lowered himself onto a child-sized chair and put a rabbit puppet on his left hand. It was the rabbit who addressed Amelia and me, as we sat surrounded by shelves of plastic dollhouses and boxes of stuffed animals.

Amelia backed into my arms when the rabbit first addressed her, but soon she was in earnest conversation with the puppet. "I don't really live here," she confided to the rabbit. "I'm just here with Ima while my mother gets better."

"What happened to your mother?" the rabbit asked. "Is she sick?"

"I'm not telling you. Wanna play house?"

That night Dr. Thompkins phoned after Amelia was asleep. I was sure he was going to tell me that when Amelia had made one doll tie the other up to the banister in the dollhouse, she was exhibiting signs of deep emotional distress. In fact he said that her violent play scenarios were natural given what she had been through. "It would be unusual if she didn't express her anger in some way," he said. His prescription was that I encourage Amelia to play with her dolls and dollhouse and that I should try not to inhibit her if her fantasies became ugly. He also asked if he could call Amelia's day care teachers to find out how she was doing there and suggested it might be a good idea for him to speak with Norma as well.

"I think it would be best for Amelia to stay with you at least through the summer," he said. "Returning her to her mother any sooner would be a setup for failure. Amelia needs time to recuperate as much as her mother does."

Maybe I had been waiting for someone to tell me that the best thing for Amelia would be to return her to Norma as soon as

Norma thought she was ready. That would be the easiest solution. Certainly it would be much simpler than a legal face-off with Norma—despite the fact that such a conclusion would mean that I would have to accept that my judgment had been seriously off base, that despite my grim assessment of the situation, Norma was now transformed into a stable, healthy woman who was well equipped to parent. The fact that I considered this to be preferable to bringing our dispute to a court of law is an indication of how strong my instinct to protect Norma, or at least to avoid provoking her, was. And strange as it now seems, I realize I was not the only one. Eli had spent a lifetime pleasing Norma, even at the risk of ruining his own marriage; and her parents had made no move to try to sway Norma or protect their only grandchild.

I remembered again: Norma in labor on that hospital bed, the nurse trying to coax me to come around and see our baby pushing through. Leave Norma's side to see the baby? Of course I wouldn't be going far away, but I didn't want to ask Norma to unwrap the iron grip of her fingers around my hand. She needed me.

I was pushing a cart through the grocery store, picking up tubs of yogurt and bricks of cheese, and letting my mind wander. Back home there were dishes stacked in the sink with dried milk and cereal clinging to the sides. There were scuff marks to clear off the wall where Amelia tapped her foot at dinner, smeared toothpaste on the bathroom sink, dried leaves tracked in from outdoors, and tangled sheets and baskets of unwashed laundry. As the chaos of our situation increased, I frantically tried to sort the simple messes in our home. In an effort to beat back the mayhem, I was trying to tidy everything: Whit's collar that was folded half in and half out of her shirt, Amelia's dollhouse with its furniture toppled and confused, her scrambled stacks of socks and shirts. "People with children just don't have pristine houses," Whit reminded me. "If you don't watch out, you'll turn into a control freak."

As I tossed cans of frozen juice into the grocery cart, I tried to think about what I had control over. I could only come up with what I'd lost: I'd lost control over my money; I had no control over how long Amelia would be with us; and I had no control over my sleep—my thoughts would shake me awake even when Amelia didn't.

As I turned my cart toward the checkout lines, I nearly collided with that of an old man. For some reason that eluded me, he had a napkin tucked into the front of his white shirt like a bib. His face was rough and stubbled, his eyes tired but twinkling. In that instant in which we froze, surprised by one another, I saw in his face the span of a lifetime. He'd lived so many decades, each one made of years and months and days and seconds like this one. "Excuse me," I said, backing up to let him pass. But I should have said thank you, instead. Because in that moment the world blew up big enough to make me feel insignificant. One day these months would blend into a long, long stream.

When I got home, Amelia and I lay outside on the deck while Whit cooked dinner inside. The sky was a perfect blue, the air cool and still, and little green buds were starting to appear on the trees. Amelia and I played a guessing game as she leaned her weight against me, grounding us both in the eternity of a passing moment.

"Where did you get Whit?" Amelia asked, gazing skyward.

"Why do you ask?"

"Because," she said, "I really love her."

As if on cue, Whit called us in to dinner.

After we ate I put Amelia to bed, but she refused to lie down. "I want more dessert," she said.

"I'm sorry. You know the rules, once we're in bed there's no more eating," I said.

"But I want more," she protested.

I told her she could bring some cake to day care with her lunch tomorrow, but she persisted. She started to cry, then to yell. I tried to hold her but she stiffened her spine as she'd done as an infant. I began to pull away when she lifted her arm and struck out at me, hitting my face. "That's it," I said. "I can't sit with you if you're going to hurt me. You can be sad and you can be angry, but you can't hit me." I handed her a pillow to pound, but she threw it off the bed.

"I want Mommy!" she yelled.

"I know you do. I know you miss her." I put my arms around her again. "Tell me what you miss about Mommy."

"I miss Mommy," she cried. And cried, and cried.

Amelia was talking to Norma on the kitchen phone one Saturday while I was washing dishes. I heard her tell Norma that I didn't give her any food she liked. My heart sank. "She's probably just used to eating different things than we do," Whit reassured me. But after Amelia went to bed I couldn't stop myself from defending my meal planning to Whit. "But I give her corn and ravioli—and sliced apples in her lunch box. She loves those."

My defense plea didn't stop there, however. Even after Whit talked me down, reminding me how Amelia was probably just lobbying for more candy, I still couldn't let the comment go. Later, in bed, I imagined myself before a judge. "Your Honor, I do give her mashed potatoes without the skins the way she likes them. But one time Whit and I wanted our potatoes baked!"

I was rehearsing for the possibility of going on trial. That's how I saw it, that *I* was going to be tried. And it was true—to an extent. Even though it was Norma's ability to parent that was really at issue, my legitimacy as a parent was at stake, as well.

II

Each week after Amelia's visit with him, Dr. Thompkins called to let me know how things were going. One night, a month and a half into her stay with us, Dr. Thompkins called to impress upon me how important it was that I fight to keep Amelia with me, at least through the summer. "Amelia needs safety, she needs continuity. She needs a guaranteed sure bet that her needs will be met. This is not a complex issue, it's not ambiguous," he said.

Meanwhile, Norma admitted to me that she was skipping sessions with her therapist, couldn't sleep, and was thinking about getting a new prescription for sleeping pills. Two days later she left a message for me at work saying she was going to pick up Amelia the next week. Before I returned her call, I called my lawyer. I left her a message, and while I was sitting at the table paying bills that evening Barbara Kaplan called back. If I didn't want to let Norma take Amelia home as she had threatened, I had to file my claim for guardianship immediately, she explained. It took seven to eight days to schedule a hearing and that was just barely enough time, given Norma's new plan. "I hope the judge will even hear the case. Technically, I suppose, it should go to New Hampshire. But there you would have even less of a chance."

I told her I wanted to try one more time to work this out with

Norma before I actually filed a motion in court. She agreed that that was still my best bet, since the law was stacked against me. Still, she said, it wouldn't hurt to have the paperwork ready "for just in case."

I asked a few questions, more to postpone the inevitable than out of any specific need for information. I already knew the answers. "I'll go ahead and get that paperwork ready then?" Barbara said.

I closed my checkbook with both hands and took a deep breath. I knew my choices. Forget the court hearing and go back to the way Norma and I had been doing things for the past two years, the emergency phone calls, the suicide attempts, the fear of what might happen to Amelia . . . or risk it all, and go before a judge. Quite possibly I would succeed in nothing more than infuriating Norma, and as a result I would lose all contact with Amelia. When I considered that possibility I could see only a colorless void. But in the end the only possibility that I truly couldn't live with was that one day a call might come telling me Amelia had been hurt because Norma had taken too many pills and had caused some grave accident, or perhaps hurt Amelia in a rage that she meant to direct at herself. So I answered, "Yes. We should get ready."

"If Norma threatens to come up any earlier, call me, then go straight to court and don't leave until you have an order from the judge granting you custody," she advised.

When she said good-bye, Barbara let out a giggle. She's nervous too, I thought.

I postponed calling Norma until after Amelia had gone to sleep. I wanted to wait until Whit got home, but it was her night to work late.

I dialed Norma's number. "I want to ask you to reconsider this plan about coming down on the eighth. I think we have to make sure you are really ready."

"It's been almost two months. I want my daughter back."

"That's not enough of a reason."

"What are you saying?" Norma asked. I was surprised that she sounded suspicious right away.

"I guess what I'm saying is that after all you've been through I really want to make sure you're well this time. I want to hear from someone other than you that you're prepared to take on parenting again. I want to hear it from your doctor, or . . ."

"Don't you try anything. Do you hear me? If you try anything . . ."

"I guess what I'm saying is I'd like to work this out with you, but if we can't . . ."

"Don't you dare . . ."

"I'll have to take it to a judge . . ."

"Don't you dare do this. I swear to God, if you try this, I am coming down there . . ."

"Norma, let's talk about this." I took the phone into the closet, praying that Amelia was still sleeping. I was sure she couldn't hear me from her room downstairs, but the upstairs bedroom is directly above hers, and I didn't want to risk it.

The calmer my voice grew the crazier Norma's became. She screamed her threats into my ear. Again and again she said the same thing, "Don't you dare!"

But I was going to dare. I had already dared. While her voice shrilled on, I felt my world split open. It folded itself inside out, and hasn't looked or felt the same way since.

I sat in the crackling quiet and waited.

Within an hour a call came from the town's police chief, who oversees law and order for our beachside hamlet. He seemed unfazed by the female-versus-female custody dispute. "A Norma Friedman just called here sounding pretty upset. She claims you've kidnapped her daughter."

"She's *our* daughter. She's here visiting."

"I see. Were you and Miss Friedman married?" he asked.

"No, sir, two women can't get married legally."

"Sure, they can," the chief argued.

"Not really, they're working on making it legal in Hawaii, but that's all. Here in Massachusetts . . ." We went back and forth on this point for a few minutes, he insisting anyone could get married, I explaining that this ought to be, but wasn't so. I was stunned by the absurdity of the situation: arguing with a police officer whether I could have married my ex, while he was supposed to be arresting me for kidnapping. Finally the chief asked for my lawyer's phone number and for my reassurance that I would appear in court in the morning to work all this out.

As soon as I hung up, the phone rang again. Norma announced that she was coming down to get Amelia. I doubted she'd really make a move before morning, but even if she left right away she'd have a hard time finding Whit's house. She'd never visited me there, so the only address she had was the post office box where we picked up our mail. I made a final call to my lawyer, then started searching my closet for an appropriate outfit for court. By the time Whit came home I was busy ironing a blue and purple floral print dress and blue jacket. I explained what had happened, and we agreed that we'd leave the house as early as possible in the morning, before Norma arrived, to avoid a scene in front of Amelia. I set the alarm clock for sometime before dawn, and we settled down to try and get some sleep.

At five o'clock I woke Amelia. "Ima, is it one in the morning?" she asked.

"No," I said, "it's just dark because it's cloudy."

Amelia dressed in her yellow dress with puffy sleeves and white sash and party shoes, as if she knew it was not just an ordinary day. Whit hurried us into the car. We raced down the back roads hoping to avoid passing Norma who could be arriving at any minute. We pictured her coming up our walk, and finding no trace of us except for the note Scotch-taped to the door glass saying we'd meet her in court. We hoped that she would not spend her rage on our windows or my car.

At the diner where we ate breakfast with the truckers, we tried to appear cheerful and behave as if we did this all the time. But I couldn't help peeking into cars with out-of-state license plates, as if Norma might come find us there.

My lawyer wouldn't reach her office in Boston for more than an hour, so with time to kill, we drove around empty roads and stopped at the beach. Whit and Amelia climbed the lifeguard tower together, while I stayed behind on the parking lot asphalt, protecting my good shoes. Finally, at the home of two of Whit's friends, I settled a sleepy Amelia in front of the television.

My lawyer had advised Whit to keep Amelia with her, someplace close to a phone in case she needed to have Amelia appear in court, or in case the judge decided to turn her back to Norma's care. I had suggested just bringing Amelia to day care, but Norma could snatch her from there, Barbara pointed out. Since Norma had never met Whit's friends, she wouldn't find Amelia at their house. Also, they would be gone all day, so Whit and Amelia would have the place to themselves. At eight o'clock I told Amelia I had a few errands to run, and left for my lawyer's office.

Driving back and forth between my lawyer's office and the courthouse in our county where the paperwork needed to be filed, I tried to notice and appreciate my surroundings. I tried to remember sandy beaches, picnics of cookies and warm juice, and all of the times I had been happy here. I slowly ate the banana and the cream cheese sandwich Whit had insisted I take. With each bite my fear and my will to go on did battle.

Behind the court clerk's desk two women were talking about the sister of one of them who was getting married. "First time?" asked a fortyish woman with red hair and an armful of files.

"First and only, I hope," the other answered. "But who's to say?"

"These days I think they shouldn't even bother to unwrap their presents right away," said the redhead, dumping the files on top of a metal cabinet.

Finally she noticed me waiting, and directed me to an office downstairs where I could get the signatures I needed.

Since our court hears cases only three days a week, and this wasn't one of them, I was told I would have to drive back to the court in the city for a hearing. I picked up my attorney and we raced through the congested streets, trying to make it to the courthouse by noon, when the judge had agreed to hear our case. Of course there was no chance we would make it, since it was already 12:20. "If I get pulled over for speeding," I told her, "I'm counting on you to get me off the hook." It was probably the only moment of levity in the day.

We ran into the courthouse at 12:40. My attorney looked simultaneously harried and perfect in her pleated navy skirt, black tights, and low heels. Her shoulder-length hair looked as though it had just caught up with her.

Norma was in the hallway. I saw her from behind, her dark hair cut close to her thin neck. She turned to see me, but didn't return my "hello." I was surprised by this cool response. Despite everything, I thought surely we would look at each other now, see the absurdity of haggling in court, and find our own way out. This would be just like all the other times one of us had pushed too hard to make the other recognize her point of view. Like the time Norma stopped the car in the breakdown lane on the Vermont highway, swearing she wouldn't resume driving if I didn't apologize for ruining her weekend. My offense, as I recall it, was that I hadn't made reservations early enough, and so the inn we'd stayed at didn't turn out to be the country getaway Norma had envisioned. I actually got out of the car and stood on the pavement, plotting ways to get home without her. Finally, Norma leaned over and popped the passenger door open. "Going my way?" she asked.

We might yell and be angry for hours, but at some point one of us always made a joke or broke out laughing, and we remembered that we loved each other, and we always made up.

When I spotted her in the courthouse, I was still clinging to the hope that at least we could make up.

But when I walked past Norma she made a spitting sound. I resisted the urge to look back to see if she had actually done this. Instead, I stopped hoping that we could patch things up with a joke and a giggle. I was finally finished trying to make nice.

My lawyer escorted me into the courtroom where Justice Saul Bernier pressed round fingers to his shiny forehead and told us we were late and now we'd have to wait. He'd go have lunch instead of reading our affidavit right then, and there were many cases in front of us.

I found a seat at the opposite end of the hallway from Norma and tried to stay calm. The monotony of waiting for the judge to get to our case was broken by my hourly phone calls to Whit, who was trying every trick in the book to keep Amelia entertained. In between, I watched people emerge from the courtroom where His Honor handed out decisions as to which parents would get which children, how to protect battered women, and who would care for the crack baby whose mother didn't even show up for the hearing. The hours crept past. I met with the court's family counselor who told my lawyer afterward that I was a "fine person" and recommended to the judge that Amelia stay with me for the next three weeks. She also suggested that a guardian *ad litem* (an impartial professional representing Amelia's interests) be appointed to check on Amelia during that time.

Back in the hallway, I prayed incessantly and made anagrams with the words "Probate Court" and "Courtroom" and the judges' names printed on placards posted on the brick walls. Finally, at four o'clock our case was heard. I never said a word and only tried to stand and sit at the right moments.

To confirm Norma's emotional state and capacity to be a parent, Judge Bernier tried to call her psychiatrist from a phone on a shelf behind his bench. But he couldn't get an outside line from the courtroom. After jabbing at the phone again and again, he asked a court officer to investigate what the problem was. The officer explained that the switchboard had closed early because of the Memorial Day weekend. The judge muttered something in disgust, then marched out to the hallway, robes flapping as he went, to make his call. All of us, plaintiff, defendant, lawyers, and court officers, traipsed out behind him. We stood and watched as the judge unceremoniously deposited a fistful of quarters into the same pay phone from which I'd been calling Whit. He motioned us away, and we shuffled back, still practically within arm's reach of His Honor as we strained to listen in.

At five o'clock the judge recessed to mull over his decision. As our lawyers, Norma, and I filed out of the courtroom I heard Norma say, just loud enough so I could hear, "I should never have signed Amelia out of the hospital. Letting them put her in foster care would have been better than this."

The janitor was mopping the empty hallways as we waited. Finally the judge called us back. He had made his decision: Amelia was to stay in my guardianship, but only for three weeks, until a judge in my own county could consider the case. The order was temporary, but when this pronouncement was made, Norma lunged at me, hands reaching for my neck. We were standing less than ten feet from the judge's bench. "Go have your own child!" she shrieked, as two uniformed guards pulled her back. As I watched her being dragged from the courtroom I began to cry.

The courtroom finally quieted again, and the judge asked that the record show that "Ms. Friedman approached Ms. Abrams in a threatening manner." Then a court officer appeared at my side to escort my lawyer and me to the parking lot "as a precaution."

As I drove home Norma's words repeated in my head: *Go have your own child,* I could hear her taunting me.

But I have my own child, I answered her silently. *But I have my own child.* Over and over.

I returned to Whit and Amelia after they'd already eaten dinner, ten hours after I had left to "run a few errands." Amelia eyed me from the window seat where she was sitting with Whit, not even feigning interest in the one-hundred-piece Barbie puzzle spread out on the table in front of her. Her look told me she was forlorn and angry. Her posture said tired.

"Sorry I'm so late."

"It's okay," Whit said, trying to speak for both of them. She offered me a cold piece of pizza she'd saved in the white cardboard box, but I shook my head.

"You must be ready for bed, little goose," I said, pulling Amelia onto my lap. I could think of nothing to tell her that would be reassuring, so I admired her puzzle and rocked her in my arms while Whit gathered our things.

Even though Amelia was asleep in her car seat on the ride home, I didn't dare discuss with Whit what had happened. I just leaned over, put my head on her shoulder, and let her try to distract me with details of their day. She described how they made slice-and-bake cookies, how they took turns snapping pictures with our friend's Polaroid, and how, every time I called, Whit pretended to be talking to someone else, so Amelia wouldn't get anxious.

Whit asked in a whisper if I was sure Norma had gone home. "She won't try anything tonight, will she?"

"If she does, she'd be the one who was kidnapping. We have the court order now. She'd be breaking the law," I said.

When our headlights found our small pink house it looked cozy and inviting in spite of everything—like something out of a fairy tale. Whit lifted Amelia out of the backseat and I gathered up our things. Amelia didn't even open her eyes before she started to protest: "Ima! Ima!" Whit and I traded bundles, and Amelia relaxed again. Inside I eased off her party shoes and socks, and put her to bed with her clothes still on.

In the morning she sniffled, coughed, and clung to me. I helped her write a letter to Norma. Then on a visit to see some friends who lived on a horse farm, Amelia had her first pony ride. And I was there to see it.

That night I lay in bed running through the chronology of events. For Whit I had repeated the details of the episode at court, recounting each minute. I had written it out in my journal as well, trying each time, I suppose, to contain my confusion. But all that came out were facts. Where, I wondered, were my emotions?

I pulled out my journal one more time and made a list of places where my feelings might be hiding: *They are in my tired feet, my sore head, my sharp tongue, my weary breath. They are in my dreams of danger, my uneaten supper, my unmade bed.* But they weren't hiding—they were just waiting.

I woke the next morning feeling powerful and calm. I knew

the litany of things that could go wrong. Norma's family might decide to intervene. I could face long court battles, lose custody, and never see Amelia again. But for the next three weeks, at least, Norma couldn't take her away from me. For the first time, she was legally mine.

That Saturday, Whit and I took Amelia shopping at tag sales. We thought we might find a new set of shelves for her room, and some more toys. At one house, Amelia spotted a blue bicycle with training wheels, just her size. All we had at home was a plastic tricycle, and when Amelia tried to ride it now her knees hit the handlebars. "Sold," I said, after giving the two-wheeler a quick once-over. We took it home and spent the afternoon oiling the chain, tightening the training wheels, and filling the tires with air. I found some pink tape for Amelia to wrap around the handlebars and it was ready to ride.

I heard the phone ring and looked at my watch. This was the day Norma was scheduled to call and talk with Amelia. For days I had been wondering what I would say when I picked up the phone and heard her voice. To my relief, a friend of Norma's, acting as an intermediary, had dialed the number and asked for Amelia. I called her to the kitchen and handed her the phone.

What Norma said to Amelia I couldn't hear, but I could tell from Amelia's responses that Norma was venting about the court hearing, and that there was talk of her driving down and sneaking off with Amelia. Whit and I exchanged angry glances. We had been doing all we could to spare Amelia the ugly details of the legal proceedings. She was already burdened with more information than a child her age should have to deal with.

When she hung up the phone, Amelia asked why I wouldn't let Norma have her. "Your mom came down to take you home because she loves you and she misses you as much as you miss her," I said. "But the doctor says she's still not ready." I suggested we take her new bike out for a ride.

"Did it scare you to hear Mommy talk like that?" I asked, as I trotted alongside Amelia.

"Mommy was scared, but I'm not," she said over the sounds of training wheels clanking from side to side as she worked to maintain her balance.

When we went back inside Amelia made a big show of loving me. She told me that I was a good Ima and sat in my lap all the

way through her *Barbar's First Step* video. At bedtime she kept
asking me to hug her tighter and tighter.

That same week, Norma's parents called. "Norma tells us
you're trying to take Amelia from her," her father said. It had
been a long time since I'd heard his voice, although Norma's
mother and I had continued to speak frequently, even after the
breakup. "Actually that's not true," I answered. I explained that I
was trying to do what I felt was best for Amelia, and that I wanted
her to live with me for a little while, at least until I had some
confirmation from Norma's doctors that she was up to the demands of parenting again. I expected a grilling and I was prepared for it. In fact, I was surprised only that I hadn't heard from
them sooner. "I knew you'd have a sensible explanation," Mr.
Friedman was saying.

"Amelia's sleeping now, but you can call her here anytime," I
said. "I'm not trying to keep her from anybody. It's just that—"

I heard Norma's mother clear her throat. "It's good Amelia's
with you," she said. Then they said good-bye.

The first thing I was aware of Monday morning when I woke up
was the blaring insistence of my sore throat. I blew my nose and
took a sip of the stale water I had set on my bedside table the night
before. It was as though the tensions of the week and a half since
going to court, the calls from Norma and her family, Amelia's
questions and concerns, had all caught up with me at once. Whit
still had an hour before she had to rise for work, so I let her sleep.
If I could get ready for work without waking Amelia, I might
actually get to the office on time.

But the day went from bad to worse. When I returned home
from work that evening, I found that Chance had had an accident in the living room. "Go play in your room while I clean this
up," I told Amelia. "And watch where you step." On my way to
the kitchen for a roll of paper towels, the phone rang. "This is
Laura, I'm a friend of Norma's," an unfamiliar voice announced.

"Oh?""

"I'd like to know what kind of a lesbian you are to do this to
another woman?"

"Excuse me?" I asked, hoping I had misunderstood.

"I want to know what kind of lesbian you . . ."

"I think I heard you. I'm afraid I can't discuss this with you
right now." Amelia appeared at my side. "Is it Mommy?" she was

asking. I hung up the phone as Laura launched into a string of insults.

"No, it was a call for me. Now go back to your room and get ready to go to work with me. Remember, I told you that after day care we had to go out on an interview?" Bringing Amelia on assignment with me wasn't my idea of professional journalism, but I couldn't figure out any other way. Besides, I'd be interviewing two women who happened to be the first lesbian couple to announce their wedding engagement in the newspaper that I worked for. Their three-year-old nephew was visiting so we agreed that we'd try to conduct our business while the children played.

I sent the dog outside while I scooped up piles of shit and threw them into the toilet. On my hands and knees scrubbing the living room carpet, I thought of all the things I wished I were doing instead: working on my poems, having dinner with Whit, talking to a friend on the phone. As I scrubbed harder than I had to, I thought of all of the things I was good and sick of, beginning with Norma's friend Laura, and ending with conversations with lawyers, psychiatrists, and day care directors.

"Ima, I'm ready," Amelia shouted, hopping into the kitchen on one foot. Wearing her bathing suit and red rubber rain boots, she twirled with a triumphant grin.

"Ready for what?" I asked, laughing just a little—but enough to console myself that I hadn't lost my sense of humor entirely.

During the interview Amelia behaved and I managed to collect enough quotes and descriptions for the twenty-inch story I had to write the next morning. And our meal at Burger King, the treat I'd promised Amelia in exchange for behaving, went smoothly as well. She ate most of her chicken sandwich, all of her fries, and even a little of the salad. Still, by the time we got home, my nerves were spent, and she was tired. Amelia was finding more things to whine about than even I could. Where were her Care Bears pajamas? Why wouldn't I help her brush her teeth? Could she have two storybooks at bedtime instead of just one?

The first of four messages that had accumulated on my phone machine had just begun to play. It was Whit saying she was sorry but she'd be home later than expected.

"Ima," Amelia called from downstairs.

"I'm busy!" I snapped, in my most impatient voice.

That sent Amelia into a round of hysterics. "Mommy, Mommy," she wailed, as if the word were a mantra. I took three deep breaths before venturing downstairs. I rocked Amelia on my lap as I listened to her cry. I imagined screaming at my lawyer, at Dr. Thompkins, at all my friends who insisted what I was doing was right: "Let's give her back! We've made our point! Enough already."

Finally Amelia calmed down enough to speak: "What if I break out crying at day care?" she asked. I told her that her teacher would hug her. "You'll never be alone," I told her. "There will always be someone there to hug you." Then she went on about how Mommy went shopping and left her home to watch a video. "Is that scary?" I asked. "No, it's fun because I can pick up Ariel." I knew how much Amelia liked to pet the bunny Norma and I had bought for her (against my better judgment) for her last birthday. Norma's track record with animals was disconcerting. There had been many trips to the animal shelter to return kittens and dogs she had adopted, then later realized she couldn't care for. Thinking about her pet made Amelia sad again. "I wish Mommy hadn't gotten a cat. I don't want a cat in our house." Before the cat Amelia had been allowed to let Ariel loose in her bedroom. With the cat's arrival that became too dangerous. When we finished talking about that, Amelia asked me to say her prayers for her.

We had been working on memorizing the prayer I used to say when I was her age. The prayer is a six-line poem asking protection through the night, followed by the Sh'ma, the Jewish prayer declaring belief in one God. But tonight I understood that it was too much for her to try reciting. So I began for her: "Before in sleep I close my eyes, to thee O God my thoughts arise . . ."

"I want to say something to God now, something I made up," Amelia said. I told her to go ahead.

"You say, 'God,' " she said.

"God, Amelia has something to say to you."

"God, I want to go home to Mommy real soon," she said. "I want Mommy to get better soon so I can go home with her." Then she said, "God, I want to go home with her because I'm so sad and I don't want to cry anymore."

I hugged her and said, "Sweetheart, you know what I think God would say to you? I think God would say, 'I love you, and I love your Mommy, and you can feel all of your sadness and cry as

much as you want to because your tears will heal your sadness."
We hugged some more. I told her we needed to get some rest and
that we could miss Mommy more in the morning. She asked if she
could cry in the car on the way to day care, and I said yes.

"You could cry, too," she said.

"I could."

"Or you could just listen to me."

Finally Amelia fell asleep, and I lay in my bed waiting for Whit
to come home. I was tired and sick of not knowing how to get
from one day to the next.

Anger, desperation, and exhaustion are a fearsome trio, I decided. Maybe I needed to talk to God, too.

A week and a half had passed, and now we were planning for the
next court hearing, in which the judge would decide whether to
extend my temporary guardianship for another ninety days.
That meant more meetings with my lawyer, and conversations
with Dr. Thompkins, who was preparing a statement for the
judge about why staying with me would be the best thing for
Amelia's psychological well-being. In between I was fielding angry phone calls from Norma and, occasionally, her friends. But
what I really wanted to focus on was Amelia, and the wonder of
watching her grow and learn. One night after we finished our
dinner at a pizza place in town, I took Amelia to the bathroom. I
turned on the faucet, but instead of thrusting her hands underneath the jet of water, she traced the letters C-O-L-D on the handle and sounded out the word "cold." I had never before thought
of the act of reading as a miracle, but there it was. She was spell-
ing out other words too; MAT, CAT, and FAT were among her
favorites.

For our car rides Amelia and I made up a new game. On our
way home from day care each night, she would ask me what I
wished for. We took turns saying our wishes. The listener would
say, "That can come true," no matter what the wish . . . with the
understanding that wishes that can't come true in real life can
come true in Wishland.

"I wish we were home already," I said.

"That's not a real wish, Ima."

"Okay, I wish we lived in a big house made of pink whipped
cream."

"That can come true," Amelia said, between giggles.

"Your turn."

"I wish I lived in a big house with a hundred million rooms and I had two babies and there were waitresses to bring the food."

"Waitresses?" I asked.

"Five waitresses," Amelia said.

"That can come true," I said.

"And Mommy would live in the house, and you, and Whit, and Ariel and everyone could all live there," she said.

Months earlier, Whit and I had put a deposit on a cottage on Cape Cod. Whit thought we should skip the vacation given the new circumstances, but I thought we should go. For one thing, if we canceled we'd lose our deposit. Besides, Amelia hadn't been on a real vacation since Norma and I had taken her to the Cape when she was nine months old. And we'd soon be back in court, and anything could happen then. We should make this time with Amelia special, I said.

As we stuffed our suitcases and bags of games and toys into the back of the car, Whit complained about how many provisions such a small child needed. On the drive down Amelia started a chorus of questions and complaints: "Are we there yet" and "I'm bored" and "I'm hungry." Whit shot me looks that clearly demanded I quiet Amelia.

"Look," I whispered, "it may not be the vacation you had in mind, but let's make the best of it, okay?"

In the morning we rented bicycles and rode to the beach. Whit quickly lost patience with Amelia's slow pace. "Ride ahead, we'll meet you there," I told her. It seemed that with Whit out of the picture, Amelia complained less and pedaled faster.

When we got home I put Amelia on her cot for a nap, and went out to the porch to talk to Whit.

Whit didn't wait until I sat down in one of the two Adirondack chairs that faced across the lawn to a row of sand dunes topped by a sagging wood fence. "I've been looking forward to this for so long, and she just takes up every inch of space with her talking and yelling and complaining."

"She's a child, you just have to be patient."

"She's not just a child. She's a demanding, bossy child."

"Okay, she's demanding. But she's going through a hard time." With my bare toes I pushed a small pile of sand through a crack between the deck's cedar planks.

"Well, I'm going through a hard time, too. And I need a vacation."

A splinter pierced my toe. "Damn!" I spat. I looked up at Whit, as impatient with her needs as she was being with Amelia's. I limped inside to get a pair of tweezers.

"I'm serious," Whit said when I returned. "She's really being hard to be with."

"So are you. Can't you see that I could use a little support myself?"

I dug out the splinter, and watched as a ball of blood followed it out.

That night Whit and I cooked dinner without saying much to one another. After we ate, I invited Amelia to come outside with me, intentionally leaving Whit to herself.

Amelia and I walked the sandy road alongside swaying green grasses that hid the spotted bunnies we loved to watch in the morning. The minute we were alone I began to remember how happy and grown up it used to make me feel when my own mother invited me to accompany her on early morning or early evening walks. The setting sun gave a rosy glow to the evening, and I imagined the soft light etching itself into Amelia's and my memories, giving us both something to look back on someday.

But Whit was right. Amelia didn't know how to be peaceful. Against the quiet evening her voice was like a siren, a television left on, a list of things to do. Her hair was a ball of tumbled twine. It would take a half hour to sort through the tangles the wind wove on the beach that day. Her eyes were two deep puddles, mirages that wouldn't stay still.

I followed behind Amelia, who was skipping and singing and calling back questions to me. She stamped along, leaving her footprints on a ridge of sand that a Jeep's tires had made. Meanwhile, I was walking in the footsteps of my own childhood—those nights when I had taken long strides in an effort to keep up with my mother, staying quiet but poised to say the thing that would make her smile. But Amelia didn't follow in the tracks of my past. She found a dirty rope in the sand, almost long enough for jumping, and tripped loudly over it, yelling commands and demands. "Look at me, Ima, look at this. Oh, you missed it." Meanwhile pink doors and weather-beaten houses slipped past with the sun behind the dunes.

What I wanted from Amelia that evening was unfair, I knew. I wanted her to be a solace to me, as I'm sure I was meant to be those evenings when my mother had sought out my company instead of my father's. I wanted Amelia to be well behaved so I could prove Whit wrong. I wanted all three of us to be on a vacation that would be as happy as the snapshots would look later in our photo album.

Back inside, I gave Amelia a bath and put her to bed. Afterward I flopped down on the couch, where Whit came and found me. "It's not her fault," I said, as she sat down.

"I know," she said. "I know what I want is unreasonable. I just can't help wanting it."

"You've been really good about all of this. I guess I don't blame you for being disappointed."

"And I don't blame you for being disappointed that I can't just be patient and helpful all the time. I guess right now we both need the same thing, but neither of us can give it."

We left the Cape a day early, and Amelia was the only one to speak fondly of that vacation, afterward.

As she wriggled out of her white feetie pajamas one morning after our trip, I marveled at Amelia's long spine. She's not a baby anymore, I thought. The print Carter's briefs on her behind were meant for age five. But her length, the snaky whole of it, let me know there was more: Her development could not be so easily defined or confined. She was growing, and I couldn't stop her, nor did I want to except for one thing: I wanted my baby. I had missed so much of my baby. She had grown through so much messiness and pain. I had imagined I'd raise a little girl in pressed pinafores; a child who wouldn't be able to tell me the things Amelia could, like, "The children in Somalia are still starving, Ima." In these months with Amelia I'd seen her grow: she was up to forty-one pounds and forty-three inches that spring. I'd heard her sound out and spell her first words. I'd held her while she cried over a doughnut she couldn't have before lunch, and over her mother who was much further out of reach.

In that moment, I regretted all my insecurities, all the time I wasted wondering if she could really love me like a mother and whether people accepted me as her parent. I regretted my impulse to go overboard, like when she was an infant and I would pull her onto my lap for photos, trying to document our bond, as if I had to prove it, to vie with Norma for equal time and equal status. But I never wanted her only for myself. I didn't ask for this, I thought, as Amelia pulled a pair of socks, stretch pants, and a T-shirt from her shelves.

I never allowed myself to hope anything grand for Amelia. I never let myself dream for her future. I kept my love rooted in each day, knowing too well that there might be nothing else. I had recently gone to hear Phyllis Burke read from her new book, *Family Values: Two Moms and their Son,* in which she writes about adopting her lover's biological son in California's first second-parent adoption. At the reading she talked about that little place we non-biological lesbian mothers have, where we keep our distance, where we hold back. It isn't fair to our children, I kept thinking.

Amelia finished dressing, and I brought her to day care. Eight hours later, when I arrived to pick her up, she was stretched out on the floor, leaning on her elbows, watching a little boy build. Her expression didn't change when she saw me, except that her eyes seemed to soften. I knelt down to say hello and she attacked me with the direct grab of a magnet. As her teacher told me about how her day had gone, I hugged Amelia and stroked her hair—in that unself-conscious, possessive way that parents do.

Amelia has had to keep on growing, unable to stop, while my ability to be her mother has raced to catch up.

III

I remember sitting in the sauna at my father's health club with him and a friend of his one day. "Taking vitamins is like pissing in the ocean," his friend said. "No effect." The expression sounded vulgar to me as I sat there between my father, who was naked except for his bathing trunks, and his friend, whose belly rolled over the waistband of a pair of blue shorts.

My current situation seemed vulgar, too: I had already thrown thousands of dollars at this problem and the ocean waves kept curling over and eating the money up. Before round 1 in court, my lawyer had consulted with her colleague while I was standing by her side. Apparently they had been discussing my case earlier. "I don't know why you think the judge would even hear this," her colleague had said.

Whatever would happen, it seemed Amelia would one day go home to a mother who left her in the house alone to watch videos while she shopped, who talked of putting her up for adoption, and who took in cats she couldn't care for, then gave them away so often that Amelia seemed to have begun to fear loving them.

More and more now I resented the fact that if I were a man who had married Norma, the judge would have handed me the child with very little hesitation, and I wouldn't be going back to court to beg for three more months. I was no longer debating what course of action would be best. Now the question was how much time would be enough, and how much money I would need to buy it.

These thoughts were winging through my mind when I looked down at the sidewalk and saw a penny, heads up. I scrutinized it for a sign that it was really filled with luck, that it might even be capable of filling a wish that I would find the two thousand dollars I needed to continue the court case just as easily as I had found the penny itself. It was warm as pavement, and one part, crushed by a train or truck, was razor-sharp. As I rubbed its surface I remembered how Amelia had said that the Lincoln Memorial on the back looks like the trolley on *Mr. Rogers' Neighborhood*. I turned it over. The hot, sharp cent was stamped with the year 1988, the year Amelia was born. I took it as a good omen. When you have a problem unlike any that shows up in Dear Abby you look for answers in strange places.

That night, in an effort to fall asleep, I listened to both sides of my Louise Hay Self-Healing tape. It was my last-resort remedy after trying every other method to stop thinking and let myself relax. "Let's take the past, all of it, and wrap it in the pink of divine forgiveness, and let it go," Louise was saying. Finally, I felt the vise grip on my heart loosen, and a wave of calm floated up in me like a rubber sandal in a pool.

It was just a matter of days before we would be returning to court when Norma called a half hour before Amelia's bedtime. "It's getting late," I told her when I picked up the phone. "Try not to keep her up too long." An hour later, still not bathed or in her pajamas, Amelia was talking on the phone to Norma.

"She's just trying to piss me off," I hissed to Whit.

"Get hold of yourself," she said, nodding toward the kitchen where Amelia was twirling the phone cord in her hand like a jump rope and describing a painting she had made in day care.

I walked out the backdoor, faced a tree in the yard, and ranted to my heart's content. I picked up sticks and flung them, hoping my anger would follow them into the thin strip of woods.

When I came back inside I heard Amelia telling Norma she didn't believe Norma wouldn't let her visit Whit and me anymore after she went home. "You'll change your mind, Mommy, you'll let me visit them again," she was saying.

When she finally hung up the phone, Amelia's lip began to quiver. "Mommy said I can't come here anymore."

I put Amelia on my lap. "I heard what you told Mommy on the phone, and I think you're right."

"Mommy will change her mind?" Amelia asked.

"I think so," I said. But that wasn't good enough and I knew it. I searched my mind for something she might understand.

"When I was a little girl, my grandpa and my daddy got really angry at each other," I said.

"Grandpa Dave?" Amelia asked.

I nodded.

"And Papa Abe?"

"That's right. Papa Abe is my grandpa and Grandma Sue's daddy."

"I know that," Amelia said, annoyed at me for stating the obvious. But she stopped fiddling with the sofa pillows and waited for whatever was going to come next. "Why were they angry?" she asked.

"I don't know exactly. But they were so angry that my daddy wouldn't let me see my grandpa for a long, long time." I didn't tell her how my mother used to sneak us off to visit her father, or how frightening it was when I would sometimes make a mistake and mention in front of my father something I'd seen or done at my grandfather's house. He never yelled at me for those slipups, but I could tell from the icy look in his eyes that my mother would somehow pay. "Sometimes my father would say really mean things to me about my grandfather, and I didn't like that because I loved both of them. Then one day they stopped being angry at each other, and I was allowed to visit my grandpa whenever I wanted." I didn't tell Amelia that I was old enough to drive before this feud, which started over business and is said to have ended my parents' marriage, was finally over. "Now Grandpa Dave and Papa Abe call each other on the phone like best friends," I said.

I had told the story so quickly that I didn't know if it had done its job. But later I overheard Amelia telling Whit: "Mommy's just saying mean things because she's angry. But I think she'll feel better like Papa Abe and Grandpa Dave," she said.

It's hard to believe I once considered the sound of a ringing phone to be a signal of happy expectation. I was always one to grab the receiver by the second ring, looking forward to the possibilities inherent in the global web of phone lines. It could be *anyone* on the other end. But by now, it seemed every time the phone rang it was a summons to disaster. The night before our second court date was no different.

Eli called to say he was filing for guardianship of Amelia. "I think this whole thing is getting out of hand," he said. "Amelia should come home."

Despite his initial reluctance to get involved, I wasn't surprised by this statement. Norma's big brother had always been there to bail her out, even when it benefited him little. If anything, I was more surprised by the fact that he had refused to help two and a half months ago when Norma first went into the hospital.

In any case, this meant there was now a blood relative, living in Amelia's neighborhood, whom a judge would find more appealing as her custodian than a lesbian ex-lover living across state lines. It might also mean that my reason for fighting was gone—that is, if my claim was true that I only wanted to keep Amelia from living with Norma while Norma was in an unstable condition.

I considered arguing with Eli. I considered fighting for the unlikely satisfaction of hearing a judge declare me, on the record and in the eyes of the state, Amelia's parent. But the reality was that I would lose now, and I probably would have lost even without Eli stepping into the ring. Now I had to think what would be best for Amelia in light of these circumstances. I had already lost Norma's cooperation. If I went up against Eli I would lose him, too. In the past, Eli had been a good support person when small battles between Norma and me flared. On occasions when Norma tried to cut back my visits with Amelia, he always sounded the voice of reason. He always had Amelia call me from his home when she stayed there for any length of time. Realistically, I needed his support if I was to maintain contact with Amelia and to keep the door open for future negotiations with Norma. Besides, it had been hard enough for Amelia to see her mother and me fighting. I didn't want her entire family to become a battleground.

After a long talk I told Eli that I would revoke my petition for guardianship, assuming he would consent to let me continue to visit with Amelia and speak to her on the phone. "We can work out the details in court tomorrow," I said.

I called my lawyer, who immediately agreed with my evaluation of the situation.

"I guess it's all right if Eli gets custody," I said. "I was only doing this to keep her while Norma was unstable anyway."

"That's not why you've been doing this," she said.

I was surprised that she was contradicting me about such a personal matter. "What do you mean?" I asked.

"You're doing this because she's yours," she answered.

A reluctant part of me was relieved that this was ending. And yet at the thought of losing her, one whole side of my body would go numb. From time to time, it still does.

What did all of the events of the past two and a half months mean? I asked myself over and over. Would all of the stress, the hardship, the "taking a stand," simply mean I would never again be able to negotiate with Norma? I'd never again be allowed to see Amelia? All I've done is slide backwards, I concluded.

Suddenly, at the brink of losing, it seemed there was nothing positive or worthwhile about what I'd accomplished by bringing Amelia home with me and by refusing to give in to Norma's demands. But I refused to succumb to utter defeat. Okay, I thought, what do I have? I had the signed document Norma gave me at the hospital, saying she was voluntarily releasing Amelia to my care. I had the court order. I had a paper trail documenting my ties. But paper aside, Amelia and I had grown in our relationship. This little girl who remembered the most trivial details of our visits would surely not leave our home without an imprint.

Two and a half months earlier when Amelia arrived, she could not say that she loved Mommy and me, or me and Whit, or Mommy and Eli. It would always be, "I love Eli but I love Mommy more." Or, "I love Ima, but I love Whit more." Now she said, "I love Ima and Whit and Mommy and Eli." Her temper tantrums had decreased, she'd become calmer and better behaved. I had protected her from the daily trauma of her mother's struggle to recover for long enough to see her settle down.

When I feel like I'm drowning, I often reach for my journal, as if it's an old log drifting by that I can cling onto to keep afloat. Writing seemed unbearably strenuous just then, but I was too stubborn to sink. Sometimes when I'm convinced that everything is bleak I force myself to list the wonderful things about the day that has just passed. It is an exercise in gratitude, in seeing the glass half full. This time, the words came out slowly, letter by letter.

Five wonderful things about today:
1. *The white flower blossoms on the tree outside Amelia's window.*
2. *Watching Amelia and her friend run as fast as tumbling barrels across the grass on the bank of the Charles River.*
3. *The cat purring and the birds singing.*
4. *Vanilla ice cream cones.*
5. *Listening to Amelia "read" a book to her doll.*

"Am I going home today?" Amelia asked when she woke up.

I had told her that this was our court day, the day that a judge would decide whether it was time for her to go home with Mommy.

"I'm not sure," I said. I didn't tell her that after she left for day care I would pack her clothes and favorite toys into the patchwork duffel bag she had come up with. Instead I reminded her that it was up to the judge.

"I think the judge will say Mommy is all better and I can go home now," Amelia said, leaning against her pillows, in no rush to get out of bed.

"What if the judge says it's time to go home? How will you feel?"

"I'll be happy because I miss Mommy."

"And what if the judge says Mommy isn't ready yet and you have to stay here?"

"I'll be happy because then I can play with my new dollhouse and finish my puzzles."

I lifted Amelia out of bed and held her on my lap for a moment.

I remembered back to the time Norma was pregnant and I had imagined what it would be like to see a baby come into the world, how I pictured a little being screaming in protest at the glare of the hospital lights and the sight of nurses in ugly green smocks.

"You know what I'm thinking about right now?" I asked Amelia.

"Mmm, about me?" she guessed.

"Exactly," I said. "I'm remembering the day you were born, and how happy you looked. If you could have talked I think you would have said, 'Wow! What an adventure' "

"But babies can't talk. I could only say gah-gah, goo-goo. Right, Ima?"

I placed my little adventurer—now fully able to stand, speak, and command the air around her—on the floor and told her to get dressed while I made breakfast. But before I let her spin into action, I sat there at the edge of her bed and admired her insistence on seeing the world in its most favorable light.

I tried to make the morning as regular as possible. For breakfast I served toast with sliced banana and cinnamon. For Amelia's car snacks I packed her blue lunch box with all-natural fruit chewies, apple slices, and a plastic cup filled with Cheerios.

"If the judge says your mom can take you home I won't see you for a little while," I said, "but I'll send you hugs and kisses every night, and I'll call you up on the phone."

"And when Mommy stops being angry I can come visit," Amelia said.

"Of course."

"We're going to be late," Whit said, but she didn't really try to rush us from a long, lingering hug that warmed me through and through. As I stepped back to let her go, Amelia in her ordinary pink-striped shirt and pants looked anything but ordinary. She seemed to radiate beauty. For an instant, I was overwhelmed with the peace of this vision of perfection, and at the same time I couldn't connect it with my knowledge that this would likely be my last glance for a very long time.

After dropping Amelia off at day care, Whit circled back and picked me up at home. This time we went to court together. I wasn't worried about Norma snatching Amelia anymore, because I was quite sure she would be taking her home with a court order anyway.

Her Honor Marilyn Rush spoke with a soft voice, stern words, and horrendous grammar. Her gray hair was lifeless, in spite of the curls that framed her frail face. My lawyer presented her with the agreement we'd reached with Eli in a quick conference we'd held just moments before in the clerk's office down the hall. It said we would transfer temporary custody to Eli, and laid out a visiting schedule between Amelia and me. All Eli would have to do was sign a bond of surety, a simple safeguard, a formality in most cases, that assures the powers-that-be that an adult is not taking guardianship of a child in order to acquire any moneys that may be in the minor's name. The judge barely let my lawyer finish a sentence. She seemed all set to deny us everything and return Amelia immediately and with no strings attached to Norma. But Norma insisted on having her say. When Attorney Kaplan asked the judge to appoint a guardian *ad litem,* Norma flew out of her chair. The judge had already reminded her several times to stay seated unless she was acknowledged to speak.

"I refuse to have some stranger snooping into my life. I am a very good mother to my child. I don't need some stranger judging my ability to raise my own daughter."

"May I remind you . . ." Judge Rush began.

But Norma interrupted. "I don't see how you can order me to accept this stranger calling me on the phone."

Eli, who was sitting next to her, stood in his sister's defense. "I don't understand this whole setup. Why do we need this guardian *ad litem?*"

"I demand to have order in this courtroom," Judge Rush practically shouted. Neither Norma nor Eli made any move to sit. In fact, Norma continued her rant, repeating her protests again and again.

"I will hold you in contempt if you do not take a seat," Judge Rush announced. Eli pulled Norma down. Judge Rush addressed my attorney. "I was inclined to deny your request, but when I see a display such as that, a red light goes off in my head, and I have to wonder if there is a reason to proceed with extreme caution after all."

Not only did the judge appoint a guardian *ad litem,* but she granted our request to award custody to Eli, not Norma, for the next ninety days. She also approved my request for visits.

Norma and Eli sprung out of their seats and headed for the door. Whit, Attorney Kaplan, and I hung back for a moment. "That's it," Attorney Kaplan said, giving her stack of papers a triumphant pat and slipping them back into her briefcase. "We did it." As we left the building she said how lucky we'd been. "That judge has a reputation," she said. "She was ready to dismiss this case before I even opened my mouth. I thought we were finished."

I felt we had won again that day, but winning had become a relative term. We got what we dared to ask for. My hair styled for the first time since it had been cut three months before, my white blouse and herringbone skirt neatly pressed, my legs shaved for the occasion, and long gold earrings stroking my cheeks, I walked out of the courthouse feeling a sense of relief. Oddly happy. Because all I was aware of just then was what I had won. I didn't yet know what I had lost.

Before I got into the car, I asked Eli for one last favor. He and Norma were headed to the day care center to pick up Amelia. "I think you should go in and get her. Norma might make a scene," I whispered. He agreed, assured me everything would be all right, and gave me a good-bye hug. I raised a hand to wave to Norma who was opening the passenger-side door of Eli's car, but she only glared at me.

This time I decided to clear Amelia's room right away, as if order could erase grief. But the smell of her red rubber boots, the sight of her Care Bear pajamas still on her bed where she had left them, overwhelmed me with a sadness pure and complete, as if someone had died.

Things That Stay

We were swimming in a pool of Caribbean blue water. You paddled toward me. Then, inexplicably, you sank: suddenly, like a stone. As I dove down, the water turned dark as a stormy sky. In the absence of sight, I groped the wet depths, until I reached you.

We broke through the water's surface and climbed out of the pool. I was holding your small, solid body, and you were crying.

In these dreams I always find you.

I

I awoke slowly, reluctantly emerging from the heavy world of sleep where I could still feel the solid weight of my child on my lap. The bright sun smacked me in the eyes, revealing the twisted covers on Whit's side of the bed, but no Whit. According to the clock, she had been gone for about an hour. Amelia had been gone for four days.

Out of habit I got up and went downstairs. If asked, I could have offered no good reason to proceed with the day. I didn't have to go to work. I was using up my precious vacation time in order to do nothing much. If I wasn't exactly vacationing, I was at least vacating. Vacating my mind, my reality, my predicament.

Since Amelia left, I had done very little that could be called productive. I had raised anchor, and was floating. But I had promised Whit I would get out of the house that day, and treat myself to something fun. I thought I would go for a swim.

The living room looked unusually large in the late morning light. The sun on the wood floor made it appear cleaner than it was, like on a furniture polish commercial. There was a conspicuous lack of clutter now that all of Amelia's books, puppets, and video tapes had been put away. The house was empty not only of her toys, but of her voice, her footsteps, the movement of air that followed her, like waves from a motorboat crossing a quiet sea.

The sea. I would need the beach chair, the cooler, a sandwich, a box of grape juice that we had bought for Amelia's lunches. Still wearing the oversized T-shirt and boxer shorts I had slept in, I began to rummage through the coat closet for some supplies. I found the folded aluminum sand chair, wedged in the space beneath the stairs and perched on top of several cartons labeled in marker "Journals." I pulled the chair free. Then without thinking, I began to dismantle the terrace of cardboard boxes. Seated on the bare floor I unpacked them. I counted more than thirty frayed books: ragged spiral-bound notebooks, black hardcover artist's books, composition books with white freckles on black backgrounds, two clothbound books with tiny locks that were filled with lists of my secret elementary school crushes. Back then I still called them "diaries." The "journals" start in five-subject notebooks and have the lyrics of songs by Bob Dylan and David Bowie inscribed on the inside covers. One is small enough to fit in the outside pocket of the backpack I took traveling across the country by Greyhound bus at age nineteen.

I am pulled into the inky tangle of lines by a suction I can't resist. In that moment those words seemed to be my only hope of salvation. "What would you think if you had known that this is how we'd end up?" I wanted to ask the eighteen-year-old me who looked out on her future and couldn't see a path. After high school graduation that "Me" had written: *I have no clear picture of this summer, or college. Everything ahead is unsettled and unknown, like those glass paperweights filled with water and snow. When you shake them up you can't see anything except for the snow. You just need to wait for it to settle, and then it makes sense.*

I loved the young girls and women I had been in these books. Angry. Smart. Determined to do her best at being human. I could trust the future a little more when I imagined another "Me," ten years up the road, reading the words between the shiny orange covers of the book I kept upstairs by my bed. Surely the Me of ten years hence would love the Me of today, as much as I was then loving the Me from ten years before.

Before she left our house, Amelia had noticed my current journal. She admired the picture of the angel on the sun-orange cover, and asked if she could open it. "Go ahead," I said, amused at how easy it was to let her snap open those sacred covers. Her inability to read acted like one of those computer scrambles that keeps nonsubscribers out of pay-TV stations.

"What is it?" she asked. "A book you write in?"

"Yes," I said. I watched as she flipped past the pages of confession and confusion to the plain white ones in the back. "That's where I'm up to."

"What does it say?" she asked, going back to the scribbled-on parts.

"I write about . . ."

"About your life?"

"Exactly. About what I do and how I feel."

The conversation felt somehow important, imperative even, because she seemed to think so. And because this habit of writing things down is a skill I have that I never thought to share with her. But she found it anyway. And maybe she'd remember.

I put away the books and drove to the beach where my toes sank into the rough sand. I listened as children squealed and parents rumbled. I pierced the box of grape juice with the plastic straw and sucked it dry. I swam because I thought I should. The cold water heaved against my chest and did my crying for me.

I crumbled onto a dock at the water's edge. Peered into the sea below, then up, and out. In the distance, across the water, a line of buildings. Cars streamed past. In the water, boats. The tides were constantly, insistently, rearranging the landscape, little bit by little bit. And right in front of me, following the line of worn wood, an ant. Because perspective is all relative, the ant appeared the same size as the cars, which in the distance occupied a parallel track. Overhead the clouds carried on to the horizon. The earth at this latitude moves six hundred miles an hour. What if it were all to stop, suddenly? My stomach lurched at the thought. And at the thought of generations dying and being born, like a great tidal swap. The ant passed. More cars in the distance. Inside those houses—what?

I closed my eyes and listened to the ocean heave. I counted off the waves until the tides obeyed and dragged me into peace. All of the invisible pulling: the moon's pull on water, the water's pull on my consciousness. And in all of this I felt no power of my own. No magnetic strength to change a single thing.

Back home I proceeded in a trance and waited for Whit. Finally I saw her blue truck turn onto our street and roll toward our house. It was like a big blue dot, the first fleck of color in my gray, lifeless landscape. Alone all day I started to feel like a bubble that could just slip off the surface and float away.

She came through the door, happy. "Where are you?" she called. I was in the kitchen, sinking a dull knife into a peanut butter sandwich—slowly, slowly. It was as if the whole room were peanut butter and I was pushing through it. The knife pressed through the bread without any bite. I looked up reluctantly from the two squares of spongy bread covered with smears of chunky peanut butter and jelly, put the quartered pieces into plastic baggies with exquisite care, and listened as Whit recited the high points of her day. She had shipped a five-hundred-dollar order to a new account at work, bought a ham-and-cheese sandwich for lunch across the street, and found a dollar bill on the sidewalk on her way out. I thought she wasn't noticing my dim tears, so we got into the car as planned and drove to the movies.

"Just let the sadness wash over you," Whit said. "It's natural."

On the way home I forgot my depression. I clung to Whit's side and let my weight be supported by her. Her hand wandered over my body, tickling a trail of desire up my thigh, over the front of my T-shirt. The night was black and my world was limited to the three feet of curving road I could see out the window. There was no room in the blackness for despair, for myself, or for the small girl I couldn't help enough. Even when the car stopped under the outside light of our house, nothing could enter. Except Whit's hand under my shirt. My foot pushing against the plastic under-side of the dashboard. A mosquito buzzing next to my ear and our breath echoing back to us from the misty windshield. When we went inside, we didn't turn on any lights.

I was eating in the kitchen, enjoying the streams of pale sunlight swooping through the window. Whit had bought bagels from the specialty store the next town over, and mine was toasted to perfection. When the phone rang I hesitated to pick it up. But when I did, the little voice screeching through the wires made me forget my bagel altogether.

Amelia was talking to me in baby talk. "I send you a hundred hugs and a hundred I Love You's and a hundred kisses. Good-bye."

"Hold on," I said. "How do you like day camp?" but she had already passed the phone to Eli who apologized for the abrupt conversation. "She's really doing fine. I guess the phone calls can be stressful, though. She knows her mother isn't happy about her talking to you."

"Has she said as much?"

"You know how Norma is."

"So she doesn't seem any better?"

"I didn't say that. I think things will work out all right. She's definitely trying."

"But she insists on turning Amelia against me."

"She's just angry now."

"And Amelia, has she been staying with you?"

"More or less."

"More or less?"

"Look, there's no need to make things weirder than they already have been. They missed each other a lot."

"But you are the guardian now. We did that because Norma was really not ready."

"Don't worry, she's spending a lot of time here, and Norma is getting a break. Absolutely." Eli paused. "That guardian thing isn't official anyway."

"What?" Anger was pumping my heart. Eli wasn't taking this court order seriously at all. He had already gone back to being his sister's servant.

"I hired a lawyer up here. He said I shouldn't sign the bond your lawyer gave me. He said that I shouldn't sign anything from your lawyer. The court should have sent it to me."

"Why not? It's just a formality saying you're not taking custody as part of some scheme to get at a child's money! Besides, none of this is legal without the bond."

"You're making such a big thing about what's legal. I'm still looking out for Amie."

"Eli, I don't think you get how important this guardianship thing is to me. I went this far because I really don't think Norma is capable of handling Amelia right now. I trusted you."

"Everything's fine the way it is. We don't need all that court stuff."

"We do need that court stuff. I need it, anyway. I need to know Amelia's best interests are being . . ."

"Look, Amelia's calling me, she needs help with the VCR."

"I'll call the court and tell them to send you the bond. Would you sign it then?"

I could hear Eli telling Amelia he was on his way, just one more minute. "Sure, if it would make you happy. I guess. Look, we can call you next Sunday. Norma doesn't want Amelia talking to you, but I told her it's my house, and in my house she can call you."

"That's nice of you. Thanks."

"So don't worry. But look, I've got to go."

Stunned by the silence, I hung up the phone. The air in the kitchen was closing in on me. Then it all seemed to evaporate. I took a quick breath and got back to my breakfast, but I couldn't eat. "Come here," Whit said, and motioned me to her lap. I collapsed into her and felt her hands tight against my back until the tears came.

Monday I waited until my editor went out to lunch so I could call my lawyer without his overhearing. "Attorney Kaplan has gone on vacation," her secretary told me. My voice cracked as I thanked her and hung up the phone. Next I dialed the number for the probate court and gave the clerk the docket number for our case. "What if the bond isn't signed?" I asked.

"Then guardianship hasn't been transferred."

"So I'm still her guardian?"

"Technically."

"But the judge ordered that her uncle is guardian for the next ninety days."

"Not if he doesn't sign the bond, he isn't."

"So will you send the bond notice to him?"

"It says here the bond was sent by Attorney Kaplan."

"But he won't sign it unless the court sends it."

"We can't do that."

"But he won't sign it otherwise."

"He has the bond already."

"But he won't sign it unless it comes directly from the court."

"I can't help you with that."

"I'm furious," I hissed into the phone.

"I'm sorry," the clerk said and hung up the phone.

I stomped out of the office, crossed the street, and cut through two parking lots to get to the store where Whit worked. "You have to calm down," she said.

"I have to explode," I answered.

Back at my office I could no longer stand the sight of my co-worker's desk, where he had a framed photograph of his two-year-old daughter wearing an adult-sized straw hat. Everyone who passed his desk always commented on how cute she was. I nudged my tissue box over the border between our desks until it knocked the picture down. Everyone was still at lunch. No one noticed.

In the afternoon I worked on a piece about a local psychologist who had written a popular self-help book. The book was inspired by his own brush with trauma. When his wife was pregnant they learned his daughter had an abnormal chromosomal makeup. She turned out to be healthy, but they lived for months not knowing whether she'd be mentally and physically disabled.

"I see so many people who give up under pressure," he said during the interview. "But that's not what fascinates me. What fascinates me are the people who survive life's challenges and are strengthened, not diminished by them."

"And what have you found to be the difference between the two camps?" I asked.

"The people who cope well are the ones who create meaning out of their experience."

"Is this book your way of doing that?" I asked him, fingering my review copy of the slight paperback as if it were a rosary, or a lock of someone's hair.

I marveled at people who could rally behind something bigger than themselves at a time of emotional catastrophe. I took my own problem extremely personally. I felt I had become invisible to God. I knew it was a self-pitying attitude but I couldn't help it. I thought of everything I'd ever lost, starting with Amelia and working back to awards I didn't win, breaks I didn't get, a best friend I lost in high school to a more popular clique. Whit told me that I deserved a prize for what I'd been through with Amelia and how I'd handled the situation. But all I could see was that I'd lost. I'd lost so much.

The psychologist was telling me the Buddhist tale of a woman who lost her child and sought out the Buddha for help. He told her to return to the village and visit every home, and when she found one that hadn't been touched by loss she should collect a seed from the people who lived there. She returned to the Buddha weeks later, empty-handed. The story was meant to illustrate the inevitability and universality of suffering. But that was no comfort to me then. I could not be comforted, and I certainly could not imagine ever being able to give comfort to someone else.

Instead I tried to hold onto what was left.

I read a newspaper article about how the magnetic pages in photo albums can destroy the snapshots stored in them. I didn't bother trying to understand exactly what it was about the sticky surface of the pages that leaked the life out of stored memories. The whole thing was nothing short of sinister as far as I was concerned. After work I went to the store and bought two new photo albums with the old-fashioned cellophane sleeves. There was still something left to rescue and, by God, I was going to rescue it.

I spent the hour before Whit got home upstairs lying on the bed with my collection of snapshots spread out like a second blanket. The article had said that images could be obliterated in as little as fifteen years. The photographs of my childhood were in the most danger, of course. Prints of me dressed in my Bat Girl costume for Halloween and snapshots of me swimming in the neighbors' backyard pool with my sister and brother could have disappeared by now according to the information in the newspaper.

But I began instead with more recent pictures. I peeled free a photo of Amelia as an infant lying naked on the changing table her first day home from the hospital. There was still a metal clip on her three-day-old belly with the stub of the umbilical cord drying around it. I recalled my anguish at trying to dislodge the clasp as the nurse at the hospital had instructed me to do. This clip, that was supposed to spring easily open, was stuck. I was nearly in tears as I tried to gently pry it apart. I couldn't stand the thought of hurting my baby. Finally, Norma's mother, who was visiting for the weekend, performed the task while I waited in the other room, covering my ears.

I slipped picture after picture into the new albums. Amelia on my lap, our dog on Norma's, and all three of us staring at one another, ignoring the camera altogether. Amelia riding on my shoulders through our kitchen. Amelia, weeks after the breakup, sitting on the chair in my new studio apartment, barely able to reach the bowl of oatmeal on the table because I hadn't yet bought a booster seat for my new bachelorette pad. Amelia opening birthday presents in the park with me and my friends on the day after her real birthday because "my side of the family" was no longer invited to the parties we held at Norma's house.

By the time Whit came up the stairs, I had finished. Taking her place on the bed beside me she turned the pages of the new albums. "I never liked this haircut, did you?" Whit asked, pointing to a picture of Amelia standing by the deer cage at the zoo.

"She looks adorable," I protested.

"Look how she scuffs her shoes," Whit commented, pointing to a picture of Amelia in her battered red party shoes.

I pulled the book out of Whit's hands. "Why bother looking if all you can do is insult her?" It was as though Whit had literally been picking my child apart. I slammed the book's covers shut and sulked out of the room. Downstairs I went through the motions of making our dinner. In fact all I did was slam cabinets and drop metal pots on the countertop.

I received a letter from Amelia's day care telling me that the books she had ordered from the Scholastic sale had arrived. From the moment I had seen the order form in Amelia's cubby at day care nearly two months earlier, I had had the uneasy feeling that even if we filled it out with all the names and code numbers for the books we wanted to buy for just a dollar or two apiece, chances were Amelia would be gone by the time the books arrived. Nevertheless, with Amelia at my side I had rustled through the newsprint catalogue so we could add our choices to the day care center's bulk order. I let Amelia keep on choosing books until her order totaled ten dollars. "Allow four to six weeks for delivery," read the final paragraph on the form. Writing out the check and depositing it along with the order form in the special box outside the day care director's office was for me an act of hope.

Now, two weeks too late, the books had arrived. I considered leaving them where they were and pretending I had forgotten all about the notice. Norma had sent back the last package I mailed to her house with an angry note threatening me with a restraining order if I mailed anything else to her address. I decided to pick up the books and send them to Eli's house with a letter explaining that they were from Amelia's day care, not from me.

When I arrived at the center, Dahlia, Amelia's former teacher, was on the playground steps supervising a group of girls who were playing "Mother May I?" As I approached, the girls scattered to the swings and Dahlia invited me to sit with her.

Dahlia was a beautiful, delicate woman. She wore a gold necklace inscribed with her boyfriend's name, "Juan," in script. She told me that five years ago her sister had dropped her son, Dahlia's nephew, at her house for a visit. Her sister never returned for the boy, and overnight Dahlia went from being an aunt to a mother.

She said Amelia seemed happier when she was here with me than she did in the toddler classroom in the years before she moved away. She said what a shame it was that Norma got to keep her. "When she came here to pick her up that last day, she sure made a big scene," Dahlia said.

"Norma picked her up? Her brother Eli was supposed to do that. He promised me Norma would wait in the car."

"Oh, no," Dahlia said, drawing her breath in and shaking her head. "Norma came in. I knew you'd been in court that day, so I thought this meant Norma won, and I thought that would make her happy. But I could see right away she was not happy." Dahlia explained that she'd offered to get Norma a copy of Amelia's evaluation, but Norma started to carry on, asking why there had been an evaluation of Amelia.

Surely Norma must have remembered that all of the children in day care get evaluations on a regular basis, I thought. They're like informal report cards. I still have the first one that we received about Amelia's progress which was dated a few months after Norma and I had split up. We were both so proud that Amelia's teachers had written that she shared nicely with the other children, played well with toys, and seemed particularly drawn to the painting table.

"By the time she was through yelling and hollering, all of the children were in tears," Dahlia was saying.

"I'm so sorry that happened," I said.

"You did what you could," Dahlia said, looking me directly in the eyes.

"I really thought Eli would come in, not . . ."

Dahlia interrupted. "Not just that. The whole thing. You did everything you could," she said.

I thanked her and went inside to get Amelia's books. Dahlia's reassurances meant more to me than seemed logical. Then again, I reminded myself, she was someone who knew what she was talking about. She'd known Amelia before and after her move, and she knew about difficult custody situations firsthand. Still, as much as I wanted to, I didn't believe her. There must have been something more I could have done.

On my way home I stopped at the public library to return a book of Chekhov's plays. Ahead of me at the book drop was a little boy with a blond buzz cut. He let me go ahead of him, and even held the metal flap door open for me. "Thank you very much," I said to him. Such a nice boy, I thought as I left. And immediately I was thinking of how I could have instilled ideals in Amelia, taught her about the importance and pleasures of reading and of letting older people go ahead of her in line. These are things you should get a chance to teach your child.

II

Summer was nearly over, but I'd hardly noticed that it had even begun. The streams of tourists pouring into town, happy in their devotion to sun and surf, were to me like images on a muted television screen. They were no more real, no more relevant, and no more distracting. In my mind then there were only two seasons: with Amelia, and without her.

One morning during that season of absence, I was dressing for work, consumed for the moment with the task of making it out the door before seven o'clock so I wouldn't be late. Then, I reached into my blazer pocket and felt a wadded-up ball of fabric. I pulled it out to find a pair of pink socks with white trim. They were Amelia's. Suddenly I remembered how she'd kicked them off in the car on our way home from day care one evening, and how after I scooped her up I'd stuck the socks in my pocket and retrieved her small saddle shoes with two fingers from my free hand. I remembered how content I'd been that evening, having Amelia's company in the kitchen as I made our dinner.

But now she was gone and I was standing stunned in my bedroom, staring down at my open palm on which balanced this artifact and the bittersweet story it told. I was sure I couldn't take another step forward. I was equally sure I couldn't put the socks down.

Whit turned over in bed, as if my sudden ceasing of movement had disturbed her rest. "Hey, aren't you going to be late?" she asked, peering at the clock. I lowered the socks onto my bureau, gave Whit a mechanical kiss good-bye, and proceeded to work as the high-pitched whirring in my head grew louder.

Even then, I knew that that evening I could talk to Whit about my feelings, that she would comfort me and let me cry. What about Amelia? I asked myself. She was carrying her own load of sorrows, but she had no way to express them, and not even a glimmer of hope that something she might do would affect a change.

It was moments like that when I stopped feeling sorry for myself and tried to clear my mind, to find the best course and take it. For now, my focus was on trying to arrange for a visit, trying to get the agreements we'd made in court to be enforced.

One sweltering afternoon I found myself in Attorney Kaplan's office, trying to avoid the frozen photographic smiles of her two young children in the portraits perched behind her. It had been a month since our last hearing, and a guardian *ad litem* had finally been appointed, but he wasn't answering my lawyer's calls, and had not contacted Eli, Norma, or myself. On top of that, Attorney Kaplan was having no success arranging a visit between Amelia and me. According to the paper we signed in court, I was entitled to see Amelia for one weekend every six weeks, as long as I didn't take her out of the state. But Norma was denying our requests, and her lawyer claimed that the court order wasn't valid across state lines. "I can threaten them with contempt," Attorney Kaplan explained. "Maybe that will shake them up."

I listened to the quiet swishing sound of the ceiling fan that was spinning above our heads. I tried not to think of how much money it would cost to "shake them up," especially if a mere threat held no sway and we had to take them back to court. Already I'd wiped out my savings account. The loans from my sister and mother, a check Whit's mother had sent when she heard what we had been up against, and the balance on my credit card were taking care of the rest. If there was some guarantee, or even just a good chance, that going deeper into debt would net a positive result, I wouldn't have minded. But I feared now I would just be paying out legal fees to dampen my fury, to harass Norma, and to get revenge. What could I win in court that would make Amelia's life better?

"Now we have to start thinking about what we want to do when these ninety days are up," Attorney Kaplan was saying. "What I would recommend is that we file a motion to extend your guardianship."

"But I still haven't decided whether I want to pursue temporary custody again. I'm leaning toward just focusing our efforts on enforcing the visits," I explained. Either way, our chances of success were dismal. A year before, the court of appeals in New Mexico had been the first to allow a nonbiological mother in a similar lesbian-versus-lesbian custody case to visit her child against her ex-lover's wishes. Beyond that, I could find no case where a lesbian co-parent had been awarded full, shared, or temporary custody. Indeed, for judges to turn down such requests was still the norm in the few dozen cases where co-parents had dared even approach the courts on such a matter. To make matters worse, New Hampshire, one of the most conservative states when it came to gay and lesbian rights, was the state where my case would likely be heard. I told Attorney Kaplan that because of all this, I wasn't feeling particularly hopeful.

She still thought we should file the papers. "It's a safeguard. This way if there is another emergency, if Norma acts in a way that shows us she's not able to take care of Amelia, you're ready to step in. If we let it go, you're back to square one."

"And if I decide not to pursue custody?"

"No harm done."

As it turned out, Attorney Kaplan was very wrong on that point. Despite her letter explaining to Norma's lawyer that we were filing only to keep our option open, and that we hoped it would not be necessary to pursue any form of custody, Norma took our actions as an all-out assault. Shortly after the request was filed, we received a letter from Norma's lawyer saying that I was no longer to send letters or packages to Norma's address, that I could no longer speak to Amelia, even at Eli's home, and that my family members should not contact Amelia either. "There's no way she can enforce that," Attorney Kaplan said. But Norma had her ways. Every letter I sent was returned unopened. She called my mother and told her she'd thrown away the gift she'd sent to Amelia.

I considered driving to New Hampshire, hiring yet another lawyer, and fighting with everything I had to get Amelia back. I fantasized about simply taking her, since legally the guardianship had never been transferred to Eli, and I could still claim she was mine. Of course, if the court in another state didn't agree, I'd be charged with kidnapping.

As fall approached, my dreams began to turn cruel. Something about the dark of early morning let the nightmares in. I would wake with my chest so heavy I couldn't breathe or move. If I had believed in ghosts I would have been convinced that one had plunked itself down on my heart and was refusing to budge.

When I woke, images of blood and sliced flesh haunted me. I would lie in bed holding my leg together with my hands as if it were falling apart, and cry, "Help, help." I would say it out loud, sitting up, eyes open. "Help me." If Whit wasn't home yet, or if she had gone to work early, my cat would look up over his shoulder from the foot of the bed wondering what it was he was meant to do. Every night it seemed I was drawing a thorn, a pin, a piece of glass, painfully out from my skin. Drawing it slowly, sickeningly, out. Whit told me I was grinding my teeth at night. I'd cracked two fillings that way in the weeks since Amelia had left. Finally, I spent two hundred and fifty dollars to have my dentist make me a plastic mouthpiece for me to clench at night instead.

I was scared of the world, and I compensated by paying bills on time or early, and balancing my checkbook to the penny. I washed and waxed my car, sanding off the rust and dabbing touch-up paint on every mark. With so many details I could not control, I was once more losing myself in those I could. I wanted to tame the world around me, cultivate the wild dirt we were planted in. I wished there was something else I could be made of. Armor would do.

There was so much fear in me I knew it wasn't natural. I began to think what a wonder it was that we weren't all as unsettled as Norma, cutting our wounds open instead of waiting.

But there was one small circle of hope. Eli continued to allow Amelia to call me from his home, even against Norma's strong objections. On random Sundays the phone would ring, and I would hear her voice. "I can't wait till I can kiss you for real," she said one weekend morning. I remembered her sleepy morning sweetness, how she would appear on the pink carpet next to my bed that spring when she lived with us.

She asked if her toys were still here, if her pajamas were still on the shelves she had helped Whit to build. I told her everything was waiting for her next visit. "That probably won't be until I'm a teenager or a grown-up," she said.

"Oh, I hope it's not that long, but if it is, all your things will still be waiting, and I'll send you kisses every night until then."

I hung up the phone, praying that we wouldn't have to wait that long. My heart, I thought, can't stretch that far.

Finally the ninety days were coming to an end. This was my last chance to act if I was really going to file to extend my guardianship. Now, with Amelia settled back into her routines in New Hampshire, and Eli saying that he was committed to looking after her, it seemed less certain that to storm in and demand to take her back was the right thing. Even if, against all odds, I was granted custody, Norma would not let such an order stand. I would simply be starting a vicious tug-of-war, and Amelia would be bounced back and forth with every new decision. Meanwhile, Eli told me that every time Norma received a message from my lawyer she became crazed. He wondered what good this fighting was doing. "Amelia is very tense about all of this," he told me.

Even if I gave up on the custody order, there was still the visitation right to fight for. But if I won that, then what? Norma would challenge that, too. We'd both be paying lawyers every time we disagreed. I would put myself further into debt, and I'd force Norma to do the same. All of our material and emotional resources would go into this fight. What would be left for Amelia? And what if Norma lost and I did get to see Amelia? Norma would be belligerent each time I showed up on her doorstep. Each encounter would be frightening for Amelia, not comforting. And that was the best-case scenario.

Stories of bravery and courage are stories of fighting for what is right and scorning surrender. But I knew that I was about to stop battling against Eli and Norma.

"I think it's time I give up," I told Whit, who was sitting at the table reading. She put her newspaper down and looked up at me, waiting for more. "It's not doing Amelia any good anymore," I said.

"You want to give up?"

"Yeah, call off the lawyers. Stop making legal threats and demands."

Whit nodded. "You're right," she said. "There's just nothing more you can do right now." I was surprised to hear her say this. She was always one to encourage me to do everything in my power.

"I can't believe I'm going to surrender. I can't believe I've lost." I sat down opposite Whit.

"You haven't lost," she said. "There's just nothing to do right now."

I sat down and wrote a letter to Norma. I explained that I would not fight her anymore. I told her I would like for us to talk to one another, and not through lawyers, and that maybe we could one day work this whole thing out. Later that evening I phoned Eli. "I'm calling it quits," I said. "I won't be filing any more motions about guardianship or visitation."

"I'm relieved to hear that," he said. "Amelia seems to be doing well."

"I hope you'll still have her call me from time to time."

"I will when she's here."

"But let's not make it an obligation. When she feels like it. Only if she wants to."

"Of course she wants to. She just feels the stress from Norma, so it's not so comfortable for her to talk to you."

"That's why I say we should wait until she's ready. Just suggest it now and then, and let her call when she really wants to."

This was the hardest part for me. The phone was all we had left. But the Sunday calls had turned into an obligatory ritual, like thanking your grandparents for the hideous shirt they bought you for Hanukkah, or visiting your senile aunt. That's not what I wanted to be to Amelia. But I was afraid of being no one.

Every night before I went to sleep I'd whisper a good night to Amelia, and send her a kiss. Beginning that night I expanded that ritual into something like a prayer: a beam of imagined light, a shower of sparkling stardust I would envision falling on her blankets and cheeks as she slept. If she could read the message in all that magic it would be a promise that in my heart I would never stop holding her.

It rained the day Amelia turned five. Whit brought home a bottle of champagne and I tried to be happy. I looked at pictures of Amelia from the previous fall when she had visited for Thanksgiving, just about a month before Norma's suicide attempt. I stared into the picture, and drank up Amelia's beautiful smile.

In the morning I went to the bank and opened an account for Amelia. In addition to refusing the gifts and letters I'd tried sending, Norma had been refusing the checks I'd been writing for "child support" for several months now. A savings account, I decided, would be a way of giving something. I could save for Amelia's future, and on all her birthdays and holidays I would make a contribution. I'd called my mother to tell her about my plan and she said she'd join the effort, adding to the account on holidays, too. As I wrote out my first check for Amelia's new fund I felt as though I was starting a hope chest of sorts.

Several weeks later, the phone rang. Miraculously, on the other end I heard Amelia's voice, clean as whistling white teeth. Our conversation bubbled like a cold, happy brook. She was in kindergarten now. She had to do tracings for homework and said her new teacher was strict.

"Where is Whit?" Amelia asked.

"Do you want to talk to her?"

"Both of you. Both of you talk at once," she commanded.

Whit picked up the upstairs phone and we all spoke at once, then we laughed.

Amelia said her mom had given away Ariel, her pet bunny, and that now Norma wanted to buy a dog. "I don't want a dog, I want Ariel," Amelia muttered. She asked me to send her a present from the swap box at the dump. Whit tried to say something then, but I interrupted. "Honey, I want to send you things from the swap box, but Mom won't let you have them. She's still angry."

Amelia repeated the pronouncement to Eli, whose house she was calling from. After a brief discussion she came back on the phone. "You send it and we'll see if Mommy rejects it," she said. Amelia had learned to negotiate nicely. Her proposal made sense, and so I agreed.

"Guess what tomorrow is?" Amelia asked.

"Rosh Hashanah. Happy New Year."

"Happy New Year, Ima. And Whit can have a Happy New Year, too, even though she's not Jewish."

Whit was chuckling as she came downstairs. I hung up the phone, still laughing, too.

The moments when I was happy were like unexpected guests. I hardly remembered what joy felt like.

But then, seemingly innocent moments could send me back to despair. A stranger might ask if I had children, or an acquaintance, unaware of what had happened those past months, would ask me how Amelia was doing. One evening I came home to find a message from Dr. Thompkins on the phone machine. He just wanted to know how Amelia was faring. I didn't call him back because I couldn't stand to acknowledge the fact that I didn't know the answer.

By December I was feeling utterly defeated. Eli and Amelia rarely called, because, Eli said, he was seeing her much less frequently now. Once again he and Lindsay were trying to move on with their lives and leave Norma to sort out her own.

The holiday lights strung through the streets seemed like an insult to me, as if the world were mocking my losses.

My editor asked me to generate some story ideas for articles that would run in the weeks leading up to the holidays. "Anything festive, family stuff, food, decorating," he suggested. After much thought I suggested a piece on divorced fathers and how they made it through this time of year without custody of their children and in the face of all the holiday hype. Not the angle my editor had been looking for, but he agreed to the idea. As long as the rest of my stories would be upbeat, he warned.

I collected names of men who were divorced and did not have physical custody of their children. I called each one, and most agreed to be interviewed. Little did they know that they would be doing more than simply contributing a few quotes for a newspaper story. They would become part of my group therapy, only they didn't know they were in the group.

"It's interesting that they sent a woman to do this story," one of my subjects said as I settled into an arm chair in his living room.

"Oh, this wasn't an assignment. I generate nearly all of my own story ideas."

"So how did you choose this particular topic?"

"I do a lot of stories about family issues," I said, trying to get out from under this line of questioning.

"Well, it's nice you're giving us fathers our say. All the media seem to want to cover are the deadbeat dads. Most divorced fathers are like me. We want to see our children but the courts still favor the mothers. I hope you'll try to understand things from our point of view."

"I will," I said. I didn't say that I already understood.

I liked spending my days talking to divorced fathers. I could relate to their stories about missing their children and accepting less than adequate visitation schedules. They said they felt unneeded except when the child support payments were due. I sympathized much more easily with them than I did with their ex-wives.

At home, I sat down to write my Hanukkah cards with little enthusiasm for the task. I wrote one to Norma's parents, to Eli and Lindsay, and one to Amelia, which I sent to Eli's house. I knew he probably wouldn't give it to her because it would just set Norma off. But not sending one would be worse. In the envelope to Eli and Lindsay I enclosed a check and asked them to buy Amelia some presents from me. This way I could give something to her, even though she wouldn't know who the gifts were really from.

"I'm going to send Norma a card," I told Whit, suddenly feeling possessed by the holiday spirit.

"What will you write on it?"

"Nothing. I'll just sign under where it says 'Happy Hanukkah.'"

"Sure, why not? If you feel up to it."

I took a card from the box and stared at the golden menorah on the cover. Inside the greeting read, "May the Hanukkah lights bring you joy and peace this season."

"Wait a minute. How can I wish her joy and peace? She won't let me see or speak to my child. Why should I wish her a happy anything?"

"I don't know," Whit said. "I'd be surprised if you could at this point."

"I'm surprised that for a minute I forgot how furious I am with her."

I finished sealing and stamping my cards and went in the kitchen to wash the dishes. I was still thinking about my anger, and how easy it had been for me to forget it. Now I couldn't stop myself from listing all the reasons I was furious with Norma, starting with her ultimatum years earlier that we have a baby or end our relationship right then, all the way up to the present.

By the time I had wiped down the counters, I was livid. And not just at Norma. Suddenly my anger focused on Whit. Earlier that week we had been driving home from work through a blizzard, and my car got stuck two miles from home. I pushed while she steered, then she pushed while I steered, and finally we met our unplowed road, and had to shovel into our driveway. I was angry at Whit because her back went out from pushing the car, and I had to bend down to pick up things that she dropped. Really I was angry because her pain was so much easier to live with than my pain.

I was angry at parents who had their children, at children who had their parents. I got angry at commercials for Pampers. Small shoes, yellow school buses, and happy endings all set me off. Like the winds that crashed against our windows that winter night, my anger rattled my edges, demanding attention. The fury settled in our small dark house. It sat in front of the fire stealing all the heat. It leaned on the kitchen counter waiting to be fed. It followed me upstairs when I thought it wasn't looking.

I had to get outside. I took the bucket of kitchen compost— pineapple rinds, old soup, and soggy coffee grinds—from the kitchen to the pile out back. I hurled the entire container, plastic and all, in the general direction of the heap. It felt good to spew the rotting food. I muttered obscenities as I kicked up a storm of crystal powder. I beat the snow harder and harder. White dust surrounded me like sound waves, making music for my wild dance.

Finally the weight of the black night stopped me. I lowered myself into the snow and looked up at the stars. I would have screamed then, but I could hear the sounds of normal conversation from the neighbors' yard across the way. They must have been shoveling, or taking out their garbage, too. I chose not to inflict my insanity on them, so I just crouched there, crying quietly, somewhere above the snow and below the stars.

The last week of work before Christmas I was walking across the newsroom to get a cup of tea when I felt myself about to faint. I wasn't tired or even hungry. I was haunted—obsessed with images from the day's news of buildings burning, people stranded and succumbing to frostbite, and children dying. Images from dreams about severed arms and legs would not leave my mind. I went back to my desk without my tea, but not daring to get up and try again. Instead, I pretended to be busy for the rest of the day.

When I returned home I told Whit what had happened. That night she held me until I fell asleep. In the morning she called in sick and insisted that I do the same. She set me up on the couch covered in blankets where I could watch while she trimmed our Christmas tree. Outside an icy gray rain plummeted from the heavens. It comforted me that the weather matched my mood.

That afternoon Whit insisted I make an appointment with a therapist. I didn't want to, but to make her happy I called the therapist I had seen off and on since I came out some ten years before. I dreaded the thought of having to talk about any of this, but I knew Whit was right, and I would never feel any better if I didn't. During the first appointment I started talking and didn't stop for the full hour. It felt surprisingly good. "Now you have to keep on talking about your feelings," my therapist told me, "with Whit, and with your friends. This is too much to hold inside."

That afternoon I was meeting Sam for lunch. On the way to the restaurant we passed a children's store. "Did I ever tell you how horrible I feel every time I pass that store?" I asked. "I hate that store. It just reminds me how sad I am that Amelia is gone."

"No, you never told me that. But it's about time you said something about how you're doing without Amelia. I always think it's strange that you never mention it."

"I don't?" I asked.

"You don't. And when anybody else asks you change the subject."

"I do?"

"Well, not anymore, I hope," Sam said.

On Christmas Eve Amelia called. "We have a tree up in the living room," I told her.

"Are there presents under it?"

"Yes, Santa brought them."

"That's impossible, Ima."

"What do you mean? It's not impossible." Was Amelia implying that Santa Claus is impossible? Or that it is impossible that Santa would bring presents to a house where a Jewish person lived?

"It *is* impossible because Santa doesn't come until midnight," she said with confidence.

Then she asked if there were any presents under our tree for her. The question was like a punch to my gut. I wanted to tell her that she had already got presents from me for Hanukkah—that the party dress Eli gave her was bought with the money I'd given him, and the paints and pads were all from me, too. Instead I reminded her that Norma still didn't allow me to send her gifts.

"Mommy says she's never going to forgive you," Amelia said.

"Well, I think she will someday. And when she does, I'll give you one present for every holiday we missed."

Amelia liked that idea. And when I hung up the phone, I let myself cry.

III

On New Year's Eve Whit and I met friends in the city for dinner in a fancy Japanese restaurant. After the meal and champagne we walked slowly down the icy streets. I was dressed in a short black dress and pumps, which didn't make it any easier to maneuver across the slippery terrain. But there was no reason to rush. The streets were packed with revelers, as well as troupes of dancers and musicians. A group dressed in what looked like rawhide with painted faces and reindeer antlers clapped wooden sticks and snaked up and down the sidewalks. We got caught between the dancers and it was like getting tangled in a fairy tale.

"Look, it's five minutes to midnight," one of our friends announced. So we went to join the crowd. It was twenty-eight degrees according to the digital thermometer glowing above us. People in the streets began to chant the seconds out loud. Whit gave me a long slow kiss, and neither of us worried who was watching. We had acquired noisemakers somehow, and we blasted our New Year's greetings into the air. I loved the feel of my breath rushing out and turning to sound. I tilted my chin to the sky and blew my plastic horn. Whit joined me and so did our friends. I watched as the steam from my breath rose and felt my chest empty again and again. As we walked on to find our car, I felt clean, cold, happy, and hopeful.

Still feeling the peace of the new year, I finally decided to send a note to Norma. I told her that I'd like to start corresponding with Amelia through the mail from time to time, but that given her strong feelings I wanted to check with her first.

Two weeks later my letter was returned, unopened, along with a letter from Norma saying that this was her final warning: if I send any more mail to her address she would file harassment charges against me. Given that that had been my first attempt at contacting Norma in months, I didn't worry too much about her threat. It was her unrelenting fury, a force of anger that left not even a slim hope of negotiating, that disturbed me.

A couple of days later Eli called. Norma said that if Amelia ever called me from his home again, she would no longer allow Eli and Amelia to see each other. "Neither of us wants that to happen, do we?" he asked.

We discussed our options for a few minutes. But it was clear he wouldn't disobey her. "I hope this doesn't last too long," I said. And I left it at that.

At work I'd been assigned to write a feature about the fact that there was a dearth of babies being up for adoption in the United States. One afternoon I found myself seated in the office of a psychotherapist who counsels birth mothers who are considering giving up children for adoption, and those who have made the choice to do so. "They suffer from psychological amputation," she said. "They always have this void where the child was, and they tend to try to fill it with something else." She explained how they have difficulty in their relationships and often turn to alcohol or drugs. I was taking notes, trying to keep my mind clear to ask appropriate questions and pursue all the relevant angles. I was sitting in an old wooden swivel desk chair, which I feared would start to spin out of control, propelled by my emotion. That term, psychological amputation, struck a deep chord. It was precisely how I felt, as if a part of me had been sliced away. But it wasn't a clean emptiness. There was that pounding ache of phantom pain.

The one-year anniversary of our first court date leered at me like a curse. I couldn't stop thinking there was something more I should have done, could still do.

"I failed," I thought, as I looked out the window where a bank of gray clouds had just rolled in. Whit was walking inside after replanting a section of lawn. She stomped the mud off her work boots as she entered the kitchen.

"How's it going?" I asked. I was sitting on the couch with folders of legal records spread around me. I had been writing columns of pros and cons, give up or fight. Listing my options had become like an obsession.

"Got it planted just in time. Rain's starting." She shook off her jacket, tossed it on a chair, and dropped down onto the couch with me.

"Watch it, you're on my decision."

"I'm on your what?" Whit leaned forward and pulled out the pad she had sat upon. "What are you deciding?"

"Same thing."

Whit glanced down at the pad and tossed it on the coffee table with the rest of the papers.

"How long's it going to take?" I asked.

"For what?"

"The grass."

"Oh." Whit pulled me into her side. I often complained that she insisted on having conversations in such close range. I like to be able to see the eyes of the person I am speaking to. But I didn't mind being nestled there just then. "Let's see, with a lot of water and a little sun, I'd say three weeks oughta do it."

Curled up with Whit like that, I wished I were one of those seeds. I wouldn't have to do anything, just be fed and cared for, and maybe in three weeks I'd burst forth, full of life and able to handle whatever was out there in the sunlight. As it was, I didn't feel ready for spring.

"That's right. Just be a seed," she said. "Then when it's time to do something again, you'll be strong and ready."

When she got up I closed my papers into their folders and put them away. Outside, the rain-soaked trees shimmered in the light, like seashells do just below the surf.

I woke from an oddly comforting dream: I was in a room, Norma's room, and it was empty except for a glass armoire. Inside the armoire was a small box. I opened the lid and a song began to play. The song told a tale about how Amelia was born so that Norma could learn to walk. I couldn't quite make out all of the lyrics, or their meaning. It was as though the words were a handful of water that kept slipping through my fingers. But the melody was so beautiful that I couldn't stop listening. Suddenly, a desperate need to understand began to mount inside me. In my frustration I shattered the armoire. Glass sprayed everywhere and I was cut badly. But this wasn't a bad dream. It was telling me something I couldn't learn any other way. That there were forces beyond me and Norma and our lawyers. That there were reasons for each of us to be in the others' lives. Maybe even a reason that I was losing Amelia now.

That same morning, Amelia called from Eli's house. As it would turn out, this would be our last conversation for many years.

"I just had a dream about you last night," I told Amelia.

"I listen to the lullaby tape a thousand times," Amelia said, as if this were a perfectly logical reply. To me it was. My dream. Her answer. We were reassuring one another that we would stay connected. Somehow.

It was a Sunday evening that summer, and Whit suggested we dress up and go out for a nice meal. "Why?" I asked. "We can't afford it and it isn't a special occasion." But Whit insisted that we couldn't afford *not* to go, and that I should just get dressed. I was willing to be convinced.

I put on a floral sundress and Whit changed into a clean shirt and trousers. Just as we were about to leave the house Whit asked me to sit down. I played along, not knowing what she had in mind. She sank down on one knee and held my hand. I could feel a cold object between our palms. Suddenly I knew what was coming. "Will you marry me?" she asked.

I didn't have an answer. How could I possibly take a chance like this again after all I'd been through? Whit was asking me to believe in happily ever afters, and I'd given up on those. Besides, lesbians can't legally marry any more than we can legally have children together. Trying to start a family didn't work for me the first time, how could I go that way again?

Then I looked into Whit's eyes and I wondered how I could possibly refuse such a chance. Our marriage would never be protected by the law, but we could protect one another.

"Yes," I said, "I will." Whit opened her hand and I saw a delicate gold band planted with diamonds and sapphires. She slipped the ring onto my finger. The center stone was a solid, soothing blue. It sang to me of things that stay. "It's perfect," I said.

One day as I walked up the path to our door, I noticed red and brown leaves crumpled in little fists on the ground. Autumn had come again.

It had been a year and three months since I'd last seen Amelia. That fact alone was more than I could bear. But it was a fact, and I had to find ways to make my life matter, in spite of it. It was time to be more than just a ghost mother, I told myself.

I decided to devote more energy to my poetry. I signed up for a writing workshop, hoping that it would cheer me up to do something I loved. The first evening the class met, the teacher read a poem by Walt Whitman. It had been so long since I'd taken the time to read poetry, and I'd always loved Whitman most of all. I nearly cried to hear familiar lines from "Song of Myself." Whitman's words reminded me how deep my love for words was and how much I had to learn in order to express myself so beautifully that even life's pain could be transformed into art.

Before we left class that night, the teacher gave us an assignment. We were to write about a fantasy party—a gathering we wished we could attend. I'm sure she expected us to spin tales of celebrity-studded affairs in Hollywood, or sensual orgies of delights. But it was the week of Amelia's sixth birthday, and I knew exactly which unglamorous party I'd give anything to attend. I began to write:

The Birthday Party That Never Was

The invitation would arrive in the mail stuck between a postcard and some bills. I'd recognize the return address, and tear the envelope open not believing I'd been included.

"Birthday Dreams are Coming True and Magic is in the Air," would be printed on a pink banner above a picture of Cinderella and her fairy godmother. Inside I would read: "Two to four p.m. Parents may stay for coffee and conversation." At the bottom Amelia would have written her name with craggy consonants and a lollipop "i."

I'd want to dress up, but I'd settle for black jeans, print cotton blouse, and vest, perhaps.

I'd try to arrive early so I could help, not wanting to seem like a guest in her home. I'd knock on the door, and Jason's mother would answer. Little Jason, who I haven't seen since he was four and all of us lived in the same neighborhood, would take one look at me, then dart back through some inside doorway to carry the news of my arrival. Meanwhile his mother and I would pretend to chat casually, trying hard not to make reference to anything less cheery than colored ice cream sprinkles.

"Amelia, your Ima's here," I would hear Jason shriek. Hearing the name only Amelia calls me would fill me with the warmth of entitlement, that comfortable claiming of a role that had been stripped away for so long.

I'd idly admire the pink and purple streamers, twisted together and taped from wall to wall across the living room. I'd be tapping one hand on a Mylar balloon held anchored by my too tightly clenched fist.

Amelia would launch herself into the room like a rocket to the moon. She would land on me and I'd fall backward two steps and let the balloon float to the ceiling. Stooping down to hug her, I'd be amazed that there was nothing between her small solid body and my sprawling adult one, except air. And then, not even that . . .

Ima
An Epilogue

I wrote this down for you in the years when we could not see or speak to each other. One day, I thought, we'd reunite, and maybe you'd ask what happened, or why I did one thing, and not another. Even if you didn't voice the questions, you would wonder.

I wrote this down knowing other people would read it, too. Because we're not the only ones who have had to go through something like this. I've begun to interview other co-mothers who lost their children for many years. And their children, of course, lost them for all that time, too. (You, and all the other children, know what that means: This missing. Then the determination not to miss anymore. The questions you don't dare ask. Learning too young about the unfairness of the world.)

Now, we refer casually to the five years absence. I ask if I can brush your hair, and you remind me you're old enough now to do that by yourself. "Come on," I say, "I haven't had a turn in a long, long time." You pass me the brush, then pick up your yellow baby brush, which I still keep in the bathroom. "Then I get to use this one," you say. We laugh as the fine bristles cave in, unable to compete with the strength of a growing girl's tangles.

You forgive me easily when I don't know what bones you've broken, what pets you've lost, whether you still love strawberries and pesto pizza. I help you out when you can't remember a name of one of our Massachusetts friends or where we keep the mixing bowls. We don't try to fill each other in, much. What's lost is lost. And miraculously, it's not as much as either of us feared.

Still, it's not as simple as turning a page, and presto! there you are. Instead, there was a long, long story in between. This is how I tell my part.

One day you'll tell yours. I want to hear it.

After I had written this book, after Amelia had been gone from our lives for three or four years, after Norma's parents and brother had long ago stopped returning my messages asking how Amelia was doing, I found myself for the first time ever longing—no, lusting—for a baby.

I wanted to be pregnant. I wanted a child of my own. I found myself trying to convince Whit, who was dead set against it. I felt the irony of my position. Now I knew Norma's frantic need, and the urge to bully the world into meeting it.

Why, Whit kept asking. Why now? Why all of a sudden? In a wash of tears I heard myself saying, "I want *my* baby. I want Amelia."

I wanted all the lost years. I wanted her to be a baby on my lap, the fuzz of her hair tickling my neck. I wanted to hear her sounding out words. I wanted her keeping me up nights. I wanted to hear her cry or talk or whine or laugh or sneeze. I hadn't allowed myself to want this in years. How many? It seemed like forever.

In gay and lesbian newspapers, I was reading about lesbian co-mothers who were becoming legally adoptive parents of their children. I read about co-mothers like me who had been denied visitation after separating from the birth mothers, who were now winning custody cases in court. Maybe I should try again.

I called a lawyer who was quoted in these articles. "I know it's unfair," she said, "but it's been several years. A judge would say you abandoned your daughter."

I took that blow and continued. "There's *nothing* I can do?"

"Nothing," she said. There was a long silence. "Well, here's something. It may not sound like much, but you could write her letters," she said.

I told her I'd been forbidden from doing so. I told her I didn't have the address. (I'd searched phone directories, on-line directories, I'd tried calling a friend of Norma's. But no luck.)

"Write anyway," she said. And I did.

Soon after, I had a dream. In it I was overcome with sadness. I was bawling, inconsolable. "Oh, God," I pleaded. "I can't take it anymore. Help me."

I woke from that dream possessed with bare desire. I walked downstairs and took a picture of Amelia off the mantel. But this time when I looked at her, my vision wasn't clouded with the pain of separation. I looked with love and longing. "Something changed inside," I told Whit. But outside, all was the same. Nothing had been gained.

And then, a month or so after that dream, the phone rang. It was Norma on the other end of the line.

The call came five years, almost to the day, from the one in which Norma told me that she and Amelia were in the psychiatric hospital.

It was about eight o'clock, I'd just returned from work, and swimming at the YMCA. Whit was stretched out on the couch, reading the newspaper.

I had heard Norma's voice a couple of times a year during those five years. Each time it was in response to an effort I had made to contact her. I made it a point to send a note or make a phone call every four to six months to let Norma know that I'd like to try to work things out if we could. I sent her a letter when my Grandpa Abe died, never knowing whether she'd even receive it. Most recently, after my talk with the lawyer a few months earlier, I'd sent her a letter telling her I'd decided to begin to write to Amelia. I said Amelia was old enough now to decide for herself whether she wanted contact with me. I mailed the letter and a few weeks later I mailed one to Amelia. I didn't know if either would ever arrive. It had been a long time since they had moved, and I only had an old address. Norma received only the letter to Amelia, and called me up to tell me not to dare try that again. Besides, she said, it was only a fluke that she'd received my mail that time. The forwarding order from their last address had expired. Soon after that, she sent me an envelope stuffed with photographs that had me in them. A clear statement that she was tearing me out of their lives. For good, I thought.

Now, here she was saying, Hello, how are you? as if we were old friends.

"Okay," I said. "I'm on the edge of my seat. Why are you calling?" I thought she must be calling to complain about something: another of my letters to Amelia had gotten through, or she needed money. Or maybe Amelia was ill, or hurt. But her voice sounded calm. Friendly, even.

Norma giggled. "You, on the edge of your seat? I can't imagine it."

"Yeah. I'm in complete suspense. Why are you calling?"

I felt impatient and angry and on my guard, but I was trying to keep my voice neutral. Then she said she was calling to apologize. To say she shouldn't have kept Amelia from me for so many years. That she didn't want this separation to go on forever.

I was waking up to the dream I'd had so many times. The call I'd hoped for each year at the Jewish High Holidays when we are asked to make amends. But there must be a catch, I thought. I looked over to Whit. "Norma," I mouthed. She raised her eyebrows. Norma was still apologizing. She wasn't groveling, she was explaining. She had been getting help for her problems. She was putting her life in order. She was in a relationship, and had been for the past four years.

I wanted to say everything. I wanted to say how much I'd been hurt, how desperate I'd been. I wanted to say I could never forgive her. I wanted to tell her all was forgiven; let's just move forward. I wanted to say, How dare you? How could you think I would just say, Okay, that's over now.

Instead I said she was brave to call. I said I appreciated her telling me these things, that I had a lot to say, too. That maybe we could have more conversations.

"I hear Amelia in her room," Norma said. "She's supposed to be asleep, but she's awake. Would you like to speak to her?"

I looked at Whit. My eyes opened wide. "She's getting Amelia," I mouthed. I sat down at my desk, in the room that had been Amelia's, in the place where her dollhouse had been. There were bookshelves now where she used to sleep. I waited while Norma went to bring Amelia to the phone.

Five years. Suddenly I could feel every turtle-backed day, the rough slide of time. The near-biblical proportions: One thousand seven hundred and forty eight days. Entire regions of my heart no longer pumping. I learned that you can survive without parts.

People asked, again and again, how can you survive it? How can you go on? Worst was when they'd say, "I couldn't." And again, I'd feel that I was not a proper mother. A real mother could not survive. Would not go on.

Meanwhile, in five years I'd earned a master's degree in writing. I'd landed a job as a newspaper editor. I'd been succeeding in the world of work. I'd been seeing my relationship grow.

A real mother would rip her own heart out of her chest rather than wait for it to decay through this long, natural process. A real mother would charge over state lines on a white mare if necessary, grab her child, and run off. Mothers kill for their young. Mothers do battle. Mothers *can't* go on.

But I *had* met mothers who did just that. I spent Amelia's eighth birthday in a run-down housing complex in Virginia interviewing Sharon Bottoms. Sharon lost her son to her own mother, who sought—and won—custody because Sharon is a lesbian. Sharon went on. She fought in the courts until she couldn't even hope for a different outcome. The hardest decision she made, she told me, was to stop fighting and accept that all she had was a schedule of weekly visits with her son.

I spoke to JAL, known that way to the press, who was waiting for the Pennsylvania courts to decide if she could, after two years, see her daughter again. Like me, JAL was a nonbiological mother involved in a lesbian-versus-lesbian custody dispute. Only she'd kept fighting in the courts. One day, between appeals, JAL was stopped at the gas pumps. She looked out her car window and saw, in a school bus one pump over, her little girl sitting in her seat next to the window. But she did nothing dramatic. Paid for her gas, and pulled away.

That summer, I sat down to a barbecue with a couple in their fifties whose son had died months before. Both mother and father cracked jokes about an item in the newspaper that day, ate prime rib, and offered to help me sell a screenplay I'd just completed.

Of course real mothers do survive. The drama is internal. It happens late at night when you're alone, or in a darkened theater when you cry so hard as the credits roll that you can't get out of your seat. Or when you leave the party and don't cry until you close the door to your own car, because someone had a new baby and couldn't stop talking about him. When you refuse your pregnant co-worker's shower invitation and make up an excuse about how you're so busy. There are the days when you remember that you used to feel something, only you can't remember what it was. When you can't feel happy for a friend and you learn what bitterness means. When you realize that survival is an involuntary reflex.

Then, when the phone rings and puts a period at the end of a very long sentence, suddenly five years feels like no time. No time at all.

When I finally heard Amelia's voice, I could have been reliving our first visit after she and Norma moved out of state. That day she nearly knocked me to the ground with her enthusiasm. Now, too, she embraced me with meteoric force. (And when I would see her in person several weeks later, she would do the same, only now she was nine and a half years old and big enough to knock me over.)

"Hello, little goose," I said.

Amelia giggled.

"Are you nervous to talk to me?" I asked.

"Just a little," she said.

"I'm a little nervous, too. But mostly I'm so happy."

So many times I had imagined our reunion. Amelia would be angry, or silent, or hurt. She wouldn't want to talk to me. I'd want to explain everything. I'd worried that she wouldn't remember me. That she'd have believed Norma's negative depictions of me. But now all the possibilities were boiling down to one reality.

Amelia giggled again. "I'm so happy, too," she said. "I have a new bunny, Ima."

Then we began to talk. And talk. I walked from room to room with the cordless phone as Amelia recounted her memories of our times together. She quizzed me about which of her toys and books and clothes I still had. I pulled boxes from the closet as we spoke and ticked off their contents. Her voice was high and beautiful. Strange and familiar. She said "cool" a lot, and asked if I still had her "perambulator." She read me stories she'd written in school. I pulled my flute out of its dusty case and played her the lullaby she'd always loved. She asked about Ahab and Chance, and I had to tell her that both had died.

"Do you wear glasses, Ima?" she asked me.

"Yes, a matter of fact I do now," I said. "I just got them about a year ago."

"Me, too," she said. "Do you have an astigmatism?"

"Hmm, I don't remember what the eye doctor said. I'll have to find out. Why?"

"Because everyone in our family wears glasses," she said. "And now you wear glasses, too."

"Do you wear your glasses all the time?"

"I have to," Amelia said. "I can't even see the phone if I'm one inch away."

"Oh, dear," I said in mock horror. "I can see the phone without *my* glasses if it's one inch away. I hope I'm still in the family."

"Don't be silly Ima," Amelia said. "You're always in our family."

Just as on the day of her birth, it was again Amelia who defined me. Who insisted I be her parent. Just as so many times along the way she'd had to tell me who I am.

All at once I felt the weight of grief for all the lies I have let myself believe. I let Norma tell me, time and again, that I was not Amelia's parent, and in the few times we'd spoken over the years, that Amelia didn't remember who I was. I let comments from my own family, from acquaintances and even strangers, convince me that Amelia had probably forgotten me, or that I'd never really been a parent anyway. I let myself be disheartened by my legal disenfranchisement, the lack of vocabulary for my familial tie to Amelia, the daily homophobia that tells me that my love is wrong, that homosexual love, our love for each other and for our children, is not equal to "normal" heterosexual love. I let myself be influenced by all the subtle and blatant ways that the world had told me that I had no right to this child, that my motherhood was a figment of my imagination.

"You know, I still send you kisses every night before I go to sleep," I told Amelia. "Do you catch them?"

"Yes," she said. "But they come a little late. Do you think you could send them express?"

That night I lay in bed, staring up past the ceiling to the heavens. I felt my heart pumping. And I felt Amelia's heart, like a physical force, beating against mine.

In the days that followed I wrote her letters telling her about the cakes I'd made for her birthdays even when I couldn't speak to her. I told her about the ring she'd left on the bathtub that last day, and how I wore it on a chain around my neck. She told me about the picture of me she'd kept by her bed all these years, and that she still kept the letters and tapes I'd sent her. We exchanged photographs by mail and I spent days adjusting to the startling fact of her new height.

Finally I could accept, not only that I am a mother—had always been a mother—but, more precisely, what kind of a mother I had been. Yes, Norma had been there for Amelia for the everyday. She made the hour-by-hour sacrifices that are associated with the term, and by which she would rightfully say that she earned this title.

I was a mother on a different plane. My job had not been the daily lunches and lessons, but a broad and amorphous task of loving, of learning and teaching the lesson (if only by my constant doubt and its constant defeat) of the heart's strength and power.

Motherhood is about (among so many other things) love and constancy. It is a net spread below our offspring—a weave of caring, concern—creating an invisible network of buoying cables.

There are so many dimensions to the word, and when I heard Amelia's voice I realized that I had found one I hadn't known existed. For one eternal moment, I understood:

Nothing had ever been lost. There had never been a question. I was Amelia's Ima, whatever that meant, whatever that means. No matter what the courts say, the laws say, the bigots say. No matter what well-meaning family members say. No matter what I let myself be convinced of.

I can't describe it in words any better now than I could on the day Amelia was born. Only now I know what my place was and is. I have found the Place of the Parent. I have lived in that place.

People who love me keep telling me that they are worried. That Norma might do the same thing again, she might take Amelia away from me. "No," I say. "She can't do that." As it turns out, she never could.